T0383062

Paul Samuelson & the Foundations of Modern Economics

Paul Samuelson & the Foundations of Modern Economics

K. Puttaswamaiah
editor

Transaction Publishers
New Brunswick (U.S.A.) and London (U.K.)

This book is printed on acid-free paper that meets the American National Standard for Permanence of Paper for Printed Library Materials.

Library of Congress Catalog Number: 2001041598
ISBN: 0-7658-0114-0
Printed in the United States of America

Library of Congress Cataloging-in-Publication Data

Paul Samuelson and the foundations of modern economics / K. Puttaswamaiah, editor.

p. cm.

Includes bibliographical references and index.

ISBN 0-7658-0114-0 (cloth. : alk. paper)

1. Samuelson, Paul Anthony, 1915- 2. Economists—United States. 3. Economics—History—20th century. I. Samuelson, Paul Anthony, 1915- II. Puttaswamaiah, K.

HB119 .P38 2001
330.1—dc21 2001041598

Contents

PREFACE

Professor Paul Samuelson, the first American Nobel Laureate (1970), is the Institute Emeritus Professor at the Massachusetts Institute of Technology, Cambridge, MA, USA. He received his second Nobel Prize after the first prize was shared by Jan Tinbergen and Ragnar Frisch in 1969. Professor Samuelson received the Nobel Prize in Economics "for the scientific work through which he has developed static and dynamic economic theory and actively contributed to raising the level of analysis in economic science."

Paul Samuelson is best known for his book, *Foundation of Economic Analysis,* which greatly increased the use of mathematics in Economics. His works are mathematically oriented and he has been very successful in putting mathematics into economics. His skill in this art of analysis is almost play for him. Professor Samuelson has contributed in many ways as a scholar who has radically changed economics analysis and as a teacher who has enriched many subjects and areas that have stimulated research. As he has stated, he has been a "comrade in arms" with his students. Friendly to one and all, he has been immensely helpful and supportive to colleagues and a warm and generous economist.

I would not be wrong in stating that Samuelson should be considered one of the greatest economists of the twentieth century. Professor Paul Samuelson "is simply superb. His conversational and writing styles are very similar: trenchant, vivid figures of speech, extensive historical references, illuminating comparative situations or ideas. He loves to improve on conventional wisdom by rephrasing, sometimes standing it on its head. For example, 'The exception that improves the rules.'"

I felt it my duty to such a noble professor that a volume honoring him and his works be published. When this idea was made known to authors of repute, there was a tremendous response. Many papers were received, from which twelve were chosen for publication. As a result of this response, I have divided the contributions into themes. "Samuelson and the foundations of modern economics" is the most important. The next important theme is "expanding economics of the twentieth century" which establishes the last theme, "Paul Samuelson—the theorist as historian of economic thought." These themes are unique and fruitful tributes to Professor Paul Samuelson and are topics that are most dear to him.

The affectionate support and cooperation of Professors Robert M. Solow, Massachusetts Institute of Technology, Cambridge, USA, and Lawrence R. Klein, University of Pennsylvania, both Nobel Laureates who have contributed to this work, are gratefully acknowledged. Professor Robert C. Merton, Harvard University, USA, Nobel-Laureate, has also given me encouragement. The other authors have also been cooperative and I owe a debt of gratitude to them.

The enthusiasm and cooperation of Irving Louis Horowitz, Chairman of the Board and Editorial Director, and Mary E. Curtis, President and Publisher of Transaction Publishers, are highly appreciated. They, with their staff, have worked with me in my endeavors, showing a keen interest in the development of academic research. Their cooperation is gratefully acknowledged.

Dr. K. Puttaswamaiah
Bangalore, India
September 2001

CONTRIBUTIONS OF PAUL A. SAMUELSON

*K. Puttaswamaiah**

Paul A. Samuelson was awarded the *Second* Nobel Prize for Economics in 1970, the *First* U.S. recipient. The Swedish Academy while declaring this award has rightly said that Samuelson has done "more than any other economist to raise the level of scientific analysis in the field of economic theories. He has rewritten considerable parts of central economic theory and has in several areas achieved results which now reach among the classical theorems of economics". He is an outstanding economist who has tried his best to shape U.S. economic and fiscal policies all through. In fact, he has done probably more than any other economist in the U.S. to recast the policy implications of the "General Theory" to suit the U.S. economic and political environment.

Paul A. Samuelson was awarded the Nobel Prize in 1970 for his "scientific work through which he has developed static and dynamic economic theory and actively contributed to raising the level of analysis in economic science." [1]

The Nobel Prize Committee on Economic Science of the Royal Academy of Sciences consisting of Bertil Ohlin (Chairman), Assar Lindbeck, Erik Lundberg, Ingvar Svennilson and Herman Wold has said in the citation while awarding the Prize to Samuelson that "Samuelson's extensive production, covering nearly all areas of economic theory, is characterised by an outstanding ability to derive important new theorems, and to find new

---

* An introductory overview of the contributions of Professor Paul A. Samuelson by the Chief Editor.

[1] *The Nobel Memorial Prize in Economics 1970,* the official announcement of the Royal Academy of Sciences, The Swedish Journal of Economics, Vol. 72, No. 4, December 1970, p. 341.

applications for existing ones. By his many contributions, Samuelson has done more than any other contemporary economist to raise the level of scientific analysis in economic theory . . . His best-known work is his *Foundations of Economic Analysis*, 1947. In this work, as well as in a large number of articles, he has rewritten considerable parts of central economic theory, and has in several areas achieved results which now rank among the classical theorems of economics. Thus, he has contributed to an integration of statics and dynamics by way of his 'correspondence principle'; he has combined the multiplier and accelerator mechanisms in a model of economic fluctuations; he has reformed the foundations of consumption theory by his theory of 'revealed preferences'; he has developed and improved several important theorems within the theory of international trade, such as the 'factor equalisation theorem'; he has created a theory of inter-temporal efficiency and formulated the 'turnpike theorem', determining the highest possible growth rate, and, finally, he has clarified the role of collective goods in the theory of optimum allocation of resources". [2]

Samuelson's rise to the top of the economics profession was very rapid. Born in Gary, Indiana, U.S.A. in 1915, he attended the University of Chicago from which he secured his B.A. degree in 1935. He took his M.A. degree at Harvard University in 1936 and Ph.D. degree in the same University in 1941.

During the next 25 years, after his education he has virtually won every honour that the profession could offer. In 1947, when only 32, he was awarded the first John Bates Clark award for the most distinguished work by an economist under 40. From 1935 to 1940 he taught 'iconoclastic' economics at Harvard with the new wave of Keynesianism and monopolistic competition. He left the Harvard University in 1940 after the completion of his Ph.D. and moved to MIT. He was elected to the Society of Junior Fellows, a position which elevated him into the upper strata of academic circles in Cambridge. His work as a graduate student includes some of his best contributions to the field: three articles on the theory of consumer choice later were expanded into a new approach to that problem. It was a graduate student in Hansen's Seminar that he developed his contribution on the Multiplier-Accelerator Principle. During 1941, he won the David A. Wells award for the outstanding economics dissertation at Harvard. In 1947, it was published as "Foundations of Economic Analysis", a classic statement of the mathematical foundations

[2] *The Nobel Memorial Prize in Economics 1970*, the official announcement of the Royal Academy of Sciences, The Swedish Journal of Economics, Vol. 72, No. 4, December 1970, p.341.

of economic theorem. In an era, when academic promotion was generally slow, Samuelson became a full-fledged Professor at MIT when he was 32. Well before the finished his work at Harvard, it was clear that Samuelson was one of the brightest young economists in the United States. By the end of the 1940's, MIT ranked with the best departments in the country. In 1948, he published the text book "Economics: An Introductory Analysis" which has become world famous and has sold over 10 million copies. In 1958, he jointly published along with Robert Solow and Robert Dorfman "Linear Programming and Economic Analysis" a path-breaking work which examined the economic implications of the concept. Joseph Stiglitz, Students of Samuelson, Robert C. Merton, Hiroaki Nagatani and Kate Crowley have published "Collected Scientific Papers of Paul Samuelson" in five volumes wherein are included about 400 articles written by their professor. One of the most original areas of Samuelson's Foundations was his treatment of consumer welfare. He was able to bring some sort of unity and cohesion to seemingly unrelated and seemingly contradictory aspects of economics and gave them a mathematical under-pinning. It was for such work that the Swedish Academy of Sciences awarded him the 1970 Nobel Prize in Economics, noting that he has done "more than any other living economist to rise the level of scientific analysis in the field of economic theory". When the award was announced, he remarked that "they don't give Nobel Prizes for writing text books". Samuelson is a man of colourful personality know for his brilliant intellect and academic thrust. He is prolific in his contribution and master of the arts of both spoken and written English.

Samuelson has been active in a number of honorary and professional organisations. He is a member of the American Academy of Arts and Sciences, a fellow of the American Philosophical Society and the British Academy; he is a member, and past-president (1961) of the American Economic Association; he is a member of the editorial board, and past-president (1951) of the Econometric Society; he is a fellow; council member and past vice-president of the Economic Society. He is a member of Phi Beta Kappa.

Samuelson is recipient of a number of honorary degrees. They include LLD (Hon.), University of Chicago (1961); LLD (Hon.), Oberlin College (1961); D.Litt (Hon.), Ripon College (1962); LLD (Hon.), Boston College (1964); D.Sc. (Hon.), East Anglia University (1966); LLD (Hon.), Indiana University (1966); LLD (Hon.), University of Michigan (1967) and; LLD (Hon.), Claremont Graduate School (1970).

His contribution range over the most divine tracts as elucidated earlier ever covered by any economist, some esoteric and some on policy question. As he said in a presidential addres to the American Economic Association: "My own scholarship has covered a wide variety of fields. And many of them involve questions like welfare economics and factor-price equalization: turnpike theorem and oscillating envelops: non-substitutability relations ... balanced budget multipliers under conditions of balanced uncertainty". His stream of output is astounding for its quality, diversity, and its stimulating and seminal nature.

How Samuelson Became an Economist?

Paul A. Samuelson has described "how he became an economist?" in his article *My Life Philosophy: Policy Credos and Working Ways.*[3] Let us start from his own words: "Many economists — Alfred Marshall, Knut Wicksell, Leon Walras, . . . became economists, they tell us, to do good for the world. I became an economist quite by chance, primarily because the analysis was so interesting and easy — indeed so easy that at first I thought that there must be more to it than I was recognising, else why were my older classmates making such heavy weather over supply and demand? (How could an increased demand for wool help but lower the price of pork and beef?)

Although positivistic analysis of what the actual world is like commands and constrains my every move as an economist, there is never far from my consciousness a concern for the ethics of the outcome. Mine is a simple ideology that favours the underdog and (other things equal abhors inequality)." [4]

His parents were 'liberals'. As a young man, Samuelson wasn't sure that he wanted to do with his life. He was interested in all of the social sciences as well as most of the sciences, and he could have gone off in any of a dozen directions. But his choice of a college presented no problem; he would attend the University of Chicago, which was within walking distance of his home.

---

[3] Samuelson, Paul A., *My Life Philosophy: Policy Credos and Working Ways*, in Szenberg, Michael., *Eminent Economists: Their Life Philosophies*, Cambridge University Press, 1992, pp. 236-247.

[4] *Ibid.*, pp. 236.

The New Deal was about to begin. America was headed into a period of intense liberal reformism, one in which the tenets of free enterprise capitalism would come under heavy and continued attack. And at the height of this movement, Samuelson would study at the school which, then as now, was the citadel of laissez-faire economic thought.

"What Harvard was becoming for Keynesianism, Chicago already was for neo-classical economics. Frank Knight, a leading figure in the attack on Keynes, was a star of the economics department and in his prime. Jacob Viner, the conservative economic historian, made his contribution too, as did Henry Simon, who rehabiliated monetary theory and used it as a weapon against Alvin Hansen and his Harvard colleagues. These men were training the next generation of neo-classicists — Milton Friedman was at Chicago when Samuelson arrived, and so was George Stigler, whose dry wit would later make him one of the few economists capable of matching Galbraith in irony and metaphor . . . Samuelson came to the University with a deficiency in economics, and so he was enrolled in an introductory course taught by Aaron Director, perhaps the most libertarian member of the faculty—who later became Milton Friedman's brother-in-law and beside whom the more famous economist seemed almost a socialist. Director and others at Chicago challenged Samuelson's innate reformism at a time when it seemed the American economic system was cracking up and change was in the air. Samuelson enjoyed the clashes but did not become a believer. Rather, as the Hoover Administration appeared to founder, he drifted further into a Keynesian orbit. Thus, he was something of an intellectual loner as an undergraduate—and he seemed to enjoy this too . . . Through most of this period he was undecided as to his major and toyed with the idea of a career in sociology, biology, or anthropology. Given a stimulating teacher, Samuelson would become a temporary convert to the discipline, if not to an ideology. This would continue until he came across the next interesting person or subject, when the process would be repeated. Apparently Samuelson continued to do well in whatever he undertook, and he remained cocky and self-confident, no small accomplishment in the depths of the Great Depression . . . Toward the end of his stay at Chicago, Samuelson decided to become an economist."[5] Chicago was a central place for study of the Keynesian economics and

[5] Paul Samuelson, in Sobel, Robert, *The Worldly Economists*, The Free Press, 1980, pp. 96-97.

Samuelson very much liked the place. To quote him: "Chicago was a good place to learn economics at that time precisely because it was a stronghold of classical economics, a subject which had reached its culmination thirty years earlier in the work of Cambridge's Alfred Marshall. Economics itself was a sleeping princess waiting for the invigorating kiss of Maynard Keynes, and if one had to spend one's undergraduate days marking time before that event, Chicago was a better place to do so than would have been Harvard, Columbia, or the London School. Cambridge University was never within my ken, but since economics was also waiting for the invigorating kiss of mathematical methods, it would have been a personal tragedy if I had become merely a clever First in the Economics Tripos there."[6]

Samuelson was a positive scientist who was certain of the results of any of his doctrinaire. He was more circumspect when interpreting specific problems. John kenneth Galbraith and Samuelson were in agreement on many economic matters, they also used to differ in certain others. Both were followers of John Maynard Keynes. Samuelson climbed the academic ladder with ease, but Galbraith has struggled to write a lot. Galbraith's contributions to science of economics and applied economics with particular reference to United States and to the under developed nations in general are plenty. His "*The Affluent Society*" and "*The Age of Uncertainty*" are the masterpieces, but these two economists, as said earlier, were at opposite poles on policy matters at times. To quote: "These two also are at opposite poles within the profession, for they stand for different roles economists might play in our culture. Galbraith presents a model for those who hope to achieve celebrity and influence the thinking of the general public; more than anyone else, he has, made the subject intelligible to laypeople. As for Samuelson, he is one of a long line of scholars who have shown students the ways to achieve professional success, the esteem of their peers, and a distinguished if limited public role."[7]

Samuelson was very much concerned with inflation in the U.S. economy and many times, he has offered his solutions. It is an economic ill which cannot be got away with easily. It is interesting to quote from Samuelson himself: "Inflation is not like small pox which if you wipe out once would be

[6] Samuelson, Paul A., *Economics in a Golden Age: A Personal Memoir*, in Brown, cary E. and Solow, Robert M., Edited, *Paul Samuelson and Modern Economic Theory*, McGraw-Hill Book Company, 1983, p. 6.

[7] Paul Samuelson, in Sobel, Robert, *The Worldly Economists*, The Free Press, 1980, p. 104.

gone. It is like reducing your weight — you have to for the rest of your life keep to the same austere programme." [8]

'Foundations of Economic Analysis' and his Book on 'Economics'

The Nobel Prize for Samuelson was, of course, awarded for his varied contributions. But it was for his original work *Foundations of Economic* Analysis which won him the Doctorate in 1941 and was published in 1947, which also gave him the Nobel Prize. It is very interesting that in the introductory note to the 14th edition (1992) of '*Economics*', Samuelson has said that: "his *Foundations of Economic Analysis* won him the Nobel Prize in 1970, 25 years later after the book was ready". When he wrote his textbook on *Economics* in 1948, some economists had remarked that the textbook is not a research work. Samuelson was not upset by this remark and says: "Linus Pauling, so great a scholar and humanist that he was to win two Nobel Prizes, had already written a leading chemistry text just as the great Richard Feynman was later to publish classic physics lectures. William James had long since published his great *Principles of Psychology.* Richard Courant, top dog at Gottingen in Germany, had not been to proud to author an accurate textbook on calculus. Who was Paul Samuelson to throw stones at scholars like these? And, working the other side of the street, I thought it was high time that we got the leaders in economics back in the trenches of general education." [9]

He further says that the first edition of the textbook was published in the Autumn of 1948, but it is noteworthy that his 1947 publication, "*The Foundations of economic Analysis*", gets the Nobel Prize, the one authored an year earlier to his first edition of his textbook "*Economics*". This book, '*Economics*' has become so popular that, since 1948, it has been published 14 times and the 14th edition is a totally revised and enlarged edition and many places rewritten, to go with the current stream of economics. This book is a monopoly of the students of the economics all over the world. It is also worthy to note that this work of his has so far been translated into 40 languages in the world.

"His first edition of *Economics* put much stress on what might be called "*Model T Keynesian macro*". With each new edition, the emphasis

[8] Ravi, N., Washington quoted in *A Serious Problem but Not a Calamity*, The Hindu, March 30, 1980, p. 5.

on monetary policy grew. And with the worst wastes of the Great Depression banished, the micro-economics of efficient market pricing has come to occupy more and more of the text's pages."[10]

At times according to the Samuelson: "Economists are accused of not being able to make up their minds. In particular the brilliant John Maynard Keynes was accused of having volatile opinions. When a royal commission asked five economists for an opinion, it was said they would get six answers — two from Mr. Keynes. Keynes himself was quite unrepentant when pressed on the matter. He would say: 'When my information changes, I change my opinion. What do you do, Sir'? He did not want to be the stopped clock that is right only twice a day."[11]

Samuelson feels that his labour spent was more than rewarded and he feels happy that John Kenneth Galbraith was the first economist, who predicted in a magazine called '*Fortune*', for which he was an editor that the "next generation would learn its economics from the Samuelson *Economics*." Samuelson says "Praise is sweet in authors' ears, but I must confess that it was the durability of the book's dominance that surprised me. As Andy Warhol put it: we live in a time when anyone can be a celebrity for about 15 minutes. Galbraith turned out to be more prescient than I. *Economics* did set a new and lasting pattern. Most of its successful rivals are written in its general mode, and it is heartwarming that much of the competition has come from the pens of good personal friends."[12]

And so it went. Hard, hard work — but ever so rewarding. Finally, came the day when tennis beckoned. To McGraw Hill I said: "I have paid my dues. Let others carry on as I enjoy the good life of an emeritus professor, cultivating the researches that interest me most and letting revisions go hang".[13] It is sweet to note what Samuelson has said: "I cannot close without remarking that the day Freeman launched me on the adventure of writing a textbook for beginners in economics was the beginning of what has been sheer fun every mile of the way." [14]

---

[9] Samuelson, Paul A. and Nordhaus, William D., *Economics*, Fourteenth Edition, 1992, p.x.

[10] Samuelson, Paul A. and Nordhaus, William D., *Economics*, Fourteenth Edition, 1992, p. xiii.

[11] *Ibid.*, p. xiii.

[12] *Ibid.*, p. x-xi.

[13] *Ibid.*, p. xi.

[14] Samuelson, Paul A. and Nordhaus, William D., *Economics*, Fourteenth Edition, 1992, p. xiv.

It is interesting to quote Samuelson again: "The years passed. My hair turned from blond to brown. Then to grey. But like the portrait of Dorian Gray, which never grew old, the textbook *Economics* remained forever 21. Its cover turned from green to blue, and then to brown and black, and to many splendored hues. But helped by hundreds of letters and suggestions to the author from students and from professors with classroom experience, the economics inside the covers evolved and developed. A historian of mainstream — economic doctrines, like a paleontologist who studies the bones and fassils in different layers of earth, could date the ebb and flow of ideas by analysing how Edition I was revised to Edition 2 and, eventually, to Edition 14. Though out of context, it is opt to quote Samuelson to explain the need for revisions of textbooks to go with the time. "Like Tobacco Road, the old economics was strewn with rusty monstrosities of logic inherited from the past, its soil generated few stalks of vigorous new science, and the correspondence between the terrain of the real world and the maps of the economics textbooks and treatises was neither smooth nor even one-to-one".[15] He has done this task of revision very easily though with a co-author and a number of collaborators. Those who have commented and offered suggestions include William C. Brainard, E. Cary Brown, Robert J. Gordon, Lyle Gramley, Paul Joskow, Alfred Kahn, Richard Levin, Robert Litan, Barry Nalebuff, Merton J. Peck, Gustav Ranis, Paul Craig Roberts, Herbert Scarf, Robert M. Solow, James Tobin, Janet Yellen and Gary Yohe. Samuelson has acknowledged their help in his Preface to the 14th edition.

As said earlier, the Prize winning book the *Foundations of Economic Analysis* is a classic treatise of Paul A. Samuelson, which is also gone into several editions. First published in 1947, the totally rewritten, enlarged edition was published in 1983.[16] This edition contains a new introduction and the mathematical appendix contains a sampling of important trends in mathematical economics that are directly related to the concerns of this revised edition. The time-phased models of production are analysed, both in their Sraffa and Leontief mainstream economics versions and in their Karl Marx versions. The 'Introduction' gives the detailed analysis of the contributions to economics and the development theories for nearly four decades, since it was published in 1947. It is masterpiece in economic literature.

---

[15] Samuelson, Paul A., *Economics in My Time* in Breit, William and Spencer, Roger W., Edited, *Lives of Laureates—Ten Nobel Economists*, Second Edition, The MIT Press, 1990, p.59.

[16] Samuelson, Paul A., *Foundations of Economic Analysis*, enlarged edition, Harvard University Press, 1983.

Samuelson remarked that "Economics never was a dismal science. It should be a realistic Science". He is often disagreed with, particularly by Milton Friedman, the Chicago University Economist, who believes that monetary rather than fiscal policy should be the dominant guide for government officials. Friedman himself has said that "disagreement among economists on public policy seldom reflects a difference in economic analysis proper, but rather in judgement about quantitative magnitude, goals to be pursued, or the time span to be considered, or political considerations outside economics". "Professional economists", Friedman points out, "know, Paul Samuelson as a mathematical economist who has helped to reshape and improve the theoretical foundations of our subject. This is the work for which this remarkably versatile man won the Nobel Prize". But Samuelson is no ivory towered Theorist and he is firmly abhored to the practical economics of the problem, despite using analogies from physics and mathematics.

Samuelson is the first economist to advocate the use of mathematics as a means to explain and explore the economic problem. It could reveal aspects of economic theory which could not be seen by institution alone. Most economic problems are concerned with the maximisation and minimisation of some variables. If the basic behaviour is postulated as a mathematical problem, then one can derive important theorems by exploring the properties of this mathematical statement of the problem.

However, he cautions against the opinion that accomplished mathematics automatically results in elegant economics. Mathematical skills without sound economic reasoning are of no utility. The objective of Foundations was to purge economic reasoning of errors resulting from imprecisely formulated theorems, operationally meaningless. Thus empiricism is at the core of Samuelsonian theorisation. His writings combine mathematics with geometric and verbal clarity in such manner as to facilitate avenues of communication to readers not over familiar with rigorous mathematical analysis.

Samuelson's earliest work was devoted to examination of the basis of the theory of consumption demand. He was critical of ability theory and the ordinalist revision by Hicks and Alum. Both are unacceptable as they are based on non-observational concepts and proportions not justifiable empirically by observation. He revolutionised the theory of consumer behaviour by putting forward the theory of Revealed preference, also known as the Samuelson postulate. By comparing the costs of different combination of goods at different price situations, we can infer whether a given batch of goods is preferred to another batch. "If an individual selects batch one over batch two, he does not at the same time select two over one". The individual guineapig, by his market behaviour, reveals his preference pattern — if there is such a consistent pattern. The central notion underlying the theory of revealed preference, and indeed the whole modern economic theory of index numbers is very simple. The theory states that any commodity for which the demand is increased with an increase in real income and no change in relative prices would also find that the demand for itself has increased when its relative price alone falls. A positive income elasticity must connote negative price elasticity; the reverse may not be said. The theory as propounded by Samuelson has sought to bridge a link between studies in respect of elasticity and pure demand theory.

This theory spawned a vast body of literature with eminent participants —Arrow, Debreu, Houthakker, Hurwicz, among others, In later papers, Samuelson dwelt upon the complementarity function and integrability conditions, these refinements arising from the lacunae pointed out in critical appraisals of the postulate. Originally unwillingly, but later purposefully, he provided a more sophisticated base for the measurement of welfare and utility.

The cost of living index and similar measures of inflationary trends in the economy are based on the measures of price changes through index numbers. Such indices are supposed to reflect changes in welfare resulting from fluctuations in the aggregate level of prices. Samuelson points out that most of the discussion of index numbers involves the statistical theory of their construction; not the economic measuring of the resulting index. Using the logic behind revealed preference, he demonstrates that there will always be some bias which will make even the most ideal index number subject to such ambiguity. The comparative studies approach of these problems does not, of course, consider the dynamic adjustments involved in reaching the new equilibrium. In the second part of his book, Samuelson turns to the dynamics of income determination in the context of the newly emerging Keynesian econometric models. It is in this area that he developed his formulation of the multiplier-accelerator phenomenon with Alvin Hansen. By establishing a more formal mathematical model, Samuelson was able to show the reaction of the income to changes in investment with a variety of values for the parameters in the model. Despite his influence in the construction of mathematical models to explain the economic problem, Samuelson has remained largely apart from the growing trend to apply statistical tools of analysis to the analysis of the economy. In addition to his preferences for theory, Samuelson's reluctance to engage in empirical work also reflects his early skepticism regarding the ability of econometric models to predict future economic events. A system is dynamical if its behaviour over time is determined by functional equations in which variables at different points of time are involved in an essential way.

Samuelson emphasized that government plays an increasing role in the modern mixed economy. This is clear from the quantitative growth of Government expenditure, redistribution of income by the state and direct regulation of economic life. Much of this regulation is in the form of planning. The principal weapons used are monetary and fiscal policies. Samuelson in his article on "The Pure Theory of Public Expenditure" in 1954, sought to integrate the existing theory of taxation with the relatively unexplored equation of allocating government expenditures. His argument starts from a fundamental distinction between two types of goods, private consumption goods and public consumption goods. Public goods are those for which more consumption by one individual does not mean less consumption by another. Defence, radio, TV, are examples. Samuelson obtained the condition of optimality of public expenditure when public and private goods co-exist. The new area of public choice in the main discipline of public finance is the direct progeny of Samuelson's famous article cited in other works over 250 times.

Samuelson's construction of a "pseudo-market equilibrium" using an abstract mathematical model is another example of the way in which mathematics can explore beyond the boundaries of intuition. He points out that theorists have provided very little additional insight into the question of collective decisions which lie behind government expenditure. He has elaborated the criteria to justify the government action as:

1. Paternalistic policies voted upon themselves by the electorate because they felt the market solution was not optimal;

2. Redistribution of income;

3. Regulation of industries which exhibit Marshallian "increasing returns"; and

4. A "myriad" of externality situations where public and private interests diverge.

Samuelson's emphasis is on a consumption externality which arises from the government's offering of a good at no price to the public.

The responsibility of the government in maintaining aggregate stability is virtually unchallenged today. This has been the important problem of the post-Keynesian world. Some of the earlier economists have indicated that "money does matter". Samuelson turns them as "monetary fanatics" and said that money along matters. He rejects extreme positions and said "Personally, I prefer to stick to the middle road of good, strong value". His views on monetary policy clearly reflects the influence of Hansen's "Synthesis" of Keynes and neoclassical thought. "The primary weapon of monetary policy—open market operations by the Federal Reserve—affects of economy . . . by lowering or raising the spectrum of interest rates, thereby increasing or decreasing the flow of investment and durable goods spending, which in turn leads to expansion or contraction in the aggregate of GNP flow". He accepts the validity of what he terms a "Depression Keynes" model of the economy, where there is a liquidity trap which renders adjustment of aggregate demand through the money supply ineffective. This model may be a reasonable approximation of the real world in the short turn.

Montetary policy is a symmetrical in its impact on the economy. Monetary policy will be more effective both in restraining and expanding credit when interest rates are high, and less effective when they are low. He emphasizes the balance of monetary and fiscal policy. This balance is greatly increased by the fact the government now accounts for over a quarter of total output. The multiplier and accelerator have a substantial effect on demand. Some of this effect can be made "automatic" through built-in fiscal stabilisers which counteract cyclical fluctuations in demand without any specific policy directives. The government should check these aspects. These policies must be formulated to employ monetary fiscal policy to both curtail and stimulate demand.

Taxes shift resources from private to public uses. Samuelson formulated a coherent theory of optimal resource allocation to public goods and optimal tax burden distribution. Since fiscal and monetary policies may have varied and conflicting effects both in quantitative and qualitative terms, an optimal mix is necessary. It would be absurd to set fiscal policy 'rules' in a dynamic setting. Public thrift could supplement private thrift by credit availability at low cost and austere fiscal policies so that capital formation can be enhanced. He vindicated neo-classical economics thus: "The neoclassical synthesis can banish the paradoxical possibility of thrift becoming abortive and can, in this sense, validate the classical notions covering capital formation and productivity". With low interest rates, monetary policy can act as an impetus towards long-term capital deepening.

Samuelson has emphasized the problem of inflation. Inflation occurred whenever the sum of consumption, investment, and government expenditures exceeded the full employment capacity of production. Samuelson regards the Phillips Curve as an important concept in the formation of modern policy. As long as aggregate demand is less than the full employment level, there is no pressure on prices. When the economy reaches full employment, when unemployment is 3 percent, idle resources have been employed and further expansion of demand will rapidly generate inflation without a reduction in the level of unemployment. Samuelson argues that to combat unemployment without inflation requires a moving of the Phillips curve. Samuelson became an advocate of a tax increase to stem from inflationary pressures from government expenditures.

Samuelson's approach to welfare economics has become part of the central core of economic theory. His analysis of the welfare interpretation of the concept of national income was fruitful. The further contributions in this field are utility-possibility frontier and the confrontation of this concept with Bergsonian Social Indifference maps for determining social optimum positions.

In the area of the theory of production, Samuelson's contributions are multi-faceted. He developed the concepts of surrogate production formation and factor-price frontier, for a constant-returns-to-scale production function using capital and labour, a technical relationship prevails between the factor prices of the rental and the wage. The scope of the relationship is the capital-labour ratio. A number of economists like Arrow, Chenery, Minhas, Solow (ACMS) and others followed up these concepts in subsequent seminal articles. He also provided the first explanation of the features of the cost function as the minimum total cost of inputs to achieve a targeted output, where the input-output relationship is shown through a production function.

Another important aspect for which Samuelson is well known pertains to the logical basis of the Leontief type input-output structure. In a world in which land and capital exist as scarce factors as say in the diminishing returns model of Ricardo or the variable-production period-length model of Boham-Bawerk, the non-substitution theorem does not hold.

In his article on "Linear Programming and Economic Analysis" written along with Solow emerged with an extremely important theorem in the pure theory of normative or optimal growth.

With regard to trade cycle theory, Samuelson worked out how income propagation would fare through time under varying sets of values of the propensity to consume and the acceleration co-efficient. He emerged with the fact that for some sets of values one exogenous shock would suffice to produce a perpetual periodicity in the cyclical model, one, therefore, need not have to resort to notions of a ceiling and a floor to explain the turning points.

Business cycle theory was constructed from two simple linear difference operations: one relates consumption to lagged income and the other hypothizes that investment is proportional to the change in consumption.

The concept of Gross National Product is now being replaced by what the Japanese have christened Gross National Welfare. The highest priority should now be given to social and economic justice, which is beginning to be seen as a verifiable input for economic growth, not only for social contentment and political stability.

Samuelson emphasized that within the advanced countries them-selves, the scene was drastically changed from the Victorian days to Laissez-faire capitalism. Capitalism had been evolving into a mixed economy with both private and public initiative and control. Following World War-II, gradually the "New Economics of the modern mixed economy" trumpeted in advance by no ideology, began to take over. At the one extreme are the anarchists, who believe in no government at all, at the other, the apologists for an all powerful, collectivised, totalitarian, communistic social order.

Today we find that many economies may be subject to the disorder of creeping inflation. Full employment and price stability are then apparently incompatible goals. When a populistic mixed economy is running badly, experiencing both inflation and unemployment at the same time, there will be disorder.

In international trade theory, Samuelson along with Stolper propounded the famous factor-price equalisation theorem which was an advance over the Heckscher-Ohlin and earlier theories on trade. The Stolper-Samuelson theorem, using general equilibrium analysis and postulating several conditions, showed that labour is hurt by tariff reduction on labour-intensive imports. Free trade equalizes international factor prices with no factor-intensity reversals. Rewards to factor will be equalized even if they are immobile domestically. Given product prices, factor prices are determined independently of factor supply. This result has had considerable significance in trade and general equilibrium theory. The Samuelson-Rybczynski theorem postulates that a rise in population raises the output of the labour-intensive product. He also clarified the transfer problem of Keynes and Ohlin. In 1977, he published a paper with Dornbusch and Fisher on the product mix of traded goods, again blazing a pioneering trail.

Samuelson points out the favourable features of the mixed economy thus: "the mixed economy is mixed. That is its strength . . . the market can be a strong horse under us. But every horse has its limits." Markets are more effective than five-years plans and a series of commands. The useful features of the market should be preserved. At the same time, public intervention is justified for social ends like the prevention of pollution and mitigation of poverty. "Economists", he says, "need to put their cool heads to the service of their warm hearts".

Students

Samuelson's contributions are not merely confined to what he writes by himself or jointly with others. He has produced a galaxy of internationally distinguished students who have carried his insights and apparatus forward. It is largely[17] because of the leadership of Samuelson that M.I.T. today ranks among the foremost of the economist-breederies in the world. His achievement

[17] Pages 201-211 are based on Brahmananda, P.R., *Economics of Paul Anthony Samuelson*, Indian Economic Journal, Vol. 18, No. 2, Oct.-Dec.1970, pp. 251-269. (Summarised with permission of author).

in this respect parallels that of Alfred Marshall of Cambridge (U.K.) around the turn of this century. When the late President Kennedy invited to join him in Washington, Samuelson refused and stuck to M.I.T. But he helped Kennedy as a 'winged' consultant.

Legends

Hardly has any U.S. economist received the adulation and even 'lionizing' that Paul Samuelson has received and receives. Nearly two decades ago, 'Fortune' acclaimed Samuelson as the 'liberator' of U.S. economics from the influence of English economics. Recently at an Econometric convention in Cambridge (U.K.) Samuelson was introduced to the audience as the greatest of the Cambridge economists! Samuelson declined the honour and termed Frank Ramsey, the brilliant mathematical prodigy of Cambridge (U.K.) who died before he was thirty as the greatest Cambridge (U.K.) economist.

Public Postures

In recent years, through his lectures, tape-recorded observations, newspaper articles Samuelson has obtained a public image in the U.S.A. (and in the financial world). It appears he has opposed the draft and argued for a disengagement of the American forces from Vietnam. In a country where the threat of persecution of intellectuals hangs like a damocles' sword, Samuelson's postures require enormous moral courage, a trait so characteristic of some of the very great scientists of the world.

The Inside View

Within the profession, Samuelson is known for a wide range of contributions to almost all aspects of pure theory. For example, in demand theory, he is known for pioneering the revealed preference approach, which in a way, has pedagogically supplanted the indifference approach. In capital and production theory, he is known for the concepts of the surrogate production function and of the factor-price frontier. In value theory, he is known for the elucidation of the non-substitution theorem. In growth theory he, along with Solow, worked out the properties of the neumann-type equi-proportionately expanding economy. In normative growth theory, he and Solow are renowned for the analytically disturbing conjecture of the turnpike theorem. In trade theory, he along with Stolper is known for the demonstration of the adverse effects of trade on real wages in a relatively capital intensive economy. The theorem of factor price equalization which Samuelson drew from the results of the studies by Heckscher and Ohlin has embellished pure trade theory. In welfare economics, Samuelson is known for the notion of the utility-possibility-frontier and for the application of Paretian welfare analysis to gains from trade.

Samuelson, very much in the tradition of Schumpeter, has contributed doctrinal appraisals on Ricardo, Marx, Wicksell, Keynes, Schumpeter, Robertson, and Lerner. He has an impressive share in the world of modern class room diagrams in economic analysis.

THEOREMS

The citation on Samuelson, known as modern 'Walras' referred to the theorems formulated or reformulated by him. In what follows, we shall touch upon his most prominent theorems.

Revealed Preference

Samuelson's earliest work was devoted to the examination of the theory of consumption demand. Along with Nicholas Georgescue-Roegen, Houthakker, Little and Hicks, he has developed over a period of years what is known as the 'Revealed Preference Approach'. No one can doubt the pioneering nature of Samuelson's contributions in this sphere. From the beginning, Samuelson has been trying to relate demand theory to empiricism. This requires minimum of dependence upon psychological postulates and the formulation of the demand law in such a manner as can be refuted by empirical data. The Hicksian indifference approach does not stand up to this requirement. Marshall's formulation left the theory in an eclectic state as he had to provide for the exceptions to the law of demand. Sir Robert Giffen had noted that in the case of poorer classes, a fall in the price of bread led to a diminution in their purchases of bread and to an increase in the quantity of meat demanded. Hicks explained this on the score that a fall in the price of bread led to so large an increase in real income that the poorer classes are in a position to buy meat and more of it in comparison to bread. The income effect swamped the substitution effect. In reality, we can observe neither the income effect of price changes nor the substitution effect. The revealed preference theory states simply that any commodity for which the demand is increased with an increase in real income and no change in relative prices would also find that the demand for itself increases when its (relative) price alone falls. Of course there are some assumptions. The law as formulated by Samuelson has bridged the link between studies in respect of income elasticity and demand theory. The full benefit of Samuelson's contribution has been reaped by Sir John Hicks who has taken the theory "forwards" and made it more elaborate.

Exit Walras

In its present form, the revealed preference approach has robbed the pure theory of demand of its link with the general equilibrium theory of Walras (and Pareto). In the latter case, the demand theory was a part of the general equilibrium theory of consumption, production, and distribution. In Walrasian general equilibrium by disturbing even a flower we can upset a star. The revealed approach can apply only to groups of consumers and not to the general economy; for, in the Walrasian static equilibrium no change in the real income of the whole system is postulated, for that would lead to dynamics. It is in Marshall that the revealed preference type of approach fulfils itself, for there we are concerned with groups and partial equilibrium states. Looked at thus, as Marshall has no general equilibrium link between demand theory, production, and distribution, he can and does conceive of relative price changes due to increasing and diminishing returns, such changes also implying changes in real income, of classes and of the community. Hicks in his Indifference Theory put demand into a strait jacket; Samuelson has liberated it but in the process has completely snapped the link between demand and general equilibrium, between Samuelson and Walras! When correctly appreciated the Samuelsonian refinements land him safely into the heart of the Marshallian analytical world.

To Marshall

But then, why should one quail against cardinality and interpersonal distributions. As Nicholas Georgescue-Roegen has cogently argued, demand theory can be approached in terms of a framework of a hierarchy of wants. Within each structure each want is irreducible. This type of approach strengthens the notion of utility as a tree and takes one further on towards Marshall with his classification of commodities into necessities, comforts, and luxuries; it also strengthens Piero Sraffa's distinction, between basic and non-basic goods. One thing is clear; the works of Samuelson, Nicholas Georgescue-Roegen, Strotz, Sraffa and of some others are taking demand theory away and away from Walras and nearer and nearer to Marshall.

Equalizing Factor-Prices

It was well known that trade would improve the well-being of each of the trading countries; but it was left for Samuelson to apply Paretian Welfare analysis technique and to prove the welfare-superiority of a trading situation to a non-trading situation. In this context, Samuelson drew upon on earlier insight of Heckscher and Ohlin to show that under standard neo-classical assumptions, trade in goods would be a proxy for trade in factors and the effect would be to equalize the relative factor-price ratios of both the countries. This is known as the factor-price equalization theorem. Its validity depends upon the relatively more capital-intensive country exporting more capital-intensive goods and importing more labour-intensive goods and the relatively more labour-intensive country exporting more labour-intensive goods and importing more capital-intensive goods. The relative price of the surplus factor in each country would go up and that of the scarce factor in each country would go down. This led Samuelson on to the theorem in the capital-intensive economy the wage-rate would tend to be depressed as a result of trade. It was natural that labour in a country like the U.S.A. should support protectionist policies.

Rewards Not Prices

The stringent assumptions under which the factor-price equalization theory can be established rob the proposition of any empirical relevance. But a more serious theoretical objection is about the validity of the link between abundance or scarcity of factors and the factor-intensification of the economies in terms of the more abundant or scarce factor. Samuelson has himself admitted that there is no valid basis for the hierarchical ordering of techniques or methods of goods so as to cause a relatively greater capital-intensity in the economy with more of capital and a greater labour-intensity in that with more of labour. The so-called Leontief paradox is a commonplace result when we deal with the disorderly impact of differences and changes in distribution upon the prices of goods, particularly of capital goods and services of technically trained labour grades. The validity of all trade theorems of Samuelson depends upon the validity and adequacy of the system of neo-classical economics. Some of the distinguished students of Samuelson like Bruno, Burmeister and Shishinki appear to be aware of the absence of any basis on which the concept of derived demand for factors can be erected.

Abstract Capital

Samuelson's contributions in capital theory are largely a reworking of the significance of the concept of abstract capital as first propounded by J.B. Clark nearly five decades earlier. J.B. Clark was prone to treat capital as a jelly like substance, a homogeneous pool of productive services embedded in concrete goods treated in the heterogeneous complex of goods known as capital which would change its form without losing the substance of productive power. Clark's concept was in direct contrast to the time sequenced structural relationship among goods termed as capital by Bohm-Bawerk. Samuelson's efforts to bridge the great gulf between the two approaches must be deemed as a failure. Neither the surrogate production function notion nor the factor-price-frontier can be deemed as analytically sustainable. Either we have to postulate that all goods have the same time-sequence of the relation between goods and labour or we must have an independent basis to measure capital, a basis independent of wages and interest, i.e. of factor-prices. The parable of J.B. Clark can hold only when all commodities are exactly similar in their time-structure relations, and which we must be capable of measuring without reference to prices, these measures being unaffected by differences and changes in wages and interest.

A Blind Alley

The alternative is to accept the approach of Bohm-Bawerk with its emphasis upon heterogeneity in the time-structure of goods. For Samuelson's to adopt this line of thinking would be to expose his analysis to the full-significance of the disorderly and non-predictable-in-advance ways in which the relative prices of individual goods are affected by differences and changes in wages and interest. It has been demonstrated by the critics of Samuelson that the very notion of factor-reward rates as scarcity-symbolising prices is a myth. Once again, Samuelson's approach lands him — or his followers — into a blind alley.

The Non-substitution Theorem

The third important theorem for which Samuelson is well known pertains to the logical basis of the Leontief type input-output structure. The Leontief type matrices can help in ascertaining of direct and indirect flow-input requirements for the production of defined quantities of any given commodity or commodities-mix. Can the Leontief-structure unravel the flow implications of shifts in the pattern of relative demand? In seeking an answer to this query. Samuelson and Nicholas Georgescue-Roegen emerged with the non-substitution theorem. If labour, undifferentiated, homogeneous, is the only scarce factor and constant returns to scale (of outputs) in each industry is assumed, relative demand shifts can be deemed to have no effects on relative prices. This theorem has important implications for the use of the Leontief type tables in applied analysis. One can now concentrate only on the scale effects of output changes and forget the effect on proportions. Samuelson noted that this interpretation of the Leontief-tables led one to a version of the labour theory of value, where the values of all commodities can be reduced to the cost in terms of labour-years. It is in this sense that Samuelson is supposed to have established a link between a supposed angle on Marx and Leontief. Samuelson himself has noted that in a world in which land and capital exist as scarce factors as say in the diminishing returns model of Ricardo or the variable production period-length model of Bohm-Bawerk, the non-substitution theorem does not hold.

Fixed Coefficients

Leontief has himself stated that his system depends upon the assumption of fixed coefficients. Technologically constant returns may rule but if land or 'capital' is deemed scarce and a choice of techniques problem exists, we have to rule out also scarcity in land and/or 'capital'. Thus fixed coefficients have to obtain both technologically and operationally. Is this enough?

Organic Composition of Capital

We don't think so. For if the different outputs in the Leontief system have differing ratios of values of direct and indirect means of production to labour the Leontief system is subject to two sorts of disturbances when there is an alteration in the distribution-mix. Relative prices change and become different; secondly, a different technical structure may be deemed more economically efficient, sectorally or globally with a different distribution-mix. There is no clue as to the direction of price changes nor to the nature of the structural alternations. Relative demand shifts must therefore not imply alternations in relative prices and hence in the commodity-wage; if this occurs, the system may have to switch over to a different technical structure.

Between Cup and Lip

There are many theoretical hurdles before we can sanction the use of the Leontief tables for applied purposes The system is unstable for alternative demand configurations and for alternative distribution mixes. To overcome the hurdles we have to assume (a) technologically fixed coefficients; (b) no scarce factors other than labour; (c) similarity in the ratios of means of production to labour in all industries. If (c) is not satisfied, we have to assume alternatively that demand shifts do not disturb the commodity wage and the labour supply and the labour demand relations.

No Marginal Productivity

The ideal case for the application of the Leontief matrices occurs when neither the wage rate nor the interest rate are determined on marginal productivity considerations, there are no supply prices of labour and of savings, and the different industries have the same ratio of means of production to labour. These are mostly similar to the properties of von Neumann system of equi-proportionately and maximally expanding economy. Of course von Neumann does not need the assumption of similarity in the means of production-ratios, as his model has the same rate of expansion year by year and the commodity wage rate is invariant through time. It may be pointed out that Leontief himself has expressed belief in the marginal productivity theory of distribution, along Walrasian lines. Samuelson himself also shares this belief. It would therefore appear that even making all the required assumptions, the non-substitution theorem cannot be of much help to justify the empirical feasibility of the Leontief system, particularly to the contemporary world. The problem is not one of the level of disaggregation but of inherent heterogeneity in the time-sequence of production of different commodities. This raises in addition the problem of the choice of an appropriate numeraire, an issue which does not appear to have been faced either by Leontief or Samuelson.

Balanced Growth and the Turnpike

We have made a reference earlier to the pioneering work of Samuelson and Solow in the elucidation of the properties of Balanced and Equi-proportionate Growth. In "Linear Programming and Economist Analysis" Samuelson and Solow emerged with an extremely important theorem in the pure theory of normative or optimal growth. The von Neumann model of an expanding economy manifests maximum growth through time. Any economy in any actual state would not be manifesting maximal growth. But if an economy wants over a very long period to augment its stock of capital assets by say, a given (large) extent, assuming no natural scarcities, a labour supply which is perfectly elastic at even a subsistence wage and no changes in technology, the above economy, if it has no economise on the time taken to attain the new capital stock situation, would find it convenient to convert itself into a von Neumann type model over at least some duration of time. This result known as a 'Turnpike Theorem' has been the subject of great deal of mathematical debate. There are now a number of Turnpike theorems. Samuelson and Solow must be credited with the pioneering work in this respect, though Samuelson himself has paid some more attention to this type of analysis in recent years. It would be fair to say that, others like Morishima, Radner, Nikkaido and Mckenzie have stolen a leap over Samuelson. It would be admitted on all quarters that even if the Turnpike conjecture can be proved to be valid, its operational significance would be limited in a dynamic world; more than anything else loom large issues of a proper choice of numeraire and the largely unknowable nature of the price vectors when growth rates are getting altered. Of course one has to reckon with dynamic changes like those in technology. An investigation that was conducted in regard to Russian growth during the crucial plan stages does not lend empirical support to the turn conjecture.

Trade Cycle Theory

For a long time it was believed that trade cycles are caused by periodic exogenous disturbances in the form of innovations or investment-bunches. Kahn and Keynes introduced the concept of the multiplier in economic analysis. J.M. Clark and Frisch among others, had introduced the concept of business acceleration earlier. It was left for Haberler and Hansen to bring about a fusion of these concepts. Under the acknowledged guidance of Hansen, Samuelson worked out how income propagation would fare through time under varying sets of values of the propensity to consume and the acceleration coefficient. He emerged with the demonstration that for some sets of values one exogenous shock would suffice to produce a perpetual periodicity in the cyclical model; one therefore need not have to resort to notions of a ceiling and a floor to explain the turning points. It was left for Hicks again to profit from the Samuelson insight and to build to a model of a trade cycle in a growing economy though Hicks chose those sets of values which would tend to lead to an explosive growth. He introduced ceilings and floors to explain the turning points.

The End Not Yet

In appraising Samuelson's contributions one must remember that he is both an economist and a mathematician. He is not just a mathematically trained economist. No wonder that abstract problems fascinate him. He would keep an open mind on any possibility that can be revealed by techniques of analysis. This should make him react more favourably to an agnostic view of the pure theory of economics. Such an agnostic view implies no faith in equilibrium and no support to the optimal nature of any existing state of affairs, and in fact no basis for the view point that any criteria for optimality can be discovered. Economics at the deepest and the highest levels makes one very humble; and as Schumpeter pointed out, "no link can be established between the politician and the pure economist". Yet it is a tragedy that most theorists in the U.S. and elsewhere should have considered him to be the modern high priest of the neo-classical, Walrasian general equilibrium version of the economic world. Samuelson's students more than Samuelson himself should be blamed for this. One cannot be both a God and an iconoclast at the same time.

Kenneth J. Arrow in a review article of Paul Anthony Samuelson's collected papers has made the following, far reaching but hardly controversial statement. "Samuelson is one of the greatest economic theorists of all time". (Samuelson's Collected Journal of Political Economy", p. 735) what then, are Samuelson's main contributions to economic science? Generally speaking, Samuelson's basic achievement during recent decades is that more than any one else he has helped raise the general analytical and methodological level of central economic theory. It is almost impossible to work in any area of central economic theory today without having to study very carefully one or several works of Paul Samuelson. Thus, as said earlier, that Paul Anthony Samuelson was awarded the first prize in economic science in honour of Alfred Nobel is hardly any surprise"[18] Samuelson has demonstrated, probably more than any one else the advantages of strict formulation, partly by way of mathematical methods,

[18] Lindbeck Assar, Paul Anthony Samuelson's Contribution to Economics, the *Swedish Journal of Economics*, Vol.72, 1970, No.4, December, pp. 342-343.

in economic analysis. He has not been satisfied by merely showing that a problem can be given a *mathematical* foundation; he has with extraordinary skill extracted the most essential theorems and implication from the assumptions, underlying his models. He also belongs to the group of economists who introduced a systematic approach to economic theory, already in his early writings on consumer theory.[19] "The death of Keynes in 1946 marked the end of the era of British supremacy in economic thought an era stretching back to Adam Smith. The inheritance passed to the United States of America and the mantle descended upon Samuelson. Thus the passing of one great Cambridge economist was accompanied by the emergence of another, for Cambridge, Massachusetts has been the intellectual home of Samuelson.

In general, in appraising Samuelson's contributions one must remember that he is both an economist and a mathematician. He is of the opinion that "economics has been getting more technical. Often that means more mathematical. From the standpoint of ultimate research at the frontier, that is probably inevitable and perhaps a good thing". He further feels that the family of economists in the world is likely to be in the danger of losing its audience as most of them are "never going to be research economists. Even those who major in Economics in college will, for the most part, go into business law or government. Such people are often allergic to mathematics and high powered statistics". Hence, statistics and mathematics should play a role in economics. There should be plenty of emphasis on principles and analysis and the students should be taught in logical reasoning. He, however, feels that mathematics should be introduced only after the students have the necessary grip on the fundamentals in economics. Samuelson has a great public image not only in United States, but in the entire world. Through his books and articles, he has impressed the world much more than any other economist of the day. He richly deserves the award for his contributions in the field of economics.

"Superlative" is the word used by Martin Bron Fendreane to describe Samuelson. This expression sums up his entire philosophy, 'par excellence'. He is a great teacher of economics with a sustained impact in very divine areas. Yet, he instills in modesty about its use.

---

[19] *Op. cit., p. 352*

The award of the Nobel Prize in Economic Science to Paul Anthony Samuelson of the Massachusetts Institute of Technology is thus not a matter of surprise to economists. Samuelson's academic achievements are taken for granted in the profession.

Robert M. Solow and E. Cary Brown have described Samuelson thus: "As a companion, Paul is simply superb. His conversational and writing styles ... vivid figures of speech, extensive historical references, illuminating comparative situations or ideas. He loves to improve on conventional wisdom by rephrasing, sometimes standing it on its head. For example: 'The exception that improves the rule'. It was only the creation of a little world, though it reached through all of economics."[20]

[20] Brown, Cary E. and Solow, Robert M., Edited, *Paul Samuelson and Modern Economic theory*, McGraw-Hill Book Company, 1983, p. xiii.

AN ESSAY ON THE ACCURACY OF ECONOMIC PREDICTION

*L.R. Klein**

ABSTRACT

Economists and other users of economic information have been dissatisfied with the precision of economic forecasts. It is inherently difficult to make usable economic forecasts for guidance to decision makers. In this essay, the present state of economic forecasting is considered, in the light of some important past events that required the use of attempts to look ahead — often in a phase of postwar planning, such as the situation that prevailed after World War II or in similar episodes that confronted US analysts who were responsible for forecasting the economy in a significantly changed environment. This paper is offered as an attempt to build on past efforts, but to look ahead by drawing on the latest developments in information technology — to harness the power of the computer, access the enlarged flow of economic information, and to process the flow with very quick response. It is felt that definite improvements in accuracy can be attained, not by an order of magnitude but by a few percentage points at a time.

CONCEPTUAL ISSUES

My first professional assignment after receiving a doctorate in economics was to forecast the prospects and needs of the United States economy in

* Department of Economics, University of Pennsylvania, Philadelphia, USA.

Dedicated research by Ju Yong Park and John Schindler has been of extreme importance in building and maintaining the high-frequency forecasting system for the USA. Weekly projections of the high-frequency model and the meaningful interpretation of results have been their responsibilities for several years, going back to the beginning of this decade.

The new thrusts into development of systems for Hong Kong and Mexico have been managed expertly by Dr. Chi-shing Chan and Dr. Alan K.F. Siu of the Hong Kong Centre for Economic Research, Hong Kong University and by Lic. Alfredo Couti-oof CIEMEX-WEFA.

conversion from War to Peace. This stood as an overwhelming objective, but the assignment was also methodological, namely to use, and thereby test, the new method of macroeconometric model building then being developed, for attacking the objectives.

The attitude then among some leading econometricians, was very optimistic that careful preparation of models, blending economic analysis (theory), with mathematical statistics, and mathematical specification of models would prove to be a powerful tool of policy formation and forecasting. Although policy formation was the stated objective for postwar economic planning, in a period of reconversion, there would be need for economic forecasting in order to implement policy programs.

Central topics of discussion were: 1. Would the postwar economy of the US return to the stage of the Great Depression that prevailed at the outbreak of the war? 2. Would American households be strongly influenced in satisfying their pent-up demands by their holdings of accumulated liquid assets? 3. Would there be strong and sustained inflationary pressure after the relaxation (or breakdown) of wartime price controls?

To answer these questions it became immediately apparent that the first step in model application would have to be the preparation of forecasts. Efforts at economic prediction were deemed to be unavoidable, except for an opposing view at the University of Chicago, where we econometricians were working together at the Cowles Commission, that there would be no problems of policy formation or need for forecasts if the economy were totally deregulated to the point of allowing markets to work freely in allocation of resources but with a steady hand from the Federal Reserve over the expansion of monetary aggregates to produce a stable price level.

The performance of economic forecasters was not good in the interwar period. Although there were some perceptive analyses, the successful business-cycle analysts did not prepare forecasts from quantitative systems, and there were notable failures of formal systems. The mathematical versions of the Keynesian system were in fashion and used to study properties of the great Depression but were not in use for advance forecasts. Several rudimentary versions were reported at academic conferences but were mainly not very optimistic about the postwar world that was about to unfold. Generally speaking, systematic economic forecasting was not held in high esteem and not able to show a favorable "track record".

This is the point at which formal models of the macroeconomy were introduced and used regularly in economic forecasting in addition to analysis of business cycles, and scenario studies. Once, the bulk of the poorly performing model forecasts had been disposed of and replaced by careful implementation of more comprehensive estimated models, a moderately favorable attitude developed and won support among several research groups, mainly in the United States, but also in the Netherlands, UK, and Canada.

Other approaches to forecasting by systematic application of quantitative methods also were developed, especially in the business cycle studies of the National Bureau of Economic Research. By and large, mathematical specification and formal techniques of mathematical statistics were eschewed at the NBER. The approach used was to construct indicators (leading, coincident, and lagging time series) among hundreds in the data files of the NBER. The emphasis was on forecasting *direction* of movement, and not its quantitative magnitude. Interwar studies by descriptive statistical analysis of time series at Harvard had been tried and abandoned.

The initial forecasting systems through the use of econometric models were mainly (but not entirely) stimulated by the interest in the Keynesian system of macroeconomics, and had several successes, from the first group of post war (II) predictions and many subsequent applications in the Korean war and the Vietnam War. In this period of the 1950s and 1960s there were many users of the models that were developed. The users were governments, large corporations, and international organizations. The forecasts that were generated had wide following for regular periodic replications. Also, there were many simulation studies of economic policies, or interesting scenarios.

Naturally there were errors, for these were *statistical* systems based on probability theory and always subject to statistical error. At first, the errors seemed quite small to the user community, and there was a readiness to use the forecasts in planning and policy formation. The errors were far smaller than we had anticipated, at the start of this kind of research activity in the United States, in the mid 1940s, thinking about the postwar world ahead. Gradually, however, demands for accuracy became more exacting and demanding.

The number of forecasts has been increasing; there are more users; but growth in forecasting of economic activity has slowed and other econometric approaches are being used, mainly statistical time series analysis, in a sense a formal mathematical treatment in place of the original NBER formulations, but without much use of economic theory for guidance. Also there are more informal judgmental approaches being used. Forecasting is as necessary and as important as ever, but is not attracting the same degree of scholarly interest and is not held in as high esteem as during its most expansive period in the decades of the 1950s and 1960s. There is general dissatisfaction with the degree of accuracy that has been attained, yet there are few promising attempts to improve the degree of accuracy. The most popular of new methods, the exploitation of time series properties of economic data, have achieved no promising lines of accuracy improvement. In fact the mathematical extension of the NBER approach, to find *leading indicators* through time series analysis, failed in its attempt to assess the 1990-91 recession.

TYPES OF ECONOMIC FORECASTS

Forecasts can be qualitative as well as quantitative, but the real needs for forecasts, are for systematic, quantitative forecasts. If possible, they should be *objective*, *non-doctrinal*, and, most of all, *replicable*. Another term, which is implied by the principle of *replicability* is *transparency*. They must be generated from systems that others can understand and appreciate. With enough mental effort, they should be capable of being generated by qualified scholar-practitioners and testable. In order to achieve these goals, the forecasts should be done by *transparent* methods that use information that is, in principal, based on available data. Of course anyone is free to generate forecasts, but in order to be convincing and useful to the world, they must be *replicable* or *transparent*.

Forecasts can be short, medium, or long. Reference, here, is to the length of the forecast horizon. List us say that some economic variable is to be extrapolated from the present (where the value may be observed) to the future.

y_t = initial value of y_t, observed

y_{t+F} = forecast value of y_t at time point t+F; the horizon is t+F, and the length of the forecast is F.

For values of F, less than 12 months, we characterize the forecast as short term. For values of F between 1.0 and 5.0 years, the forecast is intermediate. A long-term forecast covers a horizon span of 5 to 10 years.

There is interest in forecasts over very long horizons, say 10.0 to 50.0 years in length. In a strict sense that horizon may be beyond the scope of formal forecasting. In many industries and for much official planning it is necessary to try to look ahead that far into the future, but it is really outside the scope of systematic, careful forecasting or extrapolation.

In demography, nation building, or even fixed capital formation, one must try to look that far ahead, but such an issue must be approached from a judgmental point of view and not from the viewpoint of formal, objective forecasting.

In order to deal with distant objectives it may be preferable to discount values back to the present as in

$$y^*_{t+50} = \frac{y_{t+50}}{(1+r)^{50}}, \qquad (1)$$

where r is an average rate of discount of the future.

A primary reason for discounting long-term forecasts back to present values is that uncertainty surrounding forecasts should grow as the forecast target has a longer and longer horizon. The inputs are uncertain, the stochastic error variances are more uncertain, and the magnitudes of the economy tend to grow as a result of (unknown) technical change.[1]

For example, the performance and *cost* of nuclear energy facilities was thought, in the late 1940s and 1950s, to have an exceedingly bright future for producing abundant, inexpensive energy — *even to move mountains*. For a wide variety of reasons this has not been the case. Forecasts of the general economy and of nuclear power supply had to be projected far into the future, given the nature of the investment and the expected product flow. If we think about present usage of nuclear power and what was expected in the

---

[1] There is a contrary view that it is easier and more accurate to forecast far ahead than in the very near future. I strongly disagree with this view, which might be drawing upon equilibrium theory, but we are not trying to forecast equilibrium values; we aim at realistic occurrences, and economic conditions are rarely, if ever, in equilibrium.

early years of knowledge about this product, it is evident that there was a very large forecast error. A good estimate of the error variance, if appropriately made at the starting point would have been extremely large — so large as to give little guidance to project planners. A discussion of the calculation of standard error of forecast, over a long horizon, for such decisions about capital formation in the nuclear energy sector could have been made much more meaningful if done in present value terms, i.e. the error variance at project planning time would have been confined to a much smaller range of values that would have confronted the decision makers. Without saying whether or not the variance would have been in a project-go-ahead-range or a project-cancel range, it would at least have been comprehensible.

Much would depend on the discount rate (r) that was used, but, of course, it is easy to experiment with different input values of (r). Large values of r, tend to lower positive expected values; while growth of input values and of their uncertainty in the distant future tend to raise the value of the standard error of forecast. The ultimate variance of discounted forecast will depend on the relative strength of these forces.

Economic forecasts may be either micro or macro. The example just referred to, concerning the investment in nuclear power, is, project-by-project, a microeconomic forecast about how a specific economic facility will be expected to function. In such cases, the general economic environment in which the facility will operate is, itself, subject to forecast error; therefore a macroeconomic forecast must often accompany a microeconomic forecast, with appropriate allowance for errors in both.

A macroeconomic forecast is for the economy as a whole, and forecasts of all its interrelated parts involve the construction and forecast-evaluation of a set of simultaneous relationships describing the various parts of the economy and how they are combined ("added up") to form the macroeconomic situation.

The reasoning processes and specification of optimal or equilibrium values in micro and in macroeconomics are different, and these differences have bearing on inter-pretation, as well as evaluation, of micro and macroeconomic forecasts.[2]

---

[2] It is evident that I do not accept the views of some economists that macroeconomics is simply the adding-up (or other elementary aggregation algorithm) applied to microeconomic relationships. The latter are claimed to be more fundamental.

It is customary to classify forecasts as unconditional or conditional, on the out-come of some assumed or independent, or non-economic events. If forecasts are made from a model, it is generally the case that they are explicitly conditional. If they are made from pure time series analysis or by some other mechanical statistical procedure they may seem to be unconditional, but in most cases they are conditional, certainly conditional on the validity of the data base, which is implicit but, nonetheless, very important and sensitive.

Let a model of the economy be expressed in general vector notation as

$$F(Y'_t, Y'_{t-1}, \ldots, Y'_{t-\theta}, X'_t, \theta') = e_t \tag{2}$$

F is a column vector of functions $(f_1, f_2, \ldots, f_n)'$.
Y_t is a column vector of endogenous variables $(y_{t1} \ldots y_{tn})'$ with finite lags up to j periods ago.
X_t is a column vector of exogenous variables $(x_{t1}, \ldots, x_{tm})'$.
q is a vector of unknown parameters.
e_t is a column vector of random errors.
For $\hat{\theta} = \theta$, we have an estimated model, and $E(e_t) = 0$.

The econometrician assembles a relevant database, and estimates $\hat{\theta}$ by statistical inference. The specification of F draws upon economic theory and knowledge of economic institutions or conventions.

For input values of $Y_{t-1} \ldots Y_{t-\varphi}$, X_t, $E(e_t) = 0$ and $\hat{\theta}$, this equation system is solved for estimates of Y_t. It is clear that the forecast values are conditional. The observed history is not precise; there are errors of measurement; there are revisions of concepts; so forecasts depend very much on $Y_{t-1}, Y_{t-2}, \ldots, Y_{t-\varphi}$. In the forecast period, there must be assumptions or external analysis, or political control of X_t. The error vector is not known and $E(e_t) = 0$ is but one of an infinity of values for the error term; thus the forecast is dependent on the input values of error, as well as upon the specification of the model, i.e. choice of F.

Time series or judgmental forecasting analysis may or may not lay out all the underlying conditions, but they are, of course, present. Some time series methods claim that there are no external factors, as in the X_t variables, but that simply lays them open to errors of omission.

DATA NEEDS

Quantitative economics generally requires a good data base, but forecasting has some special needs. They are not all unique to forecasting because many applications of economic analysis share some of the same requirements. For the most part, forecasting draws upon time-series, but sample surveys (cross sections of data) are important for some aspects of forecasting, although not generally for the economic system as a whole, all by themselves.

First, I shall take up the time series issues. In reference to the general model (2) cited above, the time series refer to vectors Y_t and X_t. They are best structured in data banks as observed matrices.

$$Y_t = \begin{pmatrix} y_{11} & y_{12} & \cdots & y_{1n} \\ y_{21} & y_{22} & \cdots & y_{2n} \\ \vdots & \vdots & & \vdots \\ y_{t1} & y_{t2} & \cdots & y_{tn} \\ \vdots & \vdots & & \vdots \\ y_{T1} & y_{T2} & \cdots & y_{Tn} \end{pmatrix} \quad \text{and}$$

$$X_t = \begin{pmatrix} x_{11} & x_{12} & \cdots & x_{1m} \\ x_{21} & x_{22} & \cdots & x_{2m} \\ \vdots & \vdots & & \vdots \\ x_{t1} & x_{t2} & \cdots & x_{tm} \\ \vdots & \vdots & & \vdots \\ x_{T1} & x_{T2} & \cdots & x_{Tm} \end{pmatrix}$$

The bank is presented as though there are T observations on n values of y_{ti} (i=1,2,..., n) and m values of X_{ti} (i=1,2,..., m). The parameters θ and the values of the errors are not directly observed, as data; they are estimated from the equation system. In the case of errors, they are not individually of interest. They are distributed in some family of probability distributions whose parameters are to be estimated.

For long range forecasting, one would want to have 50 or more years of data, and, if possible, calendar quarters or even months. In short run forecasting, it is unwise to try to do a suitable job with fewer than 20 years of data.

In a later section, I will take up *very* short-run forecasting from high-frequency data where monthly units of observation are required. Some high-frequency modeling can be done with weekly or daily data, but there is no economy of the world now where *comprehensive* data series are available for higher frequency than monthly, although segments of systems can be constructed from available weekly, or daily, or hourly, or real-time data. In a practical sense, however, it is extremely difficult to find *comprehensive* economic data at a higher frequency than monthly.

Since economists cannot "create" their own data in controlled experimentation, except for very limited test cases, we must organize the data that are available in highly structured accounting systems.

Most businesses keep their own records by standardized systems. International standardization has not been achieved yet, and that has been a contributing factor to international financial crises. In preparing data that describe the entire economy, or parts of the entire economy, we must follow the rules for *social* accounting, which impose many restrictions on how the data are presented for use. Three accounting statements define the structure of an economy. They are:

(i) National Income and Product Accounts (NIPA)
(ii) Input-output systems (I-O)
(iii) Flow-of-funds accounts (F/F).

The first set (NIPA) have been used widely, round the world, and are able to produce estimates, for practically any country, of such magnitudes as GDP, National Income, inflation, average wage rates, profits and thousands of other entries, all tied together systematically.

To use the entries of the data matrices to construct the NIPA itself or any combination of the three social accounting systems in a timely manner is not at all simple, and there is room for many errors that give rise to violations of the accounting balances of a double-entry system. The United States is known to have the best of such systems in terms of detail, timeliness, and accuracy, yet we know that the estimate of GDP obtained from the summation of factor incomes in the NIPA differs from the summation of final expenditures. These two estimates of GDP can differ by as much as $100 billion.

This is not a trivial sum even though the total GDP exceeds $9,000 billion. The quarter-to-quarter changes (at annual rates) that provoke serious policy action is often much less than $100 billion. That degree of observation error is, indeed, serious. There are many other respects in which the data are known to be defective:

Inventory change (investment) is notoriously difficult to estimate
Worker productivity presents many pitfalls
Profits are much in doubt
Inflation is not measured precisely
Depreciation of fixed capital involves a great deal of judgment

These issues are important because forecasts are made from models, and the results depend on the inputs for y_{t-1}, y_{t-2}, ..., and often these numbers get revised after a forecast has already been based on them. That is why we should emphasize *conditionality* of forecasts, and allowance for error variance — in this case error in measurement of the initial inputs.

Very long-range forecasts may rest on observation of the economy over very long time spans, but with data being revised continually, we often find it hard to pin down forecasts, to determine later, if ever, how accurate they were.

The problems in short-run forecasting that depend on observation of the most recent economic performance are closely related to timeliness. The first estimates of major economic magnitudes undergo reconsideration and consequent revision at least every month, in the United States, and in other countries, as well. With relatively short data bases for the near term, high-frequency forecasts of the revision of errors, every month, or even more frequently, can have quite significant effects.

International forecasting is especially sensitive to data quality, availability, and timeliness because the resources of developing countries are much more meager for meeting the needs of econometricians. In the case of the *transition* economies (from "plan-to-market") the data situation has been very chaotic in finding suitable information. This includes the former states of the Soviet Union, China, Vietnam, North Korea, and others to come. In such cases, modeling has not been purely from observed data, but from à priori theory or from patterns in similar economies elsewhere. Among these countries, China has gone further than others in putting resources into preparation of statistics and in improving the work of the State Statistical Office. In the early stages, refinement to quarterly or monthly estimates on a comprehensive basis is usually out of the question.

If we think of a target as being significant improvement of economic forecast accuracy, then we must confront realistically, the issues of data deficiency, but also to try to make do with what is available, scale back our modeling plans, and keep trying to move ahead, by small steps.

All data for forecasting are not in the structural lay-out of social accounting and not factored-in to the construction of econometric models. There is much to be done by partial analysis of cross-section data. Indeed, where economies are changing rapidly, as in the cases of the transition economies, we may overcome some of the time delay by estimating some of the models' equations from cross-section data, collected very recently and quickly from sample surveys. These data may be used to help estimate parameters in structural equations of models, *and* they may be used in order to determine values for expectations of firms or of households. The expressed expectations may be used as input values for high frequency-short-run forecasts, or they may be put to extended use beyond the immediate horizon of forecasts by estimating equations that are capable of *generating* future values of expectations, by relating them to objective time-series data of the economy.

The fitting of data to models, places stricter requirements, especially of *uniformity* across data series in the bank, than if one were using pure time series methods of forecasting without definite model specifications. Data in the NBER time series treatment need not be of the same historical length among various series of the total collection because the cross-variable needs are not comprehensive; that is to say y_{tj} may be related to $y_{t-1,j}$, $y_{t-2,j}$, ..., $y_{t-1,k}$, $y_{t-2,k}$, ... without having the same requirements in each equation for variables other than j and k. Each equation or small group of equations can be treated differently. The data need not satisfy all the accounting identities of a larger equation system. The data must be classified but not into a strict social accounting mold.

As we shall see below, in discussing new ventures in forecasting the economy at very short term, it is important to have the data as soon as they are available, and to allow the latest information to have its appropriate influence on parameter estimation. At the same time, there is always pressure to shorten the period between actual economic activity and the statistical reports of such activity. In financial markets, many, but not all, of these data are known (around the globe) within fractions of a second after transactions take place. These data are not highly processed for economic content (e.g. seasonally adjusted, or estimated free of changes in capital value, or adjusted for legislative changes). Many economic data need time for processing and compilation. These time lapses are gradually being reduced, as is delivery time after processing.

It is interesting that Canada is able to produce a value for GDP every month and that quarterly NIPA accounts for the US are released about 3 weeks after the end of a quarter. Other countries might need many months to report historical NIPA data, whether for quarters or years. Generally speaking, data improvement contributions to economic forecasting depend significantly on the reduction of the reporting delay, and the trend is certainly moving in a favorable direction, but disparities across countries, in this respect, are very large, and we cannot expect the ultimate in data availability *and* quality immediately. To a large extent the international crises are associated with the false assumption that all systems should be treated alike and expected to perform alike in globalized markets.

THE ROLE OF ECONOMIC THEORY

Of the three disciplines that constitute econometrics (mathematics, statistics, and economics), economic theory, in a strict sense, is not used in an essential way in much of time series modeling. That was the basis for the debate between T.C. Koopmans and A.F. Burns and W.C. Mitchell over the concept of "Measurement without Theory". The origins of the debate arose from Koopmans' review of Burns' and Mitchell's classic work on *Measuring Business Cycles* (NBER) 1946.

In putting together an econometric model, in the style of equation (2), an important conditionality is that F expresses the correct family of mathematical specifications. There is no such formula guidance used in much of time series analysis; it is mainly a data search for systematic patterns of relationship. There is no particular equation (or system of equations) specification. This may be thought to give more freedom to the statistician, but it is dangerous in that it may violate the underlying restrictions on economic movement that are at work, regardless whether the statistician recognizes it or not. What are thought to be established empirical regularities often break down in crucial forecasting situations, where the historical patterns are ruptured because of the neglect of certain nonlinearities or particular variables.

When large changes occurred in relative prices, after the oil embargo and subsequent oil-pricing events in 1973-74, forecasts of relevant energy sensitivities were better estimated from expenditure systems with explicit structure of many cross-elasticities that were derived explicitly from economic theory than from simple correlations between energy use and oil price, alone.

Large models with many indirect international effects were better in projecting the Peace Dividend after the Cold War than were simple correlations between military expenditure and social spending. The time series properties of crude quantity equations of money broke down in the face of financial innovation after the end of the Gulf War and were less informative than theoretical specifications of the flow of funds, introduced into more complicated models. Estimates of *potential* growth of the US economy from time series extrapolations of population, labor force, and productivity were much too low for several years after 1994 and proved to be inferior to theoretically based models that were estimated from data.

There were no reliable or useful data bases in the transition economies; so empirical time series analysis was not a possibility for several years in many cases. As a substitute, until more adequate data bases could be constructed one could use theoretical equation systems, supported by weak parameter estimates for an interim period. Gradually, appropriate data bases have been put in place.

Purely empirical systems can rely heavily on impressive mathematics, yet that does not bring the appropriate kind of theory into the analysis. It is more a case of absence of economic theory than of mathematically based statistical theory, without accompanying economic analysis, that is being questioned. The traditional non-mathematical cyclical analysis that formed the basis of NBER research on leading-lagging-and coincident indicators was put into mathematical form, especially for leading series, but it has not yet demonstrated superior forecasting ability and failed to predict an important business cycle turning point in its first serious test, namely the recession of 1990. Of course, one failure does not constitute grounds for discarding an approach, but it does shift the debate to the shoulders of those who neglect economic theory in the study of econometrics.

NEW FRONTIERS

In a search for new approaches in the quest for improving the accuracy of economic prediction, the central aim of this essay, it seems to me that developments in the field of *information* — delivery, processing, presentation, communication — offer some new opportunities. I am not speaking in terms of a breakthrough, but in terms of gradual improvement. As I shall argue below, it does not seem possible to reduce forecasting error by a large magnitude, say by 50 percent or even by one-third or one-fourth, but systematic painstaking research may bring us toward average errors that are typically better than prevailing errors by a few percentage points, at most by 10 percent or maybe 5 percent at the present time.

When econometricians started *systematic, replicated* forecasting efforts, mainly in the second half of the 20th century, we were surprised at how well we did, yet that did not satisfy the user-community for long, but now the way is open for fresh attempts at improvement, and the opportunity comes through exploitation of the new developments of the information age.

Having gone from electromechanical computing hardware to amazingly powerful, fast, economical computers, I can truly appreciate the sea-change. In this transition, the role of the large mainframe computer was enormously helpful, but no match for today's good lap-top or desk-top computers, with the possibility of linkage to as much computer power as could possibly be needed at this time for econometrics, in the form of the "super computer". At the present stage, however, practical econometric work has not generally been that demanding of hardware.

Elegant and flexible software accompany the improvements in hardware. The plethora of software facilities enable econometricians to process large bodies of data with comparative ease and speed, comparative in the sense of data management of the last five decades, starting with the 1940s.

The software enables the econometrician to handle the most sophisticated techniques for estimating θ in equation system (2), although the most successful techniques in serving the quest for forecast improvement need not be the most sophisticated or complicated.

But the software permits the calculation of many more diagnostic statistics, far beyond overall correlation and serial correlation. Tests for exogeneity, randomness of error terms, and structural breaks in underlying relationships are handled with comparative ease, again in comparison with such procedures in the period before the new information age.

Equally important, perhaps more important than hardware and software, are the flows of statistical data. They are much more frequent, more comprehensive in scope, reported with greater speed, and communicated globally. There is no doubt that the entire user-community is much better off than ever before, in terms of information in its many dimensions, yet there is one respect in which there has been deterioration; that is the depth of knowledge and care that former data custodians or data processors put into their materials. Data managers had a much better understanding of each statistic and knew more about its potential or its limitations. A great deal of TLC ("tender loving care") was put into the more meager data sets of yesteryear. They were more painfully and painstakingly produced and less importance was attached to their sheeer size. Except in that respect, however, we econometricians are better off and better served by present facilities.

What potentialities are there in prospect with the enhanced volume and speed of information, together with the facilities for processing it? Several general hunches support the idea that economic forecast error can be reduced, at the macro level, by carefully using the data and facilities of the information flow. These are:

1. There is significant serial correlation in macroeconomic time series. It is mainly positive, but there are some significant negative correlations. Techniques that use and build on these tendencies can contribute to forecast improvement. This hunch is motivated by economic theory. The *solution* of macro-dynamic models is known to generate its own serial correlation.

2. The information flow follows a pattern over the course of a calendar

quarter, and as the flow builds up, we learn during each quarter more and more about the quarter's outcome; therefore we look to techniques that will enable one to use information as soon as it becomes available. Building up a forecast becomes a dynamic, time-structured process.

3. In generating forecasts over more than one-quarter, say for 12 or more quarters, it is important to have good *initial conditions* for the whole projected sequence of future quarters and a formal model to develop such *initial conditions* is extremely useful, especially for rendering *transparency* for the process, enabling one to be purely objective and to build in the possibility of forecast *replication* by others. One of the most important aspects of scientific method in empirical econometric research is to have peer-replicability.

There are many approaches to short-run forecasting that use the daily information flow and up-to-date facilities for processing, but in this essay, I shall concentrate on one particular approach that appears to hold promise and is quite manageable, with modest resources.

To be very specific, this approach will aim at forecasts of a time horizon of six months. That provides estimates of *initial conditions* and an extrapolation that depends heavily, but not entirely on the serial properties of economic data. In a very practical sense, I claim, on the basis of 50 years of forecasting experience that the limit of future information contained in available data is about six months (the "shelf-life" of current economic information). In some circumstances, the horizon may be stretched to nine months or a year, but for the United States and other industrial economies, the six-month limit seems to be plausible. That is why the proposed methods are good for supplying *initial conditions*, and that implies that they should be specified to be compatible with prevailing structural models that seek to forecast for one to three years.

The method does have some characteristics of a data search for empirical regularities, but it is not as purely data-intensive as are most time series methods, especially those that take pride in being "*a-theoretical*" or those in the tradition of Burns and Mitchell.

A certain amount of economic theory, the kind that forms the basis for NIPA research or more broadly, social accounting, guides the structure of the high-frequency model. Since the system is cast in a NIPA framework, to start, it is perfectly natural that the model builder, for the purposes of very short-run forecasting, ought to draw as much as possible on the work of the social accountants who construct NIPA and use the same kind of source materials that go into the preparation of the most recent quarterly set of NIPA values.

For example, NIPA statisticians estimate quarterly consumer spending from the estimates of monthly retail sales (by type), capital formation from monthly construction statistics, public expenditures from monthly fiscal reports on national and local budgets, exports and imports from monthly statistics on international trade (customs clearance, balance of payments accounts), surveys of inventory holdings for inventory change (wholesale, retail, manufacturing, and primary sectors). Given established lead times, such monthly statistics as building permits, housing starts, deliveries of industrial equipment, and orders for industrial equipment are very useful in estimating capital formation.

All these correspondences between high-frequency source data (monthly or more frequent) and quarterly NIPA data try to stay in touch with the work of NIPA statisticians in preparing their highly detailed tabulations. The fact that some data, in the United States and also elsewhere, became available at different time periods, means that the quarterly schedule of publication of GDP and its many constituent parts must, in the *earliest approximations*, make use of fragmentary source information. The first US reports each quarter do not have source material for three months of foreign trade; so, one or two months must be estimated, and this is often highly subjective or speculative. The same is true of inventory information, and, as we shall see below, of profit information. In the interests of transparency (replicability and objectivity) I accept the initial NIPA report as "correct" because the population at large is going to act upon it in making their economic decisions. I, therefore, establish statistical relations between NIPA quarterly entries and available monthly source data that follow, as closely as possible, the source data used by the NIPA statisticians.

The first set of econometric equations to be estimated for high-frequency modeling consist of equations such as:

$$\Delta \ln N_{it} = \alpha + \alpha_0 \Delta \ln I_{it} + e_{it} \qquad (3)$$

N_{it} = quarterly NIPA values for entry N_i in the NIPA accounts. I_{it} = quarterly averages of monthly (or more frequent) indicators that are used for constructing N_{it} in the NIPA account. A typical example is:

$$\Delta \ln C_{it} = \alpha + \alpha_0 \Delta \ln RS_{it} + e_{it} \tag{4}$$

C_{it} = i-th type of quarterly consumer expenditures in NIPA

RS_{it} = i-th type of quarterly averages of monthly (or higher frequency) reported retail sales estimates.

Monthly, or weekly, or daily retail sales will be reported sooner than quarterly estimates of similar consumer expenditure data.[3]

This equation is called a *bridge* equation; it bridges the time and average gap between some NIPA entry and a closely related indicator at higher frequency. Basically, the bridge equation in this form states that percentage changes in N_{it} follow percentage changes in I_{it}. On a priori grounds, one would look for a relationship with a high correlation, an estimate of α_0 that is not significantly different from unity, and an estimate of α that is not significantly different from zero. These are desirable properties, but the overriding property is that e_{it} should be a random variable, behaving like "white noise".

Time series statisticians manipulate the basic economic series (N_{it} and I_{it}) until they have some preconceived properties, certainly not realistic properties, that are in the minds of decision makers when they act upon information contained in N_{it} or I_{it}. It is my preference to place the probability properties in e_{it}, which is not directly observable, but whose distribution characteristics can be estimated from the statistical residuals, preserving the informational content of the original N_{it} and I_{it}.

---

[3] A complete pairing of NIPA entries and corresponding monthly indicators (that are to be averaged into quarterly values) is given for the version of the model that existed in 1995 in Lawrence R. Klein and J. Yong Park, "The University of Pennsylvania Model for High-Frequency Economic Forecasting", *Economic & Financial Modelling*, Autumn, (1995), 95-146. (See esp. 100-107.) In continuing research, this listing has been enhanced, but the principles remain the same.

The guiding feature is the isolation of "white noise", and the bridge equations that are finally selected need not be of the bi-logarithmic type specified above, but they should involve observable values of N_{it} and I_{it}, perhaps in more general lag distributions.

There are other NIPA properties to be used in model specification. The headline features of the NIPA accounts are the GDP and some major components, and, as I have stated above, it is well-known that GDP in a dual (or multiple) entry accounting system can be estimated from more than one data set. The most familiar is the sum of *final* expenditures by all agents participating in the national economy. It could equally well be estimated from the sum of all payments to factors of production for their respective roles in generating the GDP. It could also be estimated from each sector's gross production less the values of intermediate goods, used up in the production process. This difference between the gross and net production values constitutes the value added, sector-by-sector, and the summation of value added, over all sectors, should also produce the GDP. The various measurements of GDP, if independently estimated (sector-by-sector; factor payment-by-factor payment; or final expenditure-by-final expenditure) will not generally agree. The US accounts, at the quarterly time frame, generate just two estimates, one from the expenditure side and one from the factor payment (or income) side. During the last few years these numbers have been as much as $\pm$ \$100 billion apart, but not much attention is paid to this discrepancy because it is a small percentage of a multi-trillion GDP. This attitude overlooks the fact that \$100 billion is still a great deal of money. It is well-known, that very different estimates of historical trends in worker productivity result from the two methods of estimating GDP and that Federal Reserve and Administration economic officials choose to use the more pessimistic version, from the expenditure side, and thus biased their estimates of potential economic growth, thereby biasing their policy decisions in an overly conservative direction based on overly restrictive policies for several years.

Accordingly, the high-frequency forecasting system, which used information from *both* the expenditure *and* income sides of the US accounts, must estimate quarterly values of the GDP residual.

The accounting identities make sense only in current prices, for nominal values, yet there is great business-cycle interest in the movement of the real economy; therefore estimates must be constructed of corresponding price indexes in order to transform NIPA entries on the expenditure side into values that sum to real GDP. Real values do not exist for the income side, only deflated values; i.e. nominal values divided by some appropriate price indexes in order to show purchasing power or some similar construct, derived from nominal values of income, such as personal income, divided by a price index.

Formerly, our NIPA system converted from nominal expenditure values to real values by dividing the nominal values by implicit deflators, which were defined as:

$$P_{it} = \frac{N_{it}}{N^*_{it}}$$

where

N_{it} = current dollar value of i-th component of GDP from the expenditure side
N^*_{it} = constant dollar value of i-th component of GDP from the expenditure side
P_{it} = implicit deflator of i-th component of GDP from the expenditure side.

In this formulation, the sums of subcomponents equal the constant dollar value of corresponding major components, but the US Department of Commerce decided, in a fundamental revision of the NIPA, to introduce chain-weighted price indexes in place of implicit deflators, claiming that the new indexes are more accurate measures than the former fixed weight measures.[4]

In any event, monthly indexes of prices paid by producers, consumers, government procurement offices, and foreigners in great detail, are related to the price indexes that are used in computing real components of GDP from the expenditure side. If a third measure of GDP were to be computed from gross values, intermediate values, and values added by sector, there should

[4] The term "more accurate" is very misleading, since the *true* values are not known. The new price index measures have some desirable and some undesirable properties. For econometric model builders it is an unfortunate choice since it ruptures some basic identities.

be additional price relationships for computing real value added by sector.

An entire set of bridge relationships between price indexes used in computing real quarterly GDP and source price indexes by months or higher frequency are needed.

$$\Delta \ln P^{*}_{it} = \beta + \beta_{0} \Delta \ln IP_{it} + u_{it} \qquad (5)$$

P^{*}_{it} = quarterly price index of i-th entry in NIPA (expenditure side)
IP_{it} = quarterly average of monthly (or higher frequency) indicator price for the i-th entry in NIPA on the expenditure side.

It should be noted that some unit factor costs such as wage rate or interest rate are used for some entries on the expenditure side that directly involve labor or financial capital inputs.

The total equation system is not closed unless there are enough equations to "explain" all the necessary NIPA entries and also all the indicator variables on the rhs of the bridge equations [(3) and (5)].

The monthly (or higher frequency) indicator values, which generate the whole system along a dynamic path of forecast values must also be explained by another equation system. A definitive way of modeling the equations for the indicator variables has not yet been chosen; various possibilities exist, but whatever method or system is used, it must be objective and transparent.

The simplest and most direct specification is to assume that I_{it} (standing for price or NIPA indicators) can be estimated from a Box-Jenkins system of ARMA equations.

$$I_{it} = B_{i}(L)\, I_{it} + J_{i}(L)\, v_{it} \qquad (6)$$

$$B_{i}(L)\, I_{it} = \beta_{i0} + \beta_{i1} I_{i,t-1} + \beta_{i2} I_{i,t-2} + \dots + \beta_{ir} I_{i,t-r}$$

$$L = \text{lag operator} \qquad L^{j} I_{it} = I_{i,t-j}$$

$$J_{i}(L)\, v_{it} = v_{it} + j_{i1} v_{i,t-1} + j_{i2} v_{i,t-2} + \dots + j_{is} v_{i,t-s}$$

$$v_{it} = \text{unobserved error term}$$

The estimation procedures advocated by Box and Jenkins are used for estimating the polynomial coefficient in $B_i(L)$ and $J_i(L)$, with a criterion that the distribution of v_{it} be represented by "white-noise" residuals.

The logical case for turning to Box-Jenkins techniques for estimating equations like those in (6) for each separate indicator variable is that the calculated equations will produce estimates of I_{it} that are serially correlated as are practically all economic variables.

A system of bridge equations and of individual Box-Jenkins equations for all the variables in a closed system has been estimated for the US economy and used for an entire decade in frequent projections — every week, on the basis of freshly reported information about the indicators of the system as laid out above.

Single Box-Jenkins equations for each variable exploits the *auto* correlation present in individual series, but test have been made for the possibility that the serial effects are both direct and indirect. Accordingly, I have placed the variables of the US model into groups with similar or related characteristics among member series within each group. For example consumer demand for durable goods may be substitutable vs. the demand for certain non-durable goods or services. Also many consumer goods are complementary.

Durables, such as cars, need gasoline and oil, an expenditure category in the non-durables grouping; therefore these two components in the total of consumer expenditures should be expected to move together in a positive cross-correlation. Several groupings have been made, all of which are quite natural, for small VAR systems in which each variable of the group is made dependent on other variables in the group, both current and lagged. The lay-out of a VAR system is:

$$\begin{aligned} I_{it} = \gamma_i &+ \gamma_{ii1} I_{i,t-1} + \gamma_{ii2} I_{i,t-2} + \gamma_{ii3} I_{i,t-3} + \ldots + v_{it} \\ &+ \gamma_{ij1} I_{j,t-1} + \gamma_{ij2} I_{j,t-2} + \gamma_{ij3} I_{j,t-3} + \ldots \\ &+ \gamma_{ik1} I_{k,t-1} + \gamma_{ik2} I_{k,t-2} + \gamma_{ik3} I_{k,t-3} + \ldots \end{aligned}$$

$$\begin{aligned} I_{jt} = \gamma_j &+ \gamma_{ji1} I_{i,t-1} + \gamma_{ji2} I_{i,t-2} + \gamma_{ji3} I_{i,t-3} + \ldots + v_{jt} \\ &+ \gamma_{jj1} I_{j,t-1} + \gamma_{jj2} I_{j,t-2} + \gamma_{jj3} I_{j,t-3} + \ldots \\ &+ \gamma_{jk1} I_{k,t-1} + \gamma_{jk2} I_{k,t-2} + \gamma_{jk3} I_{k,t-3} + \ldots \end{aligned}$$

$$
\begin{aligned}
I_{kt} = \gamma_k &+ \gamma_{ki1}I_{i,t-1} + \gamma_{ki2}I_{i,t-2} + \gamma_{ki3}I_{i,t-3} + \ldots + v_{kt} \\
&+ \gamma_{kj1}I_{j,t-1} + \gamma_{kj2}I_{j,t-2} + \gamma_{kj3}I_{j,t-3} + \ldots \\
&+ \gamma_{kk1}I_{k,t-1} + \gamma_{kk2}I_{k,t-2} + \gamma_{kk3}I_{k,t-3} + \ldots
\end{aligned}
\tag{7}
$$

A finite array of significant coefficients is chosen much as with the Box-Jenkins search techniques, to find a "white-noise" residuals in each of the three equations of the VAR cluster, encompassing i, j, k. The VAR extension of single equation ARMA systems is potentially useful if there are strong natural relationships among I_{it}, I_{jt}, I_{kt}, as in purchases of cars, oil, and gasoline.

The idea of VAR systems has plausibility, but it has the drawback, as do most non-structural models, that it cannot accommodate a very large number of interactions simultaneously. For that reason, VAR models usually consist of just a handful of variables, fewer than ten. A good forecasting system must spread risk appropriately and therefore be decomposable into small groups, within the NIPA, consisting of no more than five-to-ten variables (not counting time delays).

There is no need to remain confined, for cross-relationships only among elements within a conventional cluster, such as components of consumption, components of foreign trade, components of capital formation, and the like. A major cross effect would be that between residential investment in the capital formation sector, and expenditures on furnishings, fixtures, and appliances to be used within a home. This is an important kind of interrelationship.

A feature of the information age in our society is *change*. If we are using the weekly flow of monthly information and finding changes of a significant magnitude in the economy's signals almost every week, it is important to be able to reassess changing situations. To do this, I follow the rule: As soon as new information becomes available, it is immediately entered into a data file, changing both latest entries and also any that may have been revised for earlier periods. Revisions are always occurring with economic information; that is why it does not make sense to claim that some complicated method of measurement is more *accurate* than another - accuracy with respect to what?

I not only use updated data that are from a data-bank that has been changed *minutes* after the release of new information for public consumption, but also re-calculate all estimates of ARMA or VAR or bridge equations immediately. Every week's forecast assessment is based on re-estimated equations that can be calculated within minutes of the change in data files. This is a point at which hardware and software of the inform-ation era play important roles in the process.

The economy is always subject to large surprises (oil embargo, war in the Persian Gulf, end of the Cold War, financial crises in Mexico and East Asia, Russian loan default, etc.). It is not likely that these events will be picked up in short-run model projections in advance, but once they have occurred and affected the economy in the very short run, the forces of serial correlation will have to carry the effects through the model — both through serial correlation in monthly movements of indicator variables and later after the next quarterly report in the NIPA variables. If the changes are very big and lasting, the recalculation of fresh coefficient estimates will gradually phase-in the structural changes into the estimated parameters.

For almost all estimates of coefficients in the time series equations to determine projected values for use with bridge equations, the systems are closed, with only NIPA or indicator variables that are, themselves, estimated from ARMA or VAR systems. But those equations can be generalized one step more (ARMA, e.g.).

$$I_{it} = B_i(L)\, I_{it} + J_i(L)\, v_{it} + T_i\, z_t \qquad (8)$$

where z_t = column vector of special variables. These special variables may be from responses to sample surveys or prices of new kinds of financial instruments such as futures prices, derivative instruments prices, forward rates of interest or currency exchange. Some of these survey responses or futures prices, or forward rates have specific horizons built-in on a contractual basis, but some have a temporal range of validity that has been established in a practical sense as a statistical regularity. If they do not fit into any of these categories, they can be treated like other indicator variables and fit into auto-regressive equations that generate their own solutions. As expressed anticipations in sample surveys, they might be given for a period as far ahead as six months, but certainly not longer.

It is an objective of the research program on construction of high frequency forecasting systems that new or hitherto overlooked subjective expectations variables be introduced, in order to keep tapping fresh new sources of anticipatory data. The most important of these are being examined for their autoregressive properties so that they can be used in models. Structural econometric models have long used variables on consumer expectations, business investment expectations, orders statistics, and housing starts. These valuable and insightful series are not simply introduced as exogenous variables, without attention being paid to their estimated values beyond the shortest of horizons. These variables in structural models are generated in stochastic behavior equations and treated as fully endogenous. In this way, they have been found to bring about improvements in forecast accuracy. The main issue at present is to unearth some entirely new and overlooked anticipatory series.

There are three important variables in high frequency NIPA systems that merit special consideration. These are equations for corporate profits, stock market averages, and the statistical discrepancy. Two of these variables, corporate profits and the statistical discrepancy, are components of the income side of NIPA. Profits are part of national income, while the discrepancy figures in the reconciliation between national income (income side) and national product (expenditure side). The theory and principles of social accounting guide the structure of the particular high-frequency indicators, and that serves as a very important distinction between this system and the economically unguided empiricism of time series analysis. Stock market averages could appear among the indicator variables that are used in bridge equations, but they are more important for a third estimate of GDP that is made for quite different reasons, that will be covered in some detail below. Also the stock market variables are significantly associated with both the profit variable (income side) and the interest rate variable (indicator for income side variables).

A basic NIPA identity (current prices only) runs as follows:

	Gross domestic product (GDP)
plus:	Receipts of factor income
less:	Payments of factor income
equals:	Gross national product (GNP)
less:	Capital consumption
equals:	Net national product (NNP)

less: Indirect business taxes
Business transfers
Statistical discrepancy (SD)
plus: Subsidies
equals: National income (NI)[5]

The components of national income are:

Wages and salaries
Other labor income
Proprietors' income
Rental income
Interest
Corporate profits

The statistical discrepancy is not a tiny random error of measurement; it is neither tiny nor random. For decades, I and my students have studied this variable and discovered that it is highly auto-correlated and also correlated with major entries in the income *and* product accounts. Some countries try to allocate the discrepancy and come to a single estimate of GDP, but the US practice is to assume (*declare*) that the expenditure side data are more correct and implicitly put all the error on the income side. In other countries, the income side data are deemed to be more accurate, as estimates of what the authorities are trying to measure. It is surely a case of needing to distribute the error all round. There are some purely statistical methods of doing this, but for the high frequency model, I have tried to estimate a meaningful equation for SD.

The discrepancy can be considered to be the difference between gross national receipts (or gross national expenditures) for final product and factor costs (the national income). Since receipts are estimated on a *final product* basis, receipts for intermediate products are automatically excluded, as they should be. This means that profits, which are notoriously arbitrary, for tax purposes and for accounting conventions, are co-mingled with the statistical discrepancy. Both are imperfectly measured residual items and some parts of profits (positive or negative) reside in the statistical discrepancy. For this reason, one should look for a correlation between profits and the discrepancy. Other variables that are empirically correlated with the discrepancy are exports

[5] National income is the "NI" in NIPA.

and government expenditures. An equation estimated from US data, 1947Q1 — 1997Q4, is

$$\left(\frac{SD}{GDP}\right)_t = \underset{(1.341)}{0.0016} - \underset{(2.915)}{0.095}\,(CP+PI - \text{trend}\,(CP+PI))/GDP$$

$$+\underset{(3.332)}{0.204}\,(X - \text{trend}\,X)/GDP + \underset{(2.287)}{0.091}\,(G - \text{trend}\,G)/GDP \qquad (9)$$

$$\bar{R}^2 = 0.99 \qquad DW(1) = 2.00, \qquad DW(4) = 1.69$$

$$AR(0) = \underset{(18.189)}{0.800}\,AR(1)$$

CP = corporate profit; PI = proprietors' income; X = exports; G = government spending.

Profits depend on receipts and costs, by an identity. The discrepancy has a similar accounting structure, but it is not identical to profits; there are many other reasons, besides improper estimation of profits, for leaving error-prone elements in GDP or in NI. A profit (bridge) equation relates quarterly corporate profit to average monthly indicators for receipts, such as retail sales (RS), industrial production (IP) and capacity utilization (rate). On the cost side, at high frequency; estimates of wage costs over prices, intermediate material costs over prices, and capital costs (10-year treasury bond rate). The estimated equation, 1967Q2 - 1997Q4.

$$\Delta CP_t = -\underset{(2.480)}{0.206}\,\Delta\,(CP)_{t-1} + \underset{(3.562)}{0.00397}\,\Delta RS_t + \underset{(2.449)}{9.503}\,\Delta IP_t$$

$$-\underset{(0.216)}{20.078}\,\Delta\left(\frac{W}{P}\right)_t - \underset{(2.030)}{277.889}\,\Delta\left(\frac{PINT}{P}\right)_t + \underset{(1.077)}{313.187}\,\Delta\left(1+\frac{r}{100}\right)$$

$$-\underset{(1.488)}{4.638}\,\Delta CU_t - \underset{(1.754)}{5.351} \qquad (10)$$

$$\bar{R}^2 = 0.269 \quad DW(1) = 2.11 \quad DW(4) = 1.71$$

CP = corporate profits; RS = retail sales; IP = industrial production, PINT = price of intermediate goods, P = consumer price index, r = interest rate of Treasury bonds (10-year), CU = capacity utilization.

All variables have the appropriate direction of effect, but some of the cost margins are not significantly different from zero. The concepts of the relevant identities and closely corresponding estimates of related variables provide guidance to these specifications.

Equity prices play a role in the high-frequency approach to modeling, and in this present era, movements of prices on equity markets have been extremely important, with some short-run impacts on spending and saving decisions. This is especially true for the US, but it is a worldwide phenomenon of our times.

For guidance, the capital-asset-pricing-model plays an important role.

$$SE_t = \sum_{i=0}^{H} \frac{CP_{t+i}}{(1+r)^i} \tag{11}$$

SE_t = NY Stock exchange index of share prices.
CP_{t+i} = expected profits in period t+i
r = discount rate

This notional equation states that the average share price is a discounted value (to the present time, t) of expected future earnings. This is a purely conceptual equation, but an operational approximation is obtained from

$\ln(SE_t) = \alpha_0 + \alpha_1 \ln CP_t - \alpha_2 \ln(1+r)_t + e_t$ estimated from monthly data

1965(1) – 1997(12) as (12)

$$\ln SE_t = \underset{(124.5)}{0.979} \ln SE_{t-1} + \underset{(3.458)}{0.0339} \ln(CP)_{t-1}$$

$$- \ 0.3726 \ln (1 + \frac{r}{100})_{t-1} \qquad (12)\ (est)$$
$$(2.861)$$

$\bar{R}^2 = 0.998 \qquad DW(1) = 1.516 \qquad D(12) = 1.997$

Equation (10) is extrapolated to obtain estimates of future earnings, and the yield on US Treasury securities is used for $(1+r_t)$.

It is evident how data for SE_t are obtained. They are available in real time, but monthly averages are used. In order to estimate a profit equation, however, it is necessary to construct monthly series for CP_t.

For individual companies, profits are reported only quarterly, and even those statistics are not as usable as desired for high-frequency analysis, because they are one or two months behind the timing for release of other NIPA data. Companies release profit data at varying times during each quarter, but all listed companies are requried to file earnings reports every quarter. The exchange statistics present the latest estimates of price-earnings ratios and these can be averaged in various ways, in particular for the S&P 500 companies. One, therefore, can have very frequent estimates of price-earnings ratios throughout the month, with the latest reports available for each company. Monthly averages can be obtained for the listed companies. The following identity holds

$$(SE)_t / (\frac{SE}{CP})_t = (CP)_t$$

price/price-earnings ratio = earnings

This provides running monthly estimates of earnings, expressed as estimates of corporate profits. This is the series that shows monthly estimates of earnings that can be used to estimate equation (11) and project future equity prices (as an average). These estimates are then used in another segment of the total high-frequency model.

In order to reduce inherent risk associated with forecasting, I propose a third estimate of GDP, namely from principal components of major indicators of real GDP and of the price of GDP. The motivation for this third approach is that averaging a variety of forecast methods spreads the risk in a very risky activity. It is basically like portfolio diversification by investors, in order to spread risk. There are, however, only a limited number of promising methods that are based on acceptable statistical procedures. This third method is not designed to generate a large number of forecast components, as in the case of NIPA-based forecasts from both the expenditure side and income side; it estimates only one equation for real GDP and for the price index of GDP. The identity

$$PGDP * GDP = GDP(\$),$$

is imposed, where GDP = real GDP and
GDP($) = nominal GDP
PGDP is the price index of GDP,

thus a third aggregate can also be estimated, if two are first estimated. Although only two headline macroeconomic aggregates are generated, many series are used for the method.

The following variables are selected as monthly indicators that are considered to convey information about real GDP:

industrial production index
shipments of manufactures deflated by the PPI
new orders for manufactures deflated by PPI (intermediate goods)
unfilled orders of manufactures deflated by the PPI (intermediate goods)
retail sales deflated by the CPI
M_1 deflated by the CPI
index of *net* business formation
non-farm payroll employment
average weekly hours worked
housing starts
exchange value of the dollar
interest rate deflated by CPI
yield spread, 10 and 1-year treasury securities
yield spread, 6 mo. commercial paper less, 6 mo. treasury bills

In the case of PGDP, the monthly indicators are:

consumer price index
producer price index, finished goods
producer price index, intermediate goods
treasury bond yield, 10-year
treasury bill rate
US import price index
index of prices received by farmers
average hourly earnings
average weekly hours

These indicators are of varying importance in explaining the movements of either GDP or PGDP, but they contain a great deal of overlapping information; i.e. they are mutually correlated. This requires that they should be used in such a way as to extract their mutually *independent* contributions to the explanation of GDP and PGDP, respectively. In each case, the *principal components* of each of the two groupings are related to the two headline aggregates.

The method of principal components is sensitive to units of measurement; therefore the calculations are made only in one measurement system, namely the statistically standardized form of each indicator variable. Each indicator, I_{it}, is transformed to

$$\frac{I_{it} - \bar{I}_i}{S_i}$$

The mean value, in the sample, is subtracted from each variable and the difference is divided by the sample standard deviation. Each indicator therefore has zero mean and unit standard deviation. The moment matrix of all the indicators becomes

$$R = \begin{pmatrix} 1 & r_{12} & r_{13} & \cdots & r_{1n} \\ r_{21} & 1 & r_{23} & \cdots & r_{2n} \\ \vdots & \vdots & \vdots & & \vdots \\ r_{n1} & r_{n2} & r_{n3} & \cdots & 1 \end{pmatrix}$$

where R is the correlation matrix for n indicators.

The principal components are linear functions of the observed indicator variables with coefficients that are elements of the characteristic vectors (eigenvectors). The characteristic roots of the correlation matrix are extracted in such a way that each principal component is uncorrelated with all other principal components. It would be possible to form n principal components, but only those that explain most (using approximately a 95% cut-off point) of the variance of the whole set are used. It is actually a data-reduction technique that uses the information contained in all n indicators so as to obtain mutually independent linear combinations of all the indicators yet, in a practical sense, using only the most important components. In most cases about five or six principal components stand for the whole set of n variables.

Each component has the form

$$PC_{1t} = \Sigma\, a_{1i}\, I_{it}$$
$$PC_{2t} = \Sigma\, a_{2i}\, I_{it}$$
$$\vdots$$
$$PC_{n^*t} = \Sigma\, a_{n^*i}\, I_{it}$$

where $n^* < n$

All the indicator variables chosen for this third method are used in order to predict GDP and PGDP, but they are used in a *restricted* way, in order to avoid the indeterminacies of multicollinearity, since the restrictions force each PC_{it} to be uncorrelated with other PC_{jt} $(j \neq i)$.

The next step is to establish a numerical linkage between the chosen few principal components and the headline economic variables. Accordingly, GDP is regressed on the leading principal components of GDP indicators, while PGDP is regressed on the leading principal components of PGDP indicators. The principal components are based on monthly values of indicators, but for correlation and for projection in forecasts, quarterly averages of the monthly variables are used.

Principal components have been used in this way before, to reduce NBER indicators (leading, coincident, or lagging) to a basic set, but they have not been generally used in forecasting. The idea of putting all variables in standardized units was used in order to lend an aspect of uniqueness to the principal components that are ultimately selected, but for ease of interpretation they are transformed back into original or conventional units, which makes them more comprehensible. The properties of multivariate linear correlations are essentially invariant under linear transformation of variables. Since GDP and PGDP for most countries are not available at time intervals more frequent than one calendar quarter, the estimated regression equations for GDP and PGDP are estimated for quarterly averages of principal components; forecasts, however, are subject to monthly revision.

If some PC_{it} are not statistically significant, they may be dropped. The significant set all have different coefficients associated with each of the principal components of the regression, and each principal component has different coefficients for each high-frequency indicator. In this way, the total effects (through the relative contributions within each component and through the relative contribution of the different components show the final marginal effect of each indicator variable on GDP or PGDP.

Having good relationships between major aggregates in NIPA and principal components of monthly indicators is not the end of the research, for the investigation must extrapolate each of the indicators over the forecast horizon. Some variations of Box-Jenkins ARMA equations or VARMA equations are needed in order to generate future inputs on the rhs of the principal components.

When building up forecasts from indicators for NIPA expenditures side information and from indicators for NIPA income side information, each NIPA entry is estimated only once. It is only the headline variables GDP and PGDP that are each estimated three times from independently treated source material. The final estimates, by quarter, are then averaged, in order to restrain risk.

There are various possible techniques for estimating different weights in averaging the three estimates of GDP and PGDP to one single estimate of each, but experience in making this kind of forecast for the last 10 years or more, suggests that sometimes the income side estimates are to be preferred; sometimes the expenditure side estimates and some times the principal components estimates; therefore I hesitate to do more than use simple, equal weights in forming the averages.

HAVE ECONOMISTS REACHED THEIR LIMITS TO ACCURACY?

As suggested in earlier sections, we econometricians are able to make much better forecasts than we had ever anticipated to be possible. Yet the user community wants much more accurate forecasts. What can be expected? Econometricians are necessarily aiming at moving and uncertain targets. Poor measurement contributes to the uncertainty, and that remains an unimproved aspect of the economy. While our in-formation sources have definitely improved, economic life has become so much more complicated that it is even harder to measure profits, depreciation, inventory change, human productivity in the services sector and many other variables.

With an enormous effort, both on the side of providing information and processing it, and on the side of interpreting the dynamic movement of the economy, we undoubtedly can reduce forecast error — not by quantum jumps, but perhaps by gains of a few percentage points.

The volume and speed of delivery of economic information have definitely increased; the quality of the resulting measurements has not necessarily improved. Developing countries that are just starting to build statistical files about their economies can certainly make great improvements. I have watched this happen in China during the past two decades, but the most advanced industrial nations have not had the same kind of improvement; they have already realized some of their greatest gains.

This puts limits on the improvement of forecasts, but I do believe that modest gains can be made through intensive efforts, and these gains should contribute to better guidance for the economy.

Among the trials of different methods of high-frequency forecasting, it is possible to detect a drop in forecast error — not hypothetically, not theoretically, not from ex-post constructed forecasts, but from truly advance forecasts executed before the event (i.e. truly *ex ante*). The accompanying graphs of forecast realization, show how the accuracy improves as more information becomes available during a quarter. This is what is to be expected and is not surprising, but the task ahead is to get the same kind of improvement without having to wait longer for more data and other indicator information to become available.

Forecast Accuracy of the University of Pennsylvania Current Quarter Mode

Annual Growth Rate, 1990Q2 to 1995Q2

MAE=Mean Absolute Error, RMSE=Root Mean Squared Error

*End-of-Month Projection

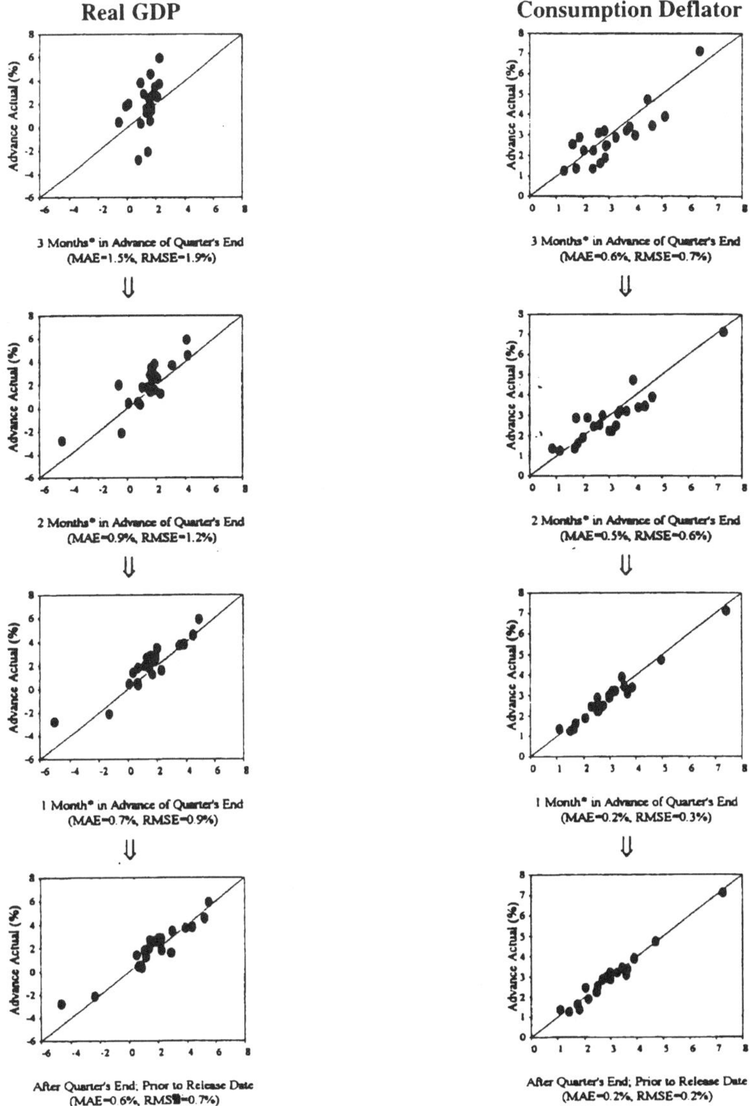

Tasks to be undertaken in order to improve forecasts.

1. From a *transparent* system based on high-frequency data, compile forecasts frequently — certainly every week or two and after major external events.

2. Introduce as many anticipatory variables as possible.

3. Revise coefficient estimates as new data become available and re-estimate the entire system when basic data changes are made by data gathering agencies.

4. Experiment with new methods and new sources of indicator information as often as possible - certainly not less than annually.

5. Do not regard the numerical estimates of the model's equations as fixed; keep doing research in international macroeconomics and try new approaches for extrapolation.

6. Do not treat the final numerical output for each forecast interval as the ultimate product by itself, but prepare a summary interpretation of every forecast.

7. Keep detailed records of forecasts and published data for the model's variables. Make extra analyses of performance at turning points - to determine where turns take place, in what volume turns occur, and maintain a history of all unusual time series patterns at turning points.

COUNTRY COVERAGE

It was natural to begin high-frequency modeling in the information age in the United States, where short-run data are comparatively abundant, usually available in machine-readable form, and published with short average time delay. High-frequency forecasting systems like that for the US have been developed by Professor Yoshihisa Inada, of Konan University, Kobe, for Japan. Curiously, Japan does not have complete income-side quarterly data, and publishes results with time delay — among summit (G-7) countries. There are, however, possibilities of making high-frequency forecasts from gross production statistics and intermediate flow statistics (the *net* is valued-added, by sector). A functioning model has been in place for several years, and contemporary research is underway, to enhance the system. Professor

Raymond Courbis of the University of Paris — X, has constructed a current-quarter (high-frequency) model for France, and it is in regular use.

In past years, exploratory models have been built for UK, and Canada. These have not been maintained, and a natural point from which to start anew is with a total Euroland system. This approach is presently under consideration.

At the level of developing countries, there are two projects that have been recently launched, namely, high-frequency modeling for Hong Kong and for Mexico. They can, if successful, serve as model cases for other developing countries. In these two cases, work is still in progress, but early indications look promising.

As starting points, the easiest way to begin, if there are to be averages from different models, is to estimate systems by use of principal components for headline aggregates. After these segments are operating smoothly, then modeling the components of the expenditure side of GDP is a natural second step. It is probably the case, for most developing countries, that quarterly (or even annual) data on the full estimation of National Income and of GDP from the income side, independently, will not exist or will be very difficult to collect fully.

Some more time is needed, to see how high-frequency modeling can be developed for emerging markets, yet the research is clearly worth the try; however the investigators must be fully aware of the data deficiencies.

A listing of the monthly indicators being used for Hong Kong and for Mexico follows.

High-frequency Model of Hong Kong, Starting date, January, 1981	**Principal Components of Monthly Indicators**
Real GDP Estimation	PGDP (deflator) Estimation
Quantum Index of Imports	Unit Value Imports Index
Quantum Index of Domestic Exports	Unit Value Domestic Exports Index
Quantum Index of Re-exports	Unit Value Re-exports Index
Visitor Arrivals (Mill.)	Exchange Rate (trade wtd.)
Building Completed (m^2)	Price Index of Retail Sales

Consent to Work, Buildings (m^2)	M1, HK$, Mill.
Consideration for Land Requisition	M2, HK$, Mill.
Incorporations (no. of cos.)	M3, HK$, Mill.
Dissolutions (no. of cos.)	Loans/Advances, HK$
Orders-on-hand, Mfg.	Dissolutions (no. of cos.)
Electricity Consumed (tera joules)	Time Deposit Internal Rate, 12 mos.
Gas Consumed (tera joules)	Savings Deposit Interest Rate
Retail Sales Volume Index	Best Lending Interest Rate
Hang Seng Share Index	Interbank Offered Interest Rate

Interest Spread, $HK 12 mos. Deposits, less LIBOR
Time Trend

The time trend is not used for the evaluation of principal components leading to calculation of eigenvalues and corresponding eigenvectors. It is used at the next step in the regression of real GDP on a subset of principal components. There are trends in GDP and in the variables that constitute the principal components. There is also a trend in the principal components, after they are transformed into original units of measurement. By the well-known Frisch-Waugh argument, it makes no difference in classical *linear* regressions (GDP on a selection of principal components) whether the variables of the estimated relationship are transformed into deviations from trend or whether variables are left in original units of measurement, while the explicit trend terms are included in the regression equation. This being so, it was deemed preferable to leave all variables in well-understood conventional units, while the trend effects are estimated from explicit variables. The only stochastic assumptions concern properties of the error term, for which tests of significance are made.

There is some similarity between the kind of variables that are used for principal component analysis of fluctuations in GDP and PGDP for the US and for Hong Kong, but fundamentally, every case can be separately considered for its own conditions and social institutions.

For Mexico, the principal components are estimated from the following monthly variables, January 1993 — December 1998.

Real GDP Estimation	**PGDP Estimation**
Manufacturing Production Index	Consumer Price Index
Construction Industry Index	Producer Price Index

Industrial Production Index
Gross Fixed Investment Index
Wholesale Trade Index
Retail Sales Index
Man-Hours Worked in
Manufacturing Index
Average Real Wages in
Manufacturing Index
Employment Rate
Maquiladora Exports (1993$)
Crude Oil Exports (volume)
Real Money Supply (M1)
Real Interest Rate (Cetes 28)
Real Exchange Rate
Tourism Balance (1993$)

Nominal Exchange Rate
Nominal Interest Rate (Cetes 28)
Nominal Money Supply: M_1
Oil Price (Mexican-mix, $)

Stock Exchange Index

Minimum Wage Index (pesos)

The same mathematical statistical procedures used for Hong Kong are used for Mexico. All the monthly data for the US and Japanese high-frequency models are seasonally adjusted. The conventional way to deal with seasonality in Hong Kong is to compare *change* over the same quarter or month, one year ago. People are used to thinking about short-run economic issues in this way; so no attempt has been made to use seasonally adjusted data, but for the Mexican statistics seasonal adjustment is more common, and the model will incorporate prior seasonal adjustment, either implicit in official data or estimated from a standard method such as X-11.

There is a long history of econometric model building, with forecast extrapolations, having been done for 30 years in Mexico. At first, the models were based on annual data, but seasonally adjusted quarterly data are now readily available and familiar for decision makers.

Hong Kong, too, has been studied from the vantage point of macroeconometric models for many years. The late T.B. Lin's annual model from the Chinese University of Hong Kong was used in Project LINK's world assessment for many years and is presently maintained. Research on the Hong Kong High-Frequency Model was started in spring 1998 and without building equations for the complete national accounting sector, but relying at first on the principal component equations for GDP and PGDP, some trial forecasts were made in May 1998, that showed estimates of GDP, before they were released officially, that were lower, quarter-by-quarter in 1998 than in similar periods of 1997. This was a good projection but not widely expected. One year later, in April 1999, the corresponding projections showed a string of positive quarters, in comparison with the year-ago quarters of 1998, of +1.0 to 3.0%. The first estimates of the same quarter released in August 1999, showed year-over-year growth of 0.5% and optimistic comments that the recovery would continue, by the same method of reckoning, with respect to year-ago values.

Oddly enough, when the Hong Kong economy was faltering, in real terms, the price deflator was expanding, as the principal components method estimated, and now the early results of 1999 show falling values of the price deflator in comparison with year-ago values.

Naturally, much more research work needs to be done on the Hong Kong Model, but the first two years' attempts, at turning-point-values - are encouraging. The Mexican Model is not yet at the same trial stage; so it will require a year's intensive research before results will be reported.

FORECASTING, POLICY FORMATION, AND VALUE JUDGMENTS

The emphasis in this essay is on the gains that are yet to be realized in economic forecasting, especially for the very near term. There is an additional aspect that merits consideration, namely, how are the forecasts to be used. Among different uses, an important application is in formulating economic policy. This is a major public sector use. Longer range forecasts are needed for many policy issues, but day-to-day guidance for maintaining *stability* in the economy rests with monetary and fiscal authorities. In this respect, much praise has been accorded to Chairman Alan Greenspan of the US Federal Reserve for maintaining the macroeconomic expansion that began in 1991 (after the Gulf War). At the beginning of the recovery, and especially through 1992, the forecasts of longer-term interest rates (i.e. longer than 90 days) were disappointing. Short-term rates (3-month bills) were lowered from 7.5% to almost 3%, but 10-year treasury securities stayed between 5.9% and 7.9%. The civilian unemployment rate stayed in the neighborhood of 7%. Inflation was kept under control, but the recovery did little for the labor market. Eventually, starting in fiscal year 1993, the federal deficit was reduced; longer-term interest rates responded, and the unemployment rate fell, until it reached values near 4%, with no acceleration in inflation.

Policy formation, at the beginning of the recovery, was set by two real-economy criteria. One was the *potential* real growth rate of the US economy, which has been placed at values between 2.0% and 2.5%, depending on which technique for measuring real GDP was adopted. The present measure in *official* favor is one based on chain-linked price indexes which has tended to make the growth in GDP a bit larger, leading to the higher end of the range for potential real GDP.

The second real criterion was the rate of unemployment, which was set at 6%, or more, to accompany the 2.5% real growth rate of potential GDP. After the economy registered month-after-month of lower unemployment, without acceleration of inflation, the authorities in government and finance suggested that a non-inflationary rate, might be lower — nearer to 5%.

These two crucial values, the potential growth rate and the unemployment rate, at full employment, have not been forecasted as well as the short-term inflation rate. The objective of the Federal Reserve with willing accomplices in other parts of the US government establishment, has been primarily to keep inflation low, near 2% or less. This has been achieved, but the correspondence between the inflation rate and the growth *potential* or the labor market *potential* has not been estimated at all well. The latter two concepts are not ordinary published statistics; they are conceptual and applicable to longer-run performance. The short-term inflation rate has been well estimated, but the medium-term *expected* rate has not. It, too, is a subjective and conceptual value, and has been consistently forecast with considerable error, in fact it is not a random error, but a biased error.

It is biased because of value judgments. Although the published directives for the Federal Reserve System encompass both a stable price level and "pursuit of full employment", there is clearly a bias in favor of maintaining a stable price level, at all cost — in this case at the cost of forgone output, jobs, and a more balanced economy.[6]

[6] The book published by the Federal Reserve System entitled *The Federal Reserve System, Purposes and Functions*, Library of Congress number 39-26719, 1994, states on p. 1 "... The Federal Reserve's Duties fall into four general cases: Conducting the nation's monetary policy by influencing the money and credit conditions in the economy in pursuit of full employment and stable prices ..."

"ANALYTICAL ASPECTS OF ANTI-INFLATION POLICY" AFTER 40 YEARS

*Robert M. Solow**

ABSTRACT

This paper reconsiders the 1960 article by Samuelson and Solow in the light of later developments in the theory of inflation and in the facts of inflation. The 1960 article was quite tentative and skeptical in tone, qualities not always to be found in current discussion. But it may have been too optimistic about the stability of the inflation-unemployment relation.

BACKGROUND

In the recession of 1948-49, the first one after the war, consumer prices actually fell. The second postwar recession came in 1953-54, and again consumer prices fell, with a slight lag. The third recession, in 1957-58, was noticeably deeper than the first two; the unemployment rate went from four percent at the peak to just over seven percent at the bottom. But prices did not fall, in fact the rate of inflation actually *rose* from 2.4 percent during the 1955-57 upswing to 2.8 percent a year during its course.

This surprising turn of events came to be called "creeping" inflation, and it set off an intense discussion of the nature of the inflationary process, both inside and outside the economics profession. The vocabulary in common use was not the same as ours today. The main divide was between those who ascribed creeping inflation to "demand-pull" and those who thought it was more accurately described as a case of "cost-push."

---

* Department of Economics, Memorial Drive, Cambridge, U.S.A.

Much subtle reasoning was devoted to refining that distinction, and thinking of ways to let facts choose between them. It is not straightforward to translate that discussion into today's vocabulary, and may be there is not much point in doing so. A demand-pull partisan might have something in common with an economist today who would say: "Simple enough if inflation speeded up during the recession of 1957-58, that just tells us that the natural rate of unemployment or NAIRU is now higher than seven percent." From that standpoint the fact that the economy seems to have plenty of slack is just irrelevant. A cost-push partisan might have been more like an economist who would look first for more or less autonomous sources of cost increases, like higher import or food prices or, more likely in those days, greater trade-union militancy. Today one might think that some cost increases might be interpreted as the very forces that cause the natural rate to rise. But those words and concepts were not available to economists who had not yet read the later works of Milton Friedman and Edmund Phelps, or Robert Gordon and George Perry.

That is the highly relevant context in which Paul Samuelson and I were asked to contribute a paper to a discussion of "the problem of achieving and maintaining a stable price level" at the annual Christmas convention of the American Economic Association in 1959. The paper we produced, with the tittle "Analytical Aspects of Anti-Inflation Policy" was read at the convention and published in the Papers and Proceedings number of the *American Economic Review* (Vol. L, no.2, May 1960, pp. 177-94). That paper is now almost exactly 40 years old, and has been much discussed in its lifetime. I thought that a look back at it would be a suitable vehicle for my tribute to my beloved friend and colleague on this occasion.

THE PHILLIPS CURVE

Perhaps the most notorious thing about the 1960 paper is that it (very likely) marked the introduction of the work of A.W. Phillips into American discussion of the inflationary process. (Phillips's paper (*Economica*, 1958) was brand new; I believe that we may have used the phrase "Phillips curve" in print for the first time.) It is sometimes said that our paper domesticated the pernicious notion of a "permanent trade-off between inflation and unemployment." I intend to suggest that there are more interesting ideas in the paper than the Phillips curve; but it is probably a good idea, in view of the history, to discuss the role of the Phillips curve first.

The most surprising aspect of Phillips's empirical work was that the relationship he found between unemployment and wage inflation in the U.K. for the long period 1861-1913 seemed to fit without change for 1913-48 and 1948-57. Samuelson and I thought that he was on to something real; but it was clear that any application to the U.S. would have to accept occasional shifts in the curve, and considerably less tight a fit. But it seemed to us that a scatter diagram of U.S. data for 1946-58 looked promising. (It is a remarkable fact that we made no attempt to fit a multiple regression. I was teaching econometrics regularly at the time, so we knew how; but we both thought that running regressions after so much eyeballing of the data would be inappropriate. Neither of us would have thought the simple bivariate relation to be an adequate representation.)

The main analytical use we made of the Phillips curve was to see if it could make sense of the cost-push vs. demand-pull debate. Changes in inflation describable as movements along the Phillips curve, presumably driven by variations in aggregate demand, could be ascribed to demand-pull; changes in inflation originating in shifts of the Phillips curve could be ascribed to cost push. But we were explicitly skeptical about that identification, and one of the reasons we gave for doubt was the possibility that the expectation of continued high employment might by itself shift the curve adversely. More fundamentally, we were doubtful in advance about the pure labor-supply interpretation of the curve that was later adopted by monetarists.

WHAT KIND OF TRADE-OFF?

Of course we were interested in the possibility that the Phillips curve might represent an exploitable trade-off between unemployment and inflation. Here I think that hindsight reveals some ambiguity. On our side, it has to be said that we were very skeptical about the durability of any such trade-off. We wrote, for instance: "But would it take eight to ten percent unemployment forever to stabilize the money wage? Is not this kind of relationship also one which depends heavily on remembered experience? We suspect that this is another way in which a past characterized by rising prices, high employment, and mild, short recessions is likely to breed an inflationary bias...." So, without formalizing it--we formalized nothing in that paper--we were obviously wondering about something like an expectations-augmented Phillips curve.

There is another, even more explicit passage: "...it might be that the low-pressure demand would so act upon wage and other expectations as to shift the curve downward in the longer run--so that over a decade, the economy might enjoy higher employment with price stability than our present-day estimate would indicate." This is not at all to say that we had the later Friedman-Phelps vertical long-run Phillips curve in mind. (Neither of us ever had much confidence in the accelerationist model when it was finally formulated and took the profession by storm.)

When we reflected on the likely consequences of a prolonged low-pressure economy, engineered in order to squeeze creeping inflation out of the system, we had other things in mind as well. "A low-pressure economy might build up within itself over the years larger and larger amounts of structural unemployment (the reverse of what happened from 1941 to 1953 as a result of strong war and postwar demands). The result would be an upward shift of our menu of choice, with more and more unemployment being needed just to keep prices stable." We were suggesting that what would later be called hysteresis might work against the favorable expectational effects of contrived low pressure. My own belief--I do not implicate Samuelson--is that Europe has still not learned this part of the lesson.

That is the case for the defense: the required qualifications are there, and the tone is appropriately tentative. But the prosecution has a case too. It is that the qualifications are just qualifications, and the reader is left with the impression that the recorded Phillips curve really does provide what the just-quoted passage calls "a menu of choice." There is certainly no hint in the 1960 paper of a "natural rate of unemployment." Even the very last sentence of the paper, speaking of the drastic institutional changes that might be needed to "lesson the degree of disharmony between full employment and price stability," describes the goal as moving the Phillips curve downward and to the left. To a true believer, the "downward" gives the game away. A reader of that paper would not have been prepared for the 1970s. There is truth in that charge. (But a small voice tells me that the same reader might have been better prepared for the 1990s.)

IDENTIFICATION AND OTHER QUESTIONS

Half of the 1960 paper goes by before the Phillips curve is even mentioned. That first half is directed mainly to the demand-pull and cost-push discussion.

The emphasis is on the kinds of empirical evidence that could hope to discriminate between theories, and the sorts of policy experiments that the two theories suggest. The general direction of the discussion is that, when account is taken of the general-equilibrium character of the inflationary process, many of the simple claims and nostrums fail.

We pointed out that both quantity-theorists and Keynesians favor demand-pull theories. Our remarks on the quantity theory were fairly standard, and mainly insisted that policy discussion could not intelligently ignore the likely interest-rate-induced variations in velocity. On Keynesian economics, our main point was that a mostly imperfectly competitive economy was its natural habitat, actually needed for some of the characteristic propositions. But it is exactly in this imperfectly competitive environment that the idea of cost-push inflation can make logical sense. But consistency is not the same thing as identification; we worried that nature and history had not provided the observations that could pin down the causality underlying events.

We rather liked a notion that Charles Schultze had proposed just then. It was that there had indeed been excess demand for capital goods in 1955-57, though not general excess demand. The natural rise in the relative price of capital goods had been converted into generalized creeping inflation by the combination of cost-push and downward-rigidity in other markets.

But we spent more time criticizing what we thought to the fallacies, in both professional and popular discussion, that tried to infer causality from simple observations. Some of these were elementary errors, like the belief that nominal wage rates rising faster than productivity implies cost-push inflation or that aggregate expenditure rising faster than real output implies demand inflation. A student of elementary macroeconomics would realize that both circumstances would characterize any inflation, whatever its originating impulse.

But we also found more sophisticated inferences to contain holes. Timing relations -- do wages rise before prices or afterwards? -- are unreliable indicators of causality. There is almost never an identifiable "normal" state of affairs from which any change must have a specific cause; and anyway effects can precede causes in situations where expectations govern behavior. More subtly, in a multi-market economy, some of the markets highly competitive and some highly imperfectly competitive, man alternative price-quantity scenarios are compatible either with demand-side impulses or cost-side impulses as the main originating force in an inflation. We did conclude, however, that sector-by-sector analysis could provide important hints about causality. But we argued strongly that causality might be different from sector to sector; there is no presumption that the right theory in any historical instance has to be monolithic.

INTERESTING RESEARCH QUESTIONS

Then we went on to suggest a couple of questions whose answers would throw light on the analysis of the inflationary process, but where we thought too little research had been done.

The first was the behavior of real aggregate demand under inflationary conditions. It is too easy and too tempting to argue from the presumption that real demands are homogeneous of degree zero in all prices to the notion that real aggregate demand is invariant to regular inflation. In any historical inflationary situation there will be distributional effects among wages, profits and fixed incomes, and there will be others that arise because, for instance, the service sector and the manufacturing sector will have different pricing practices. Other non-homogeneities arise from tax progression and the variety of tax bases. But we wondered it recent quasi-institutional developments, e.g., the existence of larger accumulations of savings, might have the effect of making real demand less subject to erosion by inflation than in the past. We thought that research might be able to provide useful answers to such questions. I am not sure that it has done so yet.

The second question that we proposed for more research was precisely the relation between nominal wage rates and inflation. That was where we made reference to the work of Phillips and introduced the discussion that filled the second half of the 1960 paper and the first half of this review of it.

CONCLUDING THOUGHTS

From the 1970s on, discussion of inflation within the economics profession had as its main focus the "natural rate of unemployment." The vertical long-run expectations-augmented Phillips curve was taken for granted. Those macroeconomists with a more institutional interest, and those with intellectual ties to labor economics, generally did not challenge the basic framework, but worked instead on the determinants of the natural rate itself. Paul Samueslon did not participate in this discussion, except perhaps casually and fleetingly. We can safely conclude that he did not find the underlying theoretical framework attractive or plausible. It was too simple-minded, and Samuelson has never found simple-minded accounts of complex economic events convincing. So he found more interesting things to do. Perhaps I should say that I shared the views that I have imputed to Samuelson. From time to time I mentioned that I found the whole natural-rate theory flimsy on both theoretical and empirical grounds. But it was, as sailors say, like spitting to windward.

Today that consensus seems to be cracking up. In just the way that, according to Robert Lucas and Thomas Sargent, the stagflation of the 1970s cut the ground from under the unvarnished Phillips curve--Sargent much later expressed a far more nuanced view--so the long non-inflationary boom of the 1990 seems to expose the weakness of the accelerationist model. Once the natural rate is endogenous--my own doubts go beyond that--the policy implications are quite different.

Forty years after, the open, eclectic, theoretical-institutional view of inflation espoused by Samuelson and his junior colleague in 1960 is looking better.

KREISLAUF AND GREAT AGGREGATES: THE MISSING LINK IN THE WORK OF PROFESSOR SAMUELSON. OR, "IN SEARCH OF LOST DYNAMICS".

*Vittorangelo Orati**

ABSTRACT

This paper is based on the two central theoretical options of Samuelson regarding the scientific heritage of his former Harvardian teacher, Schumpeter. Specifically, this paper details the intrinsic limits of the macroeconomic approach to the dynamic nature of capitalistic economy and its periodical instability. An alternative approach is proposed, based on a disaggregate model and the theory of opportunity/value, which leads to a "Dynamic Discriminating Equation" able to distinguish between physiological and pathological interruptions of the capital accumulation process. This is the difference which macroeconomics, with its fatal "blindness" with respect to dynamic process, is unable to distinguish. A "blindness" that Schumpeter in his time had correctly diagnosed but never rigorously explained.

The following essay is about the two different theoretical options which can be found in Professor Samuelson's extensive, significant work, whose importance is such when considered in the light of Schumpeter's scientific heritage. As is well-known, Schumpeter was one of Samuelson's professors at Harvard, in the 30s (Silk, 1978, 13-14; Swedberg, 1991, 113-114).

The first option is positive and concerns the defence of conceptualised quantity, the core of the Schumpeterian theory of the economic development: the *Kreislauf*, or *circular flow*. This has been one of the most criticised aspects

---

* Instituto Economico, Universita degli Studi della Tuscia, del Paradisco, Italy.

of Schumpeter's theory.[1]

The second option which is negative, in that Samuelson, in common with the "Keynesian revolution"[2], has not followed Schumpeter's suggestion as far as the misleading and deceptive logics of the economy of great aggregates is concerned, with respect to the essential task of finding the origin of the cyclical unstable capitalistic dynamics. Such a lack of esteem comes from the radical, even though diplomatic, aversion by Schumpeter to the *General Theory* and the increasing popularity of the macro-economics by Keynes (Orati, 1988, 15-16, 135-154; Swedberg, 1991, 118-119).

It is our intention here to show how, between the two above mentioned choices, there is a theoretical incoherence, when considered in the light of an analytical-Schumpeterian framework, and that this has remarkable implications on the present *state of the art of the dismal science*.

The presence — *inter alia* — of a null rate of interest in the vector of relative prices, which marks the *static stationary equilibrium* represented by the *Kreislauf* (Schumpeter, 1934, chapters I, V; 1951a), has given rise to a series of criticisms that brought Samuelson, on several occasions, to defend his former Professor (Samuelson, 1943, 1951, 1971).

In particular, Samuelson faced the following criticisms: that a zero rate of interest would push economic agents to consume the whole capital as its user cost is zero, taking for granted that the rate of time preference is in favour of present goods, rather than future goods (Robbins, 1930; Haberler, 1951).

---

[1]Leaving out those aspects which are, objectively, less important — theoretically speaking — together with the *circular flow* (*Kreislauf* is the original, German word), and the connected polemic on the null rate of interest, the other aspect of the Schumpeterian development theory, which has been most criticised, was that one which criticised the implicit, cyclical appearance of innovations or the entrepreneurs-innovators. Robbins (Robbins, 1930), Knight (Knight, 1930) and Haberler (Haberler, 1951, 205, n. 1) criticised the first aspect. Robins gives, in addition to his opposition, a list of other critical positions towards Schumpeter published in Germany. Samuelson (Samuelson, 1971) shows more recent formulations of the criticisms to "Schumpeter's zero rate of interest" (McCrae, 1968).

[2] In addition to the historical-biographical essays (Silk, 1978; Swedberg, 1931), Samuelson himself explains his adhesion to the "Keynesian revolution" (Samuelson, 1946) and more in particular, to his version known as the "neo-classic synthesis" (Samuelson, 1963).

A more recent criticism retained that there is a new and crucial problem: if in the *circular flow* there is a regime of decentralised decisions, then the economic subjects, hedonistically motivated, would freely exchange their goods, without altering the vector of the prices (Samuelson, 1971; McCrae, 1968).

However, looking closer at both they are in fact two different ways of criticising Schumpeter for the same aspect, that is for his connoting the *circular flow* in meta-economic terms, thereby contradicting the basis of *his* theory of economic development.

The first case, illustrates how the *Kreislauf* corresponds to the land of milk and honey! If we consider K_0 as the present value of the capital, Y_0 as the constant perpetual income related to it, i the rate of interest, we have:

$$\lim_{i \to 0} K_0 = \frac{Y_0}{i} = \infty$$

On the other hand, if the law of the demand and supply is not respected, the "prices" would not represent an index of scarsity. For each price level there would be a plurality of corresponding quantities. Consequently the stationary state at i=0 would result outside of any representative equilibrium.

In both the cases, the *circular flow*, being an essential element of the Schumpeter's economic theory, would be based outside the epistemological dimension of economics, which is the "kingdom of necessity and scarsity (*rareté*)".

Therefore, the contradiction would not only be evident but also paralysing, and Schumpeter's model would result deprived of its scientific meaning.

What is missing in the interpretation of the *circular flow*, which is the base of these criticisms brought to their extreme logical consequences on the formal level, is an appreciation of the strategic importance of the *Theorie der Wirtschaftlichen Entwicklung* within economic theory, as a whole.

On the syntactic level, where his worth is indisputable, Samuelson would rebuff both the imputations in their specifics.

However, as Samuelson does not seem to realise that Schumpeter's development theory operates, inside economics, by a mechanism that involves "creative destruction" — which leads to the phenomenon of development itself — he ends up making use of his well-known analytical abilities to defend his former professor in a way which is nothing more than a *beau geste.*

Robbins's scholastic reaction, as well as that of all those who share his idea is that a null rate of interest means the transformation of a necessary dis-incentive, to the gratuitous possibility of "... *turn income into capital or capital into income*" (Robbins, 1930, 213). In this Robbins maintains the rule of orthodoxy, by which the rate of interest is the user cost of capital.

Hence, the criticism towards Schumpeter who is, considered in error, with regard to the "official liturgy", instead of being followed in the design of his "research programme".

Trusting in the superiority of his knowledge of the algorithms compatible with the theodicea of the neo-classic paradigm, Samuelson "recovers" to the *ecclesia* his former professor, reproaching, in their turn, those priests who have not been rigorous in judging the "lost sheep".

He contraposes the *leit motive* of the criticism: "Why should capital be maintained at a zero rate of interest?", with this simple answer: "Why should it not? If an ... interest rate is needed to keep the stationary state, why should it not be a zero rate?" (Samuelson, 1943, 62), whilst having previously stated that "the *circular flow* is a stationary solution of a dynamical process" (Samuelson, 1943, 60-61). This last statement is essential for our purpose as it means that, starting from a dynamic model, it is possible to achieve a stationary model, considering the variables which represent the dynamic factors as equal to zero. In other words, for Samuelson, Schumpeter's *circular flow*, with i=0, corresponds to one of the many possible states of equilibrium, which can be generated by the variables that define it. In this case, this means: "a condition of perfect certainty and an economy consisting of one or more individuals" where "we further assume ... that there is no intrinsic rate of time preference" (Samuelson, 1943, 62).

In reality, the condition of perfect knowledge would have been enough to provide a rational basis for the attitude of the economic agents not to consume the capital, once it has been admitted that, as Schumpeter maintains, the *circular flow* connotes a *static stationary* economy (Schumpeter, 1951a, 158). In other words, a unique level of equilibrium in which the economy is, and to which it should return, at any time and for any reason, in case of every small disturbance. Each subject would know that he is paying for his greatest satisfaction, related to his present consumption of capital, with the corresponding reduction of future production. On the other hand, Samuelson, in his first defence, affirms that the level of the *circular flow* with *i*=0, is only *one* of *all* the possible levels of equilibrium from a situation where, given a certain amount of resources, the consumers' taste is already known and the production techniques are constant.

This is, a situation that can be compared to that represented by "Edgworth's box" (where everything is given), where "Schumpeter's zero interest rate" is only one of the points on the related "contract curve". To be more precise, this point is where — *coeteris paribus* — there is a general indifference between present and future consumption, and there are no exchanges, depending on time preferences. However, as Samuelson admits (Samuelson, 1971, 36), this position falls under the objection to the fact that, with *i*=0 at a given level of prices, the subjects could exchange unlimited amounts of commodities (no more related to the prices); all this, of course, delineates a position of equilibrium which can not be represented. At this point Samuelson, ignoring Schumpeter's position with respect to the general economic equilibrium, as well as, in particular, the presence of surplus under the form of profit, resorts to a sophisticated, even though ethereal, mathematical formulation, which reminds one of the forgotten roles of perfect competition.

With this "formula", and considering as primitive competitive behaviour, in terms compatible with the *circular flow* and *i*=0, he demonstrates — in contradiction to his earlier thoughts— that the *Kreislauf* with *i* tending to *zero*, is not *one* of the possible levels of equilibrium but the only possible level, in this configuration of the economy (Samuelson, 1971, 37). Although Samuelson radically changed his mind on this crucial issue — though, not enough to logically sustain the Schumpeterian concept of *circular flow* within the development "model", as it is, as this requires *i* equal to, and not simply *tending to zero*, he did not change his mind on the "research programme" of his former professor. This "research programme" derives from the very central, though unacknowledged, reasoning with which Schumpeter showed how the *circular flow*, being a stationary economy in a static equilibrium, with a null rate of interest — and not tending to zero — represents the only possible formulation of the Walrasian General Economic Equilibrium (G.E.E.).

Bearing in mind the assumptions of G.E.E. which are:

1. a given amount of resources and their relative allocation;
2. the production techniques (which are constant);
3. the consumer preference functions;
4. a surplus which exceeds the amount of resources necessary for the simple reproduction of the economic system. Without this surplus, it would be impossible to realise forced saving which are necessary to start development;
5. the highest possible level of employment;
6. a state of free and perfect competition.

The incidental presence of a surplus in the form of profit would be nullified. Those who realise this kind of income, that is entrepreneurs, would be compelled, by perfect competition, to reduce the prices gradually, until the rate of profit[3] is nullified, *ergo* the *productive* rate of interest, defined by Schumpeter as a fraction of the rate of profit (Schumpeter, 1934, chapters 4-5; 1939, 123 and following, vol. I). In consequence, one must take into account what Samuelson himself acknowledges when he quotes Walras when the latter says: "In the economic literature we are quite accustomed to an *entrepreneur faisant ni benefice ni perte*" (Samuelson, 1943, 62 — Samuelson's italics).

Schumpeter refers to these words by Walras, underlining that it is contradictory to admit that in the model of the general economic equilibrium, the entrepreneurs' earnings and losses compensate each others and at the same time confirming the presence of a positive rate of interest (Schumpeter, 1934, chap. I, 46 and footnote 1).

---

[3]The clearest formulation of such reasoning that, indeed, pervades the whole logical structure on which *The Theory of Economic Development* is based, besides being implicit in the "Preface" of 1937 (Schumpeter, 1951, 158 and follows), can be found in the chapter entitled *Karl Marx*, in the book *Ten Great Economists from Marx to Keynes* (Schumpeter, 1951b), retaken from *Capitalism, Socialism and Democracy* (Schumpeter, 1950). The analytical context is that which, wrongly, brings Schumpeter to criticise the *Einfache Reproduction* (simple reproduction), in the same way as he did the G.E.E. by Walras. In other words, for Schumpeter there is coincidence between the *circular flow* and the marxist simple reproduction where, here too, we could not have a positive profit. We have elsewhere confuted Schumpeter on this point (Orati, 1988, 127-134).

It is not just the result of a judgement and a note expressed *en passant*, but the *ratio* which moves the whole Schumpeterian "research programme", explicitly disclosed in the "Preface" to the Japanese edition of his *Theory of Economic Development*, of 1937.

Both these circumstances legitimise the suspicion that there has been a huge manifestation of that phenomenon described by Festinger as "cognitive dissonance".[4]

This is true especially if we consider the whole logical scaffolding, as well as the heuristics which nourishes the masterpiece of the great Austrian economist (Orati, 1988).

Also the *querelle* on the null rate of interest, for example, reveals a substantial misunderstanding, as to the distinction made by Schumpeter between *productive* interest and *consumptive* interest, as well as the functional distinction — which is, actually, historical — between the means of production and capital (Schumpeter, 1934, 116, 122, 177-178, 184).

Quoting literally from Schumpeter's important document of self-interpretation of his own work, represented by the "Preface" of 1937, for the Japanese readers , where — *inter alia* — he said:

> "To Walras we owe a concept of the economic system and a theoretical apparatus which for the first time in the history of our science effectively embraced the pure logic of the interdipendence between economic quantities. But when in my beginnings I studied the Walrasian conception and the Walrasian technique ... I discovered not only that it is rigorously static in character (this is selfevident and has been again and again stressed by Walras himself) but also that it is applicable only to a stationary process. These two things must not be confused. A static theory is simply a statement of the conditions of equilibrium and the way in which equilibrium tends to re-establish itself after every small disturbance ... A stationary process, however, is a process which *actually* does not change of its own initiative, but merely reproduces constant rates of real income as it flows along in

[4]An author (Sievers, 1962, 44), rather than a phenomenon of "cognitive dissonance" (Festinger, 1962), ascribes to an excessive acuteness in Schumpeter's thought the fact that his work did not have the prosecution it deserved (see, Elliot, 1983).

> time. If it changes at all, it does so under the influence of events which are external to itself, such as natural catastrophes, wars and so on. Walras would have admitted this. He would have said and, as a matter of fact, he did say it to me the only time that I had the opportunity to converse with him) that of course economic life is essentially passive and merely adapts itself to the natural and social influences which may be acting on it, so that the theory of a stationary process constitutes really the whole of theoretical economics ... Like the classics, he would have made exceptions for increase in population and in savings, but this would only introduce a change in the data of the system and not add any new phenomena. I felt very strongly that this was wrong, and that there was a source of energy within the economic system which would of itself disrupt any equilibrium that might be attained. If this so, then there must be a purely economic theory of economic change which does not merely rely on external factors propelling the economic system from one equilibrium to another. It is such theory that I have tried to build and I believe now, as I believed then, that it contributes something to the understanding ... of the capitalist world and explains a number of phenomena, in particular the business cycle ..." (Schumpeter, 1951a, 165-166).

The long quotation is justified by the great importance of its content. It is, in fact, an authentic guide to Schumpeter's theory of economic development. It states — *inter alia* — that:

1. unlike that which Samuelson retains, the theory of economic development is not a *prius* of the concept of *Kreislauf*. This would not represent a special case of the first, for the simple reason that the economic theory does not encompass a theory of development or a theory of economic dynamics;

2. the development is not merely a chapter of economic science, but represents substantially the same object of this science: the capitalist process is the greater part of that object;

3. economics has always cultivated the idea that the neo-classic paradigm, based on the theory of the General Economic Equilibrium, could treat economic development as a chapter of such a theory; instead, it is only and irremediably adequate to an economic system in a stationary condition and in a static equilibrium: in other words, in a situation corresponding to the *circular flow*;

4. it is impossible to reach a theory of development (and therefore a theory of cyclical character of such developments) by building models which involve dynamic stimuli, external to the *circular flow*.

In other words, the process of capitalist accumulation can not be explained by independent or *autonomous* quantities or *exogenous* variables. It is necessarily an *endogenous* development theory which originates from the *circular flow* and finds the necessary "energy" to initiate the take-off by those (potential) forces which are present inside the *circular flow* itself. This is the case of the *effort* related to innovation, that is to the introduction of new production techniques — *alias* — to the entrepreneur-innovator, and therefore to the middle-class which gave origin, historically, to capitalism, according to Schumpeter's theory. Although predicting the fortune of all the writings and publications concerning the business cycle and in general economic development, for Schumpeter the only possible way to explain the capitalist process is by taking into consideration not only the development process but also its cyclic *modus operandi*.[5] Moreover at the end of the essay from which the previous quotation is drawn, the Author warns against the dangers represented by the pseudo-explanations, as these are based on mere, even though new, formal instruments:

> "But it should be observed that the results due to these new method (reader could inform himself about some of them by *reading Professor Tinbergen's Suggestions on Quantitative Business Cycle Theory* in <Econometrica>, vol. 3, n. 3) do not constitute an alternative theory of business cycle or the process of economic change in general. They describe repercussions and propagations without saying anything about the forces or causes that set them into motion. Whatever those causes, the way in which they operate and in which the system reacts to them

---

[5]As if he wanted to highlight his disagreement on the "vogue" of the "macro-economy", that is the attempt to make dynamic the "static" apparatus of Keynes's *General Theory*, and so re-establishing the fact that the capitalist dynamics can not but be explained by dividing the simple movement of income in the time from the cyclic nature of such a movement, Schumpeter begins his "Preface" to *Business Cycle* as follows:

> "Analysing business cycles means neither more nor less than analysing the economic process of the capitalist era. Most of us discover this truth which at once reveals the nature of the task and also its formidable dimensions. Cycles are not, like tonsils, separable things that might be treated by themselves, but are, like the beat of the heart, the essence of the organism that displays them (Schumpeter, 1939, V, vol. I); (see also Orati, 1999, 10).

is elucidate by the new methods. But they do not touch the question whether the force actually at work is correctly described by the principle of innovation or not" (Schumpeter, 1951a, 168; 1934 XI).

This last note means that one must be careful not to consider as explanations of the capitalist process — and therefore of its peculiar oscillatory movement, with *irregular regularity* — some representations which mime the phenomenon but which are without a profound comprehension of their real nature and laws, as the *ratio* of the scientific research requires. In particular, without taking into account the change in production techniques ("new combinations") that, as we know, are the main cause of blocking the general economic equilibrium in the continuous, static-stationary ebbs and flows of the *Kreislauf* or *circular flow*. In this way, competition is compelled to transfer the surplus to the consumers, surplus that can be conceived under the form of profit *ergo* of interest.

We have seen what is meant by the theoretical and methodological connection between the stationary process and the dynamic process. From this, we have Schumpeter on one side and Samuelson, with the whole official economic theory, on the other side. Schumpeter insists that economics can not develop a dynamic theory (and therefore "realise" its main object: capitalism), based on the paradigm of the General Economic Equilibrium.

According to Schumpeter, the theory of economic dynamics must be built *ex novo*, even though starting from that *prius* which is the Walrasian model, properly amended in its form without contradictions, and represented in terms of *circular flow*. This form *inter alia* requires that the (*productive*) rate of interest is zero, not as one of the possible values which it can assume in the vector of the prices which ensures the static equilibrium, but as the *only* value which can ensure such an equilibrium.

Such a position of great relevance, can accommodate everything apart from *un fin de non recevoir*. This is not only relevant to the logical-narrative context of the *Theorie*, but to the "research programme" in its entirety already presented in Schumpeter's early work *Das Wesen und der Hauptinhalt der Theoretischen Nationalökonomie* (1908).

The "research programme" is not overlooked in the later *Business Cycles*, or in the posthumous *History of Economic Analysis* (Schumpeter,

1939, V; 1954, 963-964).

In the last chapter (V), of the last part (the 5th) of *Das Wesen*, entitled *The possibilities of development of the theoretical economy*, with respect to the limits of the "pure economy":

> "Our starting point, which need not be demonstrate, is the existence of some problems, beyond our system... . The accumulation of the capital, the interest on capital, entrepreneurial profit and crises, are phenomena in front of which, nowdays, pure economic science fails. Therefore, they must take into consideration all these under one name, *dynamics*" (Schumpeter, 1908, 489-490).

The continuity of the *Theorie* with the tasks of the future research with which *Das Wesen* ended, is evidenced in the "Preface" to the first German edition of the *Theorie*:

> "This book is the sequel of another published by the same publisher in 1908 entitled *Das Wesen und der Hauptinhalt der Theoretischen Nationalökonomie*. The aim of this book is to maintain most of the promises made in the previous work... . Little by little I felt the need to treat, in a new and original way, increasingly important theoretical problems, until I realized that it was always involved with the basic idea. This idea concerned, on one hand, the whole field of the theory while, on the other hand, made possible to develop the limit of the theoretical knowledge, in the direction of the economic development" (Schumpeter, 1911).

As far as *Business Cycles* is concerned, it is Schumpeter who states:

> "Nor do I think that there is anything novel in my combination of historical, statistical and theoretical analysis... . The professional reader will have no difficulty in seeing their relation to the scaffolding which I have published nearly thirty years ago... (Schumpeter, 1939, V).

In the *History of Economic Analysis*, even though Schumpeter assumes, in the abstract, that the "statics" (indeed, the stationary level of the economy) is a particular case of dynamics, he confirms that "*this has not been so in any field of scientific endeavour whatsoever*: always static theory has historically preceded dynamic theory ... . The history of economic analysis is no exception" (Schumpeter, 1954, 964).

In the light of all this, Samuelson's position in favour of Schumpeter is evident, on the issue of the zero rate of interest in the *circular flow*, — subsequent to this reasoning Samuelson says: "this concludes the refutation of professor Robbin's belief that there is a contradiction in the existence of a zero rate of interest in the *circular flow*" (Samuelson, 1943, 63) — delineates a logical fallacy: the *ignoratio elenchi*.

In fact, Samuelson's defence of his former professor aims at another aspect rather than the meaning of the zero rate of interest in the *circular flow*, according to Schumpeter's theory. Beyond the criticisms addressed by Schumpeter on this issue, there is the preservation of the neo-classic paradigm from the "attack" against the General Economic Equilibrium *via* circular flow and its related null rate of interest.

If Schumpeter is incorrect, the rate of interest *can not be zero* even in the *circular flow*, then by definition this leads to the possibility of capital accumulation. In which other way would it be possible to remunerate the savers who want to consume more in the future, if not through resources which will be added to the level of the present and global production? It is the "chapter" concerning Development which explains the ways in which the resources become available.

In other words, the economic theory would not be incomplete or interrupted at its first stage, the "static" stationary economy. And it would not be deprived of its object: the dynamics *alias* the capital accumulation process in time, that is the *raison d'être* of capitalism.

Finally, the "dynamics" does not need to be founded *ex novo*. If so, then not only has Samuelson defended the *clou* which is behind the Schumpeterian concept of *Kreislauf*, but on the contrary, he showed the less talented critics — even though faithful to the marginalist orthodoxy — that their "paradigm" is more general than they realised, and that it can also explain that extreme and particular case where there are no time preferences.

However, Schumpeter's *repechage* to the neo-classic *milieu*, could only be considered successful if it had been proved to him that his *circular flow* with a null interest, is not the *only* rigorous — even though amoebic — formulation of the General Economic Equilibrium, *en sich* and *für sich*, unable to generate a "dynamic" process. But things have not gone this way, not with

Samuelson nor with others, even to-date at the very end of the century and millennium.

But before dealing with this crucial issue, some more considerations are necessary.

Although we do not share the *construens* part of the Schumpeterian scientific heritage, and therefore his proposal to restore economic science with *his* theory of the economic dynamic, that is that of unstable capitalist accumulation. However, we totally share with him the stigma that he thinks a proper theory of capitalist process must have. In particular, we agree with Schumpeter when he says that such a theory must be able to explain, at the same time, the movement of the accumulation and its cyclical *modus operandi*, and therefore the necessity of a theory of crisis recurring with *irregular regularity* (Schumpeter, 1939, 33, vol. I).

Careful consideration of the *Theorie* would have proved the sterile formalism of both its critics, and the defenders of Schumpeter on the battlefield of the *querelle* concerning the topic of zero interest rate.

The first point which we must absolutely emphasize concerns another essential characteristic of the *circular flow*. This is the presence of the surplus within the *circular flow*, which, *pour cause*, does not come out in this *affaire* to the consequential of the embarrassment of economics as far as the surplus is concerned. The discomfort of the "dismal science" is total because it does not explain the surplus, but assumes it, *versus* the "law of Lavoiser".

In particular, the given and repetitive level of the *circular flow necessarily* implicates, a surplus, even if it is entirely consumed.

With Sraffa's terminology, the *circular flow* can be defined as an economic system that satisfies the condition of a *re-integrative state*, and admits the existence of a surplus; for this reason, it is potentially "progressive": the economy produces more than the minimum required for its re-integration or reproduction.

This characteristic is essential to foster the dynamic power of the innovation inside the *Kreislauf*; as it is a net increase in the investments that this requires. Net investments that in their turn require forced savings. But such a surplus is also apt to maintain the rate of interest that, in the *circular flow*, according to Schumpeter, can exist as an expression of the *consumptive* interest, because it is opposed to the *productive* interest (Schumpeter, 1934, 177-183).

The "accountable" damages, caused by a null rate of interest to which a world immersed in abundance would correspond, — of which Schumpeter's critics as well those who are faithful to the neo-classic orthodoxy are afraid of — are not inevitable.

The *consumptive* rate of interest, that which fosters the incidental presence of asymmetric preferences amongst individuals, concerning present and future consumption, is absolutely compatible with the *circular flow*. Even if Schumpeter does not make use of categorisations, one can easily respect his distinction between *consumptive* and *productive* interest, by defining the first as an interest which can exist only within an economic system where the resources, transferred by the rate of interest, are at "zero sum", compared to a specific given and constant surplus, within a stationary system. Vice versa, the productive rate of interest is the rate of interest at which resources are transferred through economic development, that results in a growing surplus within a system in a dynamic phase.

Schumpeter knew Shakespeare's *The Merchant of Venice* and the kind of interest charged by Shylock. But he did not mean to foster the "equivocation" with which his *Theorie* had been welcomed, when it first was published: the commentators, in fact, thought it was a book of economic history. Such a misunderstanding offended Schumpeter's declared positivism as well the professionalism, to which he officially subscribed. And it was this misreading that induced him to eliminate the last chapter of his theoretical *magnus opus*, which had a theoretical-historical character, in all the subsequent editions of his work (Swedberg, 1991, 37).

Moreover, his "model" requires the *circular flow* not simply as a starting point of the development process: the development, in fact, always proceeds from a lower towards a higher level of *Kreislauf*. That is why his defence of this issue is not adequate or sufficient, but this does not mean that he is "guilty", as far as this specific case is concerned (Orati, 1997, 284-287, vol. I).

But if all this is true, one could use "Ockam's razor" with respect to Samuelson's defence of his old professor, if it was not for the fact that his choice of defence is full of very important implications, regarding the state of economic theory; as well as the fact that economic theory still has a debt towards Schumpeter and his neglected "research programme". This forms the foundation of an authentic "dynamics" (Swedberg, 1991, 1): in other words, that which represents the greatest part of the real subject of economic science.

Among Samuelson's important studies, thanks to which he has a place in the Gotha of the great contemporary economists, there is that which gave a very important contribution to the rise of the modern theory of economic fluctuations (Samuelson,1939, Balogh, 1956).

This essay specifically showed Samuelson's inconsequence, in a Schumpeterian sense, concerning the explanation of the cyclic *modus operandi* of the capitalist dynamics. This inconsequence, as such, we must remember, if we look at his sharing the concept of the *zero rate of interest* inside the *circular flow*, as well as at the implicit denunciation related to this, of the static-stationary character of the General Economic Equilibrium. A character that Samuelson and *tout le monde* of the "profession" never officially rejected.

On the other hand, if Samuelson's defence of Schumpeter did not concern such important implications on the side of the scientific value of the neo-classic paradigm, the whole *affaire* of the Schumpeterian null rate of interest would be without intellectual *charme*. This is clearly in contrast with the rank of the participants to that debate, as well as to his objective merit, whose problematical boundaries are marked by the presumptive "heterodoxy" (indeed, it is anti-dogmatism and the attempt to make the economic analysis evolve upon neo-classic bases, beyond the static-stationary limits of the official paradigm) of the great Austrian Economist (Orati, 1988, 99-105).

Further one may consider the model with which Samuelson, through the interdependence between multiplier and accelerator investigated the capitalist "dynamics", none of Schumpeter's precepts on this regard is maintained.

First of all, as far as the passage from the *circular flow* to the "dynamics" is concerned, there is no indication of a possible origin of the preceding static-stationary state.

Secondly, the Archimedic lever of "dynamics" is considered as an independent variable, an *external* quantity. According to this the whole process begins out of "nothingness", a sort of *fiat lux*, as if the capitalist development process were the beginning of the world and the economy, a *sub speciæ æternitatis*.

This is the opposite of an *effort* which belongs to and originates within the *Kreislauf* itself.

Effort which, generally overlooked anticipates — without the present theoretical difficulties on this matter — for its links with the figure and the economic function of the innovator — entrepreneur, the micro-economic foundation of "macro-economics".

Another missing ingredient is the "innovation" or "new production combination", which is the only thing able to get over the suffocating limits of the General Economic Equilibrium, in the respect of the *full employment* inherent in the *circular flow*.

When the model we are talking about admits a cyclical movement of the national income growth — as does the whole modern theory of the cycle — it miraculously eliminates the problem concerning the explanation of the crisis, which represented a crucial, unsolved or falsely solved *topos*, in the economic theory (Orati, 1998).

In fact, instead of it being the crisis which explains the cycle, it is the contrary. This is possible because the cycle is "built", so to speak, by hypothesis and becomes similar to an "analytical toy", mathematically constructed and involving the effect of lags. These lags, properly conceived, give rise to "commutators", able to configure the upper and lower turning points of the "cycle", once the dynamics *tout court* has been admitted. In this way the algebra of the macro-dynamics excludes the crisis where it conceptualises a "cyclical" movement; therefore, it logically excludes the "cycle" itself: the absence of the actual crises.

The combination of the parameters defining the "dynamics", configures an oscillatory movement of the national income in time. This happens thanks to the constant inequality between aggregated demand and supply. To be more precise, the first exceeds the second one in the "growing" phases and the contrary happens during the phases of "recession".

If the "crisis" represents *ex definitione* a remarkable dynamic disequilibrium, this means that the context where it happens must admit an equilibrium, or an equilibrium of a dynamical nature.

But this equilibrium or dynamic norm is absent, and it can not be derived from the syntax which presides the macro-dynamics. This is not compatible, as it can not be derived from the functions upon which macro-dynamics is based.

The crisis is the *principium individuationis* of the cycle, in addition to the crisis that is missing, paradoxically, in the modern theory of the cycle, the cycle itself is also missing.

The corresponding identity of the dynamics and its cyclical form is broken, and the cycle is diagnosed only as one of the possible configurations of the economic "dynamics", and not as *its* inborn morphology. It is, therefore, denied the "tragic" character of capitalist development established by Schumpeter, in the indissoluble dialectic connection between *creation* and *destruction* ("creative destruction"), related to innovation, which is the real *deus ex machina* of development.

In a Keynesian way (but not in the sense of Keynes's criticism of the neo-classic orthodoxy, and together with the neo-classic synthesis of the *General Theory*, which is its only possible acceptable formulation), the *cycle ergo* the "crisis" are not linked together by some necessary "legality" inside the capitalist logics, but are the result of a vicious combination of the *parameters*, upon which the more or less virtuous relationship between the aggregates, determining the national income and its profile in time, is based.

So, Keynes's interventionist philosophy is confirmed in the "long run" too, but it is limited only to the cases in which the economic harmonies are not working.

Being an important exponent of the "neo-classic synthesis" — together with Hicks and Hansen, Samuelson does not join merely for his modesty

(Samuelson, 1980, appendix to chap. 18; 1936a, 381-384) — his contribution here is clear. Keynes claimed that the non-full employment was a situation of equilibrium achieved in "general" by the economic system. This situation is opposed by the Hickesian, static model IS/LM, showing that we do not get the full employment only in the case of unpredictable rigidities (of fact), in the workings of the market. Whereas Samuelson is in agreement with this last model. He does so, by proposing again the *clou* of the "synthesis" on the dynamic side, concerning the non "general" need of intervention on the mechanisms of the market.[6]

Another incongruity of Samuelson's "dynamics", concerns the characteristics that real dynamics, according to Schumpeter, should have. In this regard one must note the important fact which represents the real proof that we are in front of a pure mathematical algorithm, which mimics the real happening of the development process in time: the cycle, when it is accommodated by the parameters' game of this model, it would be *deterministic.*

Therefore, we have here Samuelson's ontological and epistemological break from his former professor who, despite his claimed positivism, has always underlined the *irregular regularity* which accompanies the cyclic syndrome (Schumpeter, 1939, 33; Orati, 1988, 137-142).

Moreover, in the case that this model should begin to work from a situation of *circular flow*, this would mean the failure of any "dynamic" impulse or effort; and this would confirm the theoretical impasse Schumpeter meant to overcome, once the capitalism and its dynamics are not conceived like an over-historical circumstance, whose début in the reality requires an act of faith or a *deus ex machina.*

However, in order to see this and other things, we must look at this work in detail, postponing the treatment of the last of Samuelson's "infidelity" towards his former professor, that concerning his adhesion to the logics of the aggregates. Beyond what, in this regard, implicitly results (already) from the fact that the "great aggregates" are the raw materials from which the

---

[6]This is implicit in the range of the possible "qualities" that the economic development can assume in Samuelson's analysis. As here the cycle, and therefore the dynamic instability, is not given in general, so, in the same way, the resort to anti-cyclic policies would not be, necessarily, "general".

model concerning the inter-relationship between multiplier and accelerator is derived.

Starting from this last point, the equation which describes the model concerned is the following:

$$Y_t = G_t + C_t + I_t \qquad [1]$$

where Y_t is the national income at time t, G_t is the state of expenditure in deficit at time t, C_t is the consumption at time t.
If now:

$$C_t = m(Y_{t-1}) \qquad [2]$$

and

$$I_t = a(C_t - C_{t-1}) \qquad [3]$$

by substituting [2] in [3] and both in [1], this gives:

$$Y_t = G_t + m(1+a)Y_{t-1} + maY_{t-2}. \qquad [1.1]$$

Now, looking at [1.1] and assuming the hypothesis of starting from a level of the given and constant income of the *circular flow*, it is evident that the full employment which marks this, makes any level of the state expenditure in deficit groundless, therefore:

G=0.

But in presence of a *Kreislauf* or *circular flow*, it is also true that $I_t=0$, as C_t-C_{t-1}=0, and Y_t=Y_{t-1} and if this is true, then [1.1] will be:

$$Y_t = m(Y_{t-1}) \qquad [1.2]$$

And, as:

$$m = \frac{C}{Y} = \frac{dC}{dY}$$

when we consider the *circular flow*:

$$Y_t = C_t \qquad [4]$$

just as in the case in which, as Schumpeter defines, the whole income is consumed and the value of the investments goods is calculated according to their opportunity/cost, in terms of consumer goods.

It is important to consider, for the general nature of this last demonstration, Hansen's variant to his model of the inter-relationship multiplier-accelerator, with respect of the model under consideration.

The variation is in the substitution of the state expenditure in deficit G_t, as an independent variable or as externally fixed, with the autonomous investments I_t (Hansen, 1951a).

It must result that the conclusion which allowed us to come to [4], would not change, even in the case of Hansen's model. In fact, as the model starts from a condition of *circular flow*, it is not possible to conceive additional net investments, even though autonomous (induced by the technical progress that, on the other hand, has not got any outcome in Hansen's model), since in the *circular flow* there is not any net save *ex ipothesis*. Therefore:

$$Y_t = I_{at} + m(Y_{t-1}) + I_t \qquad [5]$$

and, as both the autonomous and the induced investments result null, and bearing in mind that $Y_t = Y_{t-1}$:

$$Y_t = m(Y_{t-1}) \qquad [1.2]$$

therefore:

$$Y_t = C_t. \qquad [4]$$

It clearly results, therefore, that Samuelson, after having shared Schumpeter's *circular flow*, not only neglects the value of its analytical position in the theory of the economic dynamics of his former professor, but also the fact that the *circular flow* is idiosyncratic to the concept of economic dynamics. This would immediately fail, as such, if it had come from the *circular flow* configuration of the economic system. This reveals the impossibility, for the modern theory of the cycle or of cyclical capitalist dynamics, to explain what would be right to ask for, logically, economically, mathematically and methodologically: the explanation of the passage from a static-stationary to a dynamic economy. After all, this means that economic theory is expected to possess its own object, which can not be supposed by hypothesis. Hypothesis that, otherwise, is ineluctably over-historical and, therefore, full of metaphysics.

On the formal-mathematical level, the legitimacy of the request lays in the possibility as well the necessity to admit that an algorithm apt to express the passage from the dynamics to the circular, uniform motion of the *circular flow*, allows the opposite passage too, in this case this does not happen.

At this point, one must say that, even though the demonstration with which Samuelson wanted to show that in the *circular flow*, a zero rate of interest as its only possible level of equilibrium can be admitted, was acceptable, then that particular case could not create the model of the dynamic instability which comes from the inter-action between multiplier and accelerator. Model that, by reducing the stationary economy to a special case of the dynamics, as Samuelson intended, would not be able to sustain the "general" theory from which it comes, as the reversibility of the algorithm which allows one to go from the general to the special case, results impossible.

So, one can not but accept the final consideration of Samuelson's article, that with his formulation of the alternate and oscillatory course of the capitalist process. Here we find that, unlike the common opinion, mathematics, if rightly used, does not put concrete things on the abstract level but, on the contrary, it helps to disentangle the most complicated expressions of reality (Samuelson, 1939).

Let us now take a closer look at the implications which come from the expressions [1], [2], [3] and [1.1] which characterize Samuelson's model. He verifies and tests four possible qualitative forms of "dynamics", in relation to the change of the parameters of the multiplier and of the accelerator, in relation to their consequential changing inter-relationships.

1. Case relative to relatively small levels of the "relation" (or "principle" or accelerator).
With a given and repetitive level of public expenditure G in deficit at the time, the national income Y will approach, asymptotically, a value that represents $\frac{1}{1-m}$ times state expenditure G, that is $\frac{1}{1-m}G$.

A single impulse of expenditure, which is not continuous, will be followed by a progressive fall of Y to its initial *null* level.

Only if the (independent) public expenditure in deficit G occurs periodically, with perfect rhythm, the fluctuations of the income also occur periodically, at the same perfect rhythm. Income that, we must add, would oscillate between an invariable minimum (0) and maximum $\frac{1}{1-m}G$ levels.

2. Case in which m= 0,5 and a=1.
A constant and continuous public expenditure in deficit G originates a "dynamic" which oscillates, but in a damped manner, around a level of Y that gradually and asymptotically comes close to the value $\frac{1}{1-m}G$.
Here too, we are in front of a roughly constant course of Y.

An episodic public expenditure, consisting of one or a finite number of impulses, gives rise, respectively, to one or a finite number of damped oscillations, around a null level of income.

Also in this case, to an expenditure G which comes at perfectly regular intervals, there will be corresponding regular oscillation of the income, between an invariable minimum and maximum.

3. Case in which m=0,6 and a=2.
A constant level of public expenditure in deficit G will give rise a growing and explosive oscillation, around a value of Y, which

asymptotically tends to $\frac{1}{1-m}G$.

A single act of expenditure or a finite number of such acts, will give rise to an explosive tendency, which oscillates around zero.

4. Case in which the marginal tendency to consumption and the accelerator are high (for ex.: m=0,8 and a=4).

In this circumstance, both a constant, public expenditure or an independent and single impulse from the net investments, give rise to an ever increasing rate of development, which comes near to the compound interest rate. At the same way, even the minimum disinvestment brings the system towards an increasing downward spiral. This system is highly unstable. This conclusion converges with Harrod's development model, apart from the evident, growing inflation or deflation, that he connects to the two possible courses of Y, just mentioned.

With regard to this last case, one must add, to that already said by Samuelson, that the process of the increasing growth will find a "bottle neck" in the achievement of the full employment, admitting unemployment at the beginning of the process.

But even the "evil" version of such "dynamic" would have a lower limit of Y: that level which, roughly, finds the equilibrium of a pure reproduction of the system.

The details of Samuelson's "dynamics", apart from confirming our previous considerations which concern it, allow us to realise an unexpected analytical result.

On the base of such a model, the range of its possible variants, in terms of inter-relationship of parameters results in a cyclical course of income which does not grow. This is because it is contained within a range of variation which goes from a minimum to a *never overcome* maximum (only the case sub 3, once assumed the minimum level of the trough, shows, a "cyclical" internal course — so as to speak — considering that the whole "analytical toy" depends on an impulse coming from an independent quantity and, for this reason, exogenously determined. In fact, in the cases sub 1 and 2, the resulting cyclic character that is deterministically predictable, is too compromised to correspond to the cyclic character of an independent variable. So this sort of "dynamic " can not be considered the right one.

Otherwise (case sub 4), one can have a process of (over) growth of Y, without any possibility of connoting it in cyclical terms.

The conclusion, therefore, is that: either a "cycle" of income that does not grow; or growth without a cycle!

This confirms Kaldor's strong belief, to whom nobody has ever replied:

> "Indeed, the development of trade-cycle theories that followed Keynes's *General Theory* has proved to be positively inimical to the idea that cycle and dynamic growth are inherently connected analytically ... . For it has been repeatedly (and in my view, conclusively) shown that a few simple addition to Keynes' own model of a general equilibrium will take the form, not of a simply steady rate of production in tíme, but of rhythmical movement of constant amplitude and period. In other words, a perpetual oscillation around a stationary equilibrium position" (Kaldor, 1960, 214).

As to this issue, let us refer to some comments which introduce us to the "Keynesian" choice by Samuelson. We must return to a crucial topic: the (cyclical) "crisis".

Apart from the impossibility of explaining the crisis with the cycle (which is like explaining to someone suffering from malaria, that it is so because he is cyclically feeling ill), rather than the contrary; apart from the fact that an economy which does not grow, and that can only see the fall of its global income, is a pre-capitalist economy, depending on the freaks of nature (including the human one of war); what makes it really impossible to talk about the crisis in the "modern" theory of the cycle. It is the fact that the models, such as those based on the inter-relationship between multiplier and accelerator, do not have nor even admit, a norm of dynamic equilibrium.

This is the only thing which allows one to talk, rigorously, about that remarkable, dynamic disequilibrium, that is the crisis.

Where economic algebra, founded on "great aggregates", does not lead to models of "steady state growth", of the absence of crisis *ex definitione*, even though it is able to configure a "systolic" movement of the income (even if, we know, it is not growth, as *Y* oscillates between a minimum and a maximum of "constant period and amplitude"), this is possible thanks to the constant — throughout the duration of the peak of *Y* — excess of the global demand on the global supply, that is in constant disequilibrium. In this way, as the crisis, is a disequilibrium coming from another disequilibrium (even though normalized in terms of a *trend* whose points would be, points of disequilibrium, as they are the average among disequilibrium points), would not have any conceptual sense.

This is, one of the possible reasons why Schumpeter gradually came to have an aversion towards the economy of the great aggregates or, in other words, towards the macro-economics of the *General Theory*.

Again, it is possible to explain relative to the *circular flow*, essential to his development theory, as it would allow for his need to find an "equilibrium norm" for this development. This is, only apparently founded upon the logics of the great aggregates, as apposed to Hansen's[7] mistaken belief, even though, *prima faciœ,* such a development is characterised, throughout all its duration, by a global demand which exceeds the global supply and is, therefore, always obtained away from the equilibrium.

This disequilibrium is unequivocally marked by the fact that the rate of inflation remains positive when a new and higher level of *circular flow* is achieved, this rate extinguishes only when the innovation and its diffusion in the system that it has made dynamic, are completely metabolized by the

---

[7] Hansen (1951, 208) declares:

> "Macro-economics began with monetary and business-cycle theory. Schumpeter was one of five Continental economists whose work on business cycles laid the foundation for modern macro-economics".

Hansen was one of the most important, influential and praised professor at Harvard, when Schumpeter was teaching there. He was also well-known as Keynes's prophet in the USA, and also co-founder, together with Hicks and Samuelson, of the "neo-classic synthesis". It is therefore emblematic that his alignment in the general misleading of the authentic, scientific Schumpeterian message, especially by those paradigms who were in "vogue" amongst the most prestigious academic environments. In this respect, we can think of Schumpeter's parallel opposition to the dogmatic preservation of the standard, neo-classic tradition, and to the "Keynesian revolution".

mechanisms of the economy (otherwise one would have a certain amount of monopoly in the economic system, against the hypothesis of the Schumpeterian framework). This involves the new achieved equilibrium between aggregated demand and supply. But to resort to aggregates in the syntax of the Schumpeterian model, is purely formal, and has nothing to do with their logics, within the macroeconomic theory.

One can, at best, talk about a micro-economic foundation (innovation and entrepreneur-innovator) of the economic development, as theorized by Schumpeter, which the great aggregates passively register but do not explain. This because, such great aggregates have not got a life of their own in the model under consideration. Consequently their inter-relationship does not cause, actively, and therefore functionally, a remarkable mechanism as far as reality, and therefore the economic analysis is concerned. This, on the other hand, corresponds to and is coherent with the never repudiated adhesion, by the economist from Triesch, to the "methodological individualism". And if it is true that it can not be ignored in the case of the micro-economic foundation, it is also true that it makes epistemologically impossible, on the side of the scientific rigour, any attempt base on the micro-economic foundation of the macro-economics — if we wish to give some theoretical-analytical independence to this. Hence, the predictable failures of this contemporary illusion that wants, harmonically, to arrange an authentic contradiction in terms[8] (holism *versus* methodological individualism).

Going back to Schumpeter's need to give an equilibrium "norm" (of reference) to his unbalanced development, in terms of great aggregates, it is clear that such a role can not but be played by *circular flow*. Obviously, not that from which the development process originates, but the *circular flow* where it ends, when the dynamic impulse finishes its energy (effort), and has transferred the increase.of productivity connected to the innovation to the consumers. Innovation is the real power which pushes the economy outside the calm waters of the *Kreislauf*.

Consider, Schumpeter's need of an equilibrium norm:

> "Hence, much more interest and importance than most of us are inclined to admit attach to the endeavours of some staticiens and

[8] Despite his aversion towards the disquisitions concerning the "methodological" aspects (Samuelson, 1963), Professor Samuelson should agree with our conclusion.

> economists to distil from statistical material of an economic world which is chronically in a state of disequilibrium, the time sequence of equilibrium values ... . But fluctuations must be fluctuations around something and, if pressed, he would probably define that something in terms ... related to our equilibrium" (Schumpeter, 1939, 70-71, vol. I).

However, Schumpeter's development "model" has in common, with those based on the economy of the great aggregates — for reasons that we can mention — an "original sin": it is without a development trend, different from the average of the points which characterise the unbalanced development. In other words, a dynamic development trend in equilibrium, as we know it, can not be useful. This is due, *en passant*, to his refusal of a *steady state growth* which would have the features of a pseudo-development of an *organic growth* (equi-proportional growth of the whole economic system). The starting point of the dynamics is the *circular flow* where, *inter alia*, there is "full employment". Consequently, due to the lack of a norm of dynamic equilibrium, in the respect of which it is possible to conceive both the beneficial disequilibrium of the development, and the negative disequilibrium of the crisis and the recession (in the bi-phase cycle), like a detachment from "something", in Schumpeter's model, we will have to be content — it sounds like a contradiction — of a tendency towards a (new) equilibrium: the final *circular flow* of the whole capitalist process (Orati, 1988, 114-115), and of an equilibrium norm able only to measure the more or less high amplitude in the neighbourhood of the equilibrium; towards which, any point of the development process can be found and defined:

> "In order to harness our equilibrium concept ... which is fundamental for our analytic technique, we will not postulate the existence of states of equilibrium where none exists, but only where the system is actually moving towards one ..." (Schumpeter, 1939, 70, vol. I).

In the attempt to escape from the funnel, that at this point leads to determination of an equilibrium norm of the dynamic process, the *circular flow*, even though this is higher compared to the previous, where that process finishes; therefore, in the attempt to escape from the contradiction to put, as an equilibrium norm for the dynamic process, an equilibrium norm of a static-stationary economy, Schumpeter defines that anodyne concept which is the "neighbourhoods of equilibrium":

> "Hence we will, for our purpose, recognize existence of equilibrium *only at those discrete points of time scale at which the system approaches a state which would, if reached, fulfill equilibrium conditions.* And since the system in practice never actually reaches such a state, we shall consider, instead of equilibrium points, ranges within which the system as a whole is more nearly in equilibrium than it is in outside of them. Those ranges, which are the operational form to which we shall apply properly modified equilibrium considerations, we call *neighbourhoods of equilibrium* (the term must not be understood in its mathematical sense)" (Schumpeter, 1939, 70-71, vol. I).

As we can see in the above quotation, Schumpeter recognizes only in *practice* that the economic system is always outside the equilibrium, because in theory his development moves between two different levels of *circular flow*. So, on the pure, theoretical level his model has only a static-stationary equilibrium norm to which he refers his own dynamic disequilibria[9].

However, this is not the right place to verify if Schumpeter's attempt to find an adequate answer for the problem he has evidenced, that of find the dynamics[10], is valid or not.

---

[9]There are many analytical reasons which, on the theoretical level, bring Schumpeter's model to recognise that the development process disentangles among different and growing levels of *circular flow*, so that this last one is not only the static-stationary economy from which all the dynamics derives. First of all, if it was not because of the tendency for the dynamic episodes to flow into the *circular flow* (static-stationary), the same dynamics would be without an equilibrium norm (where the aggregate demand and supply are in equilibrium). Secondly, if the development would not flow, in theory, between two *circular flow*, the coherence with the hypothesis of a general situation of free and perfect competition would fade: we should admit a certain degree of "imperfect competition". In fact, if the starting *circular flow* had the characters of a static-stationary economy, the Schumpeterian "model" of the capitalist process would come to have some historical connotations which, in a certain way, are in conflict with the "positive" Method, Schumpeter always professed. In order to underline the substantial incomprehension of the Schumpeterian analytical categories, as far as the *circular flow* is concerned, Kuznets (Kuznets, 1940, 260) believed that Schumpeter measured the cycles from *circular flow* to *circular flow* only as a (neutral) alternative to the current practice, according to which they are measured "from trough to trough or peak to peak", because there too, like here, there would be a "turning point". Also Samuelson alludes to the analytical necessity of a zero interest inside the Schumpeterian *circular flow*, as for him a simple tendency towards such a value is enough (Samuelson, 1943, 678; 1971, 36-37).

[10] It is important to say that there is no alternative to the lack of a real, dynamic equilibrium norm in Schumpeter's model, despite the opinion of authors like Date (Date, 1961, 22-34). The *trend* can not be such a norm because, as it can only be derived from the data relating to the development process entirely outside the equilibrium (the aggregates of the demand and the supply are equal only

We have tried to show that, in any case, he tackled the question of an equilibrium norm related to disequilibria connected to the accumulation process. On the other hand, there is nothing with regard to satisfying such a need, or of determining a dynamic equilibrium norm, in macro-dynamic theory.

The counter-indication suggested by Schumpeter with respect to the logics of aggregates, and in particular macro-dynamics, can make sense in the light of that just seen. This goes beyond his opposition to any kind of philosophy whose corollary is the interventionism anti-*laissez faire* (Schumpeter, 1950, chapters V-VI; Orati, 1988, chap. V), philosophy which moves the macro-economic *appeal*, even in the *reductio* of the neo-classic synthesis.

As for the negative judgement by the economist from Triesch, on the decisive limits of the aggregate analysis, especially in its developments concerning the cycle, little is said explicitly, or examined closer than in *Business Cycles*. Here the judgement is peremptory and *tranchent*:

> "From the standpoint of aggregative theory, it is in the nature of paradox to say that partial disequilibria — innovation and response to innovation create in the first instance nothing else — produce what obviously is a general disequilibrium in the system as a whole. But we realize now in what sense that is so, how it comes about, and how aggregative quantities are thereby changed. Perhaps it is only common sense to recognize that, in order to produce effects on aggregates, a factor or event need not itself be an aggregate. It follows on the one hand that, relations between aggregates, being entirely inadequate to teach us anything about the nature of the process which shapes their

---

in the *circular flows* which follow one another), it would be a *trend* whose points are points of disequilibrium, as they are the average among disequilibrium points. We could think that the *trend* comes from the line which connects two subsequent levels of *circular flow*. Even if we do not consider the fact that these *circular flows* are not dynamic, we can not but notice that they are marked by the course of the development process; therefore, the line which connects them can not but be the average of the data from which the process is made: again these are outside the equilibrium just like their average. In turn a *steady state growth* coming from (autonomously) the starting *circular flow* is impossible, because as Schumpeter refused to consider it as a development process. Moreover, we must consider the impossibility of getting such a *steady state* starting from the given and constant levels of the variables which define the starting *circular flow*: in particular, the constant techniques and the full employment.

> variations, aggregative theories of the business cycle must be inadequate too" (Schumpeter, 1939, 144, vol. I).

In this extract, Schumpeter puts in evidence the supposed virtue of his micro-economic approach, and the defect of the approaches based on great aggregates, in their macro-dynamic version regarding the crisis, that is the "general disequilibrium in the system as a whole". The recurring accusation focuses on the fact that, not only is "new economics", not in its dynamic version, unable to reveal the mechanisms of the crisis, but it tends to hide them!

Regarding the above mentioned inability, as well as the guilt of hiding, that which should be put in evidence and explained about the crisis, Schumpeter underlines that only his approach to the *creative destruction* can succeed where as the other approach is doomed to fail, alien as it is, considering the "tragic" nature of the economic development due to the innovation:

> "For some of the *old* firms new opportunities for expansion open up ... but for others the emergence of the new methods means economic death ... . Aggregative analysis, here as elsewhere, not only does not tell the whole tale, but necessarily obliterates the main (and the only interesting) points of the tale" (Schumpeter, 1939, 134, vol. I).

This last circumstance is particularly serious, with regards to that remarkable disequilibrium represented by the crisis, if it is true that the relationship among the aggregates, and in particular their equilibrium:

> "is compatible with most violent disequilibria ... It is therefore misleading, to reason on aggregative equilibrium as if it is displayed the factor which initiates change and as if disturbance in the economic system as a whole could arise from those aggregates. Such reasoning is at the bottom of much faulty analysis of business cycles ... It keeps analysis on the surface of things, and prevents it from penetrating into the industrial process below, which is what really matters" (Schumpeter, 1939, 43-44, vol. I).

In fact, Schumpeter never succeeded in explaining the crisis as *principium individuationis* of the cycle, whereas he well knew how important it was to do so, from the scientific point of view[11].

With regard to this, he has been an unware Hegelian, having over-estimated the dialectics of the *creative destruction.*

As we have already seen (Orati, 1988), such a contradictory variable can not show, at the same time, both the development phenomenon and its critical interruption. We can have either the prevailing of one or the prevailing of the other phenomenon, but not both, otherwise a series of irremediable contradictions arise.

We have demonstrated, that his criticism of the macro-dynamics has a foundation, even though Schumpeter has only denounced in general its insufficiencies and defects. These, deprive economic theory of a well formed, congruent and satisfying theory of economic dynamics, or theory of alternate *modus operandi* of capitalism.

After this demonstration of the foundation of Schumpeter's distrust towards macro-dynamics, we would like to try to give a meaning to his repeated but only enunciated accusation, concerning the fact that the "algebra" which subtends the macro-economic paradigm concerning the cycle, not only would not give account of the crisis, but it would also hide the presence, and therefore the rise of the crisis itself.

We will use a "parable" with the comfort that Professor Samuelson also often used it (Samuelson, 1943, 61; 1962). And I hope, as Samuelson once hopped, that this would stimulate the production of a guide to Schumpeter by his orphans. In fact Samuelson once written, metaphorically, that Keynes' *General Theory* required a guide in the same way and for a similar purpose, to that which should be written for Joyce's *Finnegan's wake* (Samuelson, 1946).

[11] Lange (Lange, 1941, 192-193) is the only commentator that perceived the absence of the crisis, through the absence of unemployment in the Schumpeterian "model". But such an intuition does not reach its logical conclusion (absence of the crisis) because it is wasted on an unconcerned and unbelievable comparison with the *General Theory*. A strict and rigorous diagnosis of the necessary absence of the crisis in the Schumpeterian "model" of the "dynamics" is given, instead, by Orati (Orati, 1988).

The guide to Schumpeter should be written in a similar manner to Proustian *À la recherche du temps perdu*, in a sense that it is the dynamics that must be recovered.

The parable begins by admitting the possibility of having a *tableau économique* comprised of two sectors, as follows:

$$\begin{array}{ll} I & C_I+V_I+S_I=W_I \\ II & C_{II}+V_{II}+S_{II}=W_{II} \end{array} \qquad [A]$$

where sector I produces the means of production, and sector II the consumer goods.

C_i, V_i, S_i, W_i are, respectively, the means of production, the wages, the surplus and the output of the ith sector. We presume that the means of production have a single rotation, so they finish entirely in a production cycle; so:

$$W_I + W_{II} = W_T$$

represents the annual GNP.

Where the institutional framework is capitalist, so that the surplus goes to the capitalists as a profit. Not considering rent, and with the system in equilibrium, so respecting both the conditions which define it at the same time, that is:

$$p_i = \frac{S_i}{C_i + V_i} \qquad [I]$$

the rate of profit, that must be equal in each sector, corresponds to the average of the system; in other words, it must be equal in I and II, as the first condition for the equilibrium[12]. The second condition concerns the equality of the inter-exchange among the sectors, so we must have the following equation:

[12] For reasons of space as well as of harmony in the treatment of the subject, we must consider as solved the issue which allows the representation of the surplus and its allocations in such a way as to ensure an equal rate of profit inside the two production sectors, even with different production techniques in those sectors. We have elsewhere developed the theory (the theory of the value/opportunity) which allows such a result (Orati, 1984). Hence, in this essay, the "parable's" purely theoretical role ends here.

$$C_{II} = V_I + S_I \qquad [II]$$

where it is implicit that the surplus is entirely consumed by the capitalists.

To measure the technical conditions in relation to the ratio capital/ labour in each sector and, in particular, one may assume:

$$\frac{C_I}{V_I} > \frac{C_{II}}{V_{II}}$$

Apart from that portion of income necessary to amortize and substitute the capital, the rest of the net income is entirely consumed, which means, *via* II, the simple reproductive equilibrium of the system.

Eliminating the improbable hypothesis concerning the consumption of the surplus by the capitalists; let's leave them to their propensity to accumulate, that they get by re-investing the whole of their profit in means of production and labour; also leave apart their consumption, assuming that this is a decreasing portion of the accumulation itself with time.

Considering the same production techniques and supposing that the workers are available at all times, it is reasonable to assume a *steady state growth*[13] whose rate coincides with that of the profit. This can represent the economic system in its dynamic phase as follows:

---

[13] That the full employment is a particular or extreme case of the accumulation process which is not able to guarantee it a condition of general equilibrium, is a matter of fact; therefore, it can be assumed as a verosimilar hypothesis. However, such an hypothesis must not be confused with the theoretical necessity to show the reason why it is not possible to maintain a state of full employment in time. Theoretical necessity which coincides with the theory that can explain the cyclical crisis; crisis that, being the cause of the cycle, can explain why the dynamic equilibrium of the full employment can not be maintained indefinitely. Consequently, we can assume that the capitalist development takes the form of a steady state growth; in turn, we can also solve the other problem concerning the dynamic equilibrium norm, represented by the same steady state, in respect of which research of that remarkable disequilibrium, that is the crisis, becomes possible. The starting point of the dynamic process from a condition of full employment has been fatal both to the macro-dynamics and to Schumpeter's development theory: this fact (inter alia (has denied to both these approaches having a norm of dynamic equilibrium.

$$\begin{aligned} I \quad & C_I + V_I + \Delta C_I + \Delta V_I = W_I^{'} \\ II \quad & C_{II} + V_{II} + \Delta C_{II} + \Delta V_{II} = W_{II}^{'} \end{aligned} \qquad \text{[B]}$$

where the increasing surplus S_i, from period of production to period of production is shared in ΔC_i and ΔV_i in each ith sector, and where, evidently:

$$\frac{\Delta C_i}{\Delta C_i} = \frac{C_i}{V_i}$$

With a given and constant rate of profit which will be the same in both sectors, the condition of equilibrium among the exchanges between the sectors, throughout the accumulation phase will be:

$$C_{II} + \Delta C_{II} = V_I + \Delta V_I \qquad \text{[III]}$$

This can be referred to any production cycle, that is for each time t, taking into account the synchronization of all the variables.

In order to make evident the production techniques, that the technical-structural aspects of the economic system with the performances of the last, the reproductive scheme [B], may also be represented as an input-output scheme; given the following technical coefficients, for each ith sector:

$$\frac{C_i}{W_i^{'}} = aC_i\,; \quad \frac{V_i}{W_i^{'}} = aV_i; \quad \frac{\Delta C_i}{W_i^{'}} = \alpha C_i; \quad \frac{\Delta V_i}{W_i^{'}} = \alpha V_i$$

it will be:

$$\begin{aligned} I \quad & aC_I + aV_I + \alpha C_I + \alpha V_I = 1 \\ II \quad & aC_{II} + aV_{II} + \alpha C_{II} + \alpha V_{II} = 1 \end{aligned} \qquad \text{[B']}$$

therefore, it will also be true that:

$$\begin{aligned} I \quad & aC_I W_I^{'} + aV_I W_I^{'} + \alpha C_I W_I^{'} + \alpha V_I W_I^{'} = W_I^{'} \\ II \quad & aC_{II} W_{II}^{'} + aV_{II} W_{II}^{'} + \alpha C_{II} W_{II}^{'} + \alpha V_{II} W_{II}^{'} = W_{II}^{'} \end{aligned} \qquad \text{[B'']}$$

From [B''] one may derive the condition of equilibrium of the *steady state growth* among the sectors; this, considering the time homogeneity of the terms on the left and right of the equal sign, is valid for any phase of the development process:

$$W_{II}^{'}\left(aC_{II}+\alpha C_{II}\right)=W_{I}^{'}\left(aV_{I}+\alpha V_{I}\right) \qquad \text{[IV]}$$

and therefore:

$$\frac{\left(aC_{II}+\alpha C_{II}\right)}{\left(aV_{I}+\alpha V_{I}\right)}=\frac{W_{I}^{'}}{W_{II}^{'}} \qquad \text{[V]}$$

Rearrangement of this with the inclusion of quantity $1\text{-}(aC_I + \alpha C_I)$ derived by [B']; therefore we will have[14]:

$$\frac{\left(aC_{II}+\alpha C_{II}\right)}{1-\left(aC_{I}+\alpha C_{I}\right)}=\frac{W_{I}^{'}}{W_{II}^{'}}. \qquad \text{[VI]}$$

Consequently, if the equilibrium norm, or condition, of the *steady state growth* can be found in the coefficient $\overline{K}$, in the sense that [VI] verifies:

$$\frac{\left(aC_{II}+\alpha C_{II}\right)}{1-\left(aC_{I}+\alpha C_{I}\right)}=\frac{W_{I}^{'}}{W_{II}^{'}}=\overline{K}, \qquad \text{[VII]}$$

then, the [VI] assumes an analytical value of great importance, defined as the "Discriminating Dynamic Equation", as it is able to indicate, if properly used:

1. The authentic, and until now unnoticed, cause of the critical or remarkable disequilibrium, which configures the crisis *qua* absolute over-production.

---

[14] This formula can be found in Lange (Lange, 1965); however, he does not perceive (for a lack of "parables" (how it could be utilised as a norm of dynamic equilibrium, therefore its "discriminating" ability, as far as the more or less pathological alterations of the capitalist accumulation process is concerned.

2. The revealing of a disproportion among the sectors evoked, up to now, as the cause of the crisis by the *General Theory* and all the Keynesians, included those of the "synthesis". The "Keynesians", at their best, confound the effect of the crisis with its cause[15].

3. The distinction between both the perturbations of the *steady state*, and also the impossibility of recuperating the first one to the dynamic equilibrium, through the semeiology of the free and competitive market. The semeiology, instead, permits the benign and physiological re-inclusion of the second, without a "critical" interruption of the development process.

4. The definitive absolution of "Say's law", in a sense that, being an authentic truism, such a "law" is not and can not be the target to be destroyed, in order to build, upon its ashes, an authentic theory of the crisis. This fact has practically misled all the attempts to understand the "arcane" generalized *glut* of the goods, that is the paradox or contradiction of the "poverty in the midst of abundance" (Orati, 1988).

Starting from the first statement. During the *steady state growth*, — in order to increase the amounts produced at the same cost — we register a "remarkable" innovation in sector I, of the "labour saving" type — this would have the same consequences if this involved the other sector and, *a fortiori*, if it involved the whole economic structure —.

As all the surplus is, gradually, re-invested at the same rate, in the production fixed by the capital/output ratio, through the formula:

$$\frac{C_I}{V_I} < \frac{C_I'}{V_I'}$$

the rate of growth of sector I, which is constant similar to sector II, would not suffer any alteration, and therefore:

$$\frac{W_I'}{W_{II}'} = \overline{K}$$

15 Largely dealt with in (Orati, 1996, 1997, 1998 2° vol., 1998).

where $\overline{K}$ is the parameter of the dynamic equilibrium.

But the first side of the equation [VII] will change as, the numerator remains constant, whilst the denominator will decrease, so giving:

$$\begin{cases} \dfrac{aC_{II} + \alpha C_{II}}{1-(aC_I + \alpha C_I)} \neq (>)\overline{K} & \text{[VIIIa]} \\ \dfrac{W_I^{'}}{W_{II}^{'}} = \overline{K} & \text{[VIIIb)} \end{cases}$$

The cause of the crisis is that which has caused the inequality [VIIIa]. In sector II, the share of the consumer goods which increased to that point at a constant rate, will then decrease, due to a minor growth in sector I of the employed workers, unlike the constant rate with which this has occurred up to that point. As a consequence of this, sector II would not be able to maintain its rate of growth, as it has not made what it requires, in order to sustain its rhythm of growth, in terms of investment goods *ergo* in terms of workers. So, *both* the two sectors will have *over-produced*, in relation to the condition of equilibrium among the sectors. This will cause a decrease in the prices of the consumer goods and in the investments, in a deflationistic spiral fostered by the market's signals and by the multiplier, which now works as a de-multiplier of the income. As both the sectors I and II have over-produced, we have the absolute over-production with deflation, that is the "crisis", freed from its arcane aura.

All this happens, let us remember, while we have [VIIIb]: the sectors I and II have by hypothesis invested resources at the same rate, which has guaranteed, up to this point, the *steady state growth.*

So, the total growth of the aggregates *does not betray any change* of the process of growth, on the contrary, it *hides* the bursting of the crisis. Q.E.D.

As for the second point, it is enough to suppose that the capitalists, instead of continuing to invest in the same sector, decide to move their resources from the usual sector to a different sector, and that this phenomenon is not compensated between the two sectors; so that one is greater than it has been up to that point, in terms of *steady state*, and therefore we have a parallel decrease of the rate of growth in the other sector. Whilst, overall, the system grows at the same rate (the propensity to invest remains unchanged), due to the fact that the production techniques remain the same, we will have:

$$\begin{cases} \dfrac{aC_{II} + \alpha C_{II}}{1 - (aC_I + \alpha C_I)} = \overline{K} & \text{[IXa]} \\ \dfrac{W_I^{'}}{W_{II}^{'}} \neq \overline{K} & \text{[IXb)} \end{cases}$$

Apart from any other consideration, [IXa] and [IXb], as they create a contemporary *relative* over-production/under-production, excludes that there is a crisis (this is missing by recent contributions based on "spillover effect"): the increasing prices where there has been an under-production and the decreasing prices where there has been over-production, while this excludes a general deflation it, will configure a physiological "error" concerning the assessment of the production sectors, which is to consider normal inside a capitalist market economy. The semeiology of the market will indicate the way to bring the economy back to its dynamic equilibrium, moving the resources coherently with the relative price signals.

As, according to the Keynesians who do not want to upset the meaning of the *General Theory,* which only in its "synthesis", finds an adequate systematization for us we would have, in the end, the supposed crisis because of a defect in the supply of money *vs* commodities or, in other words, for a surplus in the supply of commodities *vs* money, as we have already said (and elsewhere seen in detail). It is evident that we are still in the case of relative over-production (surplus in the supply)/under-production (defect of supply). The explanation of the crisis is due to its limit in the cyclical character of the "classic" crisis; this would involve the cyclical, insufficient supply of money as an exogenous quantity (quantitative money theory) or, in other words, the contradiction of an independent variable, which behaves in a cyclical manner!

There is no doubt that the explosion of the crisis involves the need of additional money in respect of the insufficiency of money up to that point, to foster exchanges and the economic growth. The general over-production means that there is a lack of realization, in monetary terms, of the supply of commodities. But this, as we do know, is the effect of the crisis, not its cause, and it is therefore what is to be explained, and not the explanation of the crisis. It is upon such a *qui pro quo* that most of the theories of the crisis have so far failed, including the Keynesian explanation (Orati, 1998). Even though Keynes was protested for being the theorist of public intervention in the economy, and therefore the antagonist of *laissez-faire*, he still remains the unprejudiced author of the "definitive" criticism of "Say's law" (Samuelson, 1946; Sweezy, 1972, chap. VI).

Whilst the third point regarding the "Dynamic Discriminating Equation", has now been clarified by the immediate previous point, it is essential to notice that the explanation of the crisis in its real terms of *general over-production*, does not need the criticism of "Say's law", which is, on the contrary, overcome[16]. And this would not be different, considering the character of truism of that law.

As showed by [VIIIa] and [VIIIb], the crisis expresses itself despite the performance of the *steady state growth*, where the global supply and demand are equal *ex hypothesis*.

In particular, "Say's law" is not denied in the case of [IXa] and [IXb] where, always by hypothesis, one has the performance of the *steady state* and there is no crisis, but also because the difference or disproportion among sectors, has never meant the falsification of "Say's law": Say never claimed the perfect identity between demand and supply from the point of view of the perfect correspondence in terms of gender of the goods between demand and supply (Schumpeter, 1954, 619). If it was not so, one could not understand of what the self-regulating virtues of the market consist.

An important corollary derives from what we have just seen, and can only be mentioned here. If this reasoning is valid, then the self-regulating virtues of the market reduce to a minor thing: to amortize the "physiological errors", which, as they are benign in theory, and are so insignificant they may be ignored.

---

[16] Schumpeter criticises Keynes (Schumpeter, 1954, 615-625) also with regard to "Say's law" and the importance of its criticism for the validity of the General Theory. Nevertheless, even though Schumpeter explains many things with regard to the supposed guilt of the "law of markets", in endless dossier on the crisis he can not go until the end, because he can not provide a rigorous explanation of the crisis and, in particular, of its aspect of absolute over-production.

On the other hand, the social and economic relevancy of collective knowledge, which expresses itself in technical progress, can not be, as such, metabolised by the market and the logics of the *laissez-faire*, unless it goes through the drama of the crises and of the contradiction of the "poverty in the midst of abundance".

Let us leave this conclusion to the considerations of those who, by supporting the *deregulation* as a sort of password of globalization, together with the *main stream* and its radical re-conversion to the *status quo ante* the rise of the Keynesian interventionist heterodoxy, put in evidence a further epistemologic anomaly[17] of the *dismal science*. The anomaly is that which denies economic science — the only one among the various science — any kind of intervention upon its own object and its pathologies. First of all, in the sense of the *economic policy;* secondly — as a parallel cause which brought to the *naturalistic* and contemplative *revival* towards this object — in the sense of lost "dynamics" by the *economic theory*.

REFERENCES

Date K. (1961), "The Relation of Cycles and Trends in Schumpeter's Model", *Waseda Economic Paper*, vol. 5.

Elliot J.E. (1983), "Schumpeter and the Theory of Capitalist Economic Development", *Journal of Economic Behavior and Organization*, December.

Festinger L. (1962), *A Theory of Cognitive Dissonance*, London and Stanford; see (1977) *The Fontana Dictionary of Modern Thought*, A. Bullock - O. Stallybrass (eds.), 109.

Haberler G. (1951), "Schumpeter's Theory of Interest", *Review of Economic Statistics*, May.

Hansen A.H. (1951a), *Business Cycles and National Income*, W.W. Norton & Co..

______. (1951b), "Schumpeter's Contribution to Business Cycle Theory", *Review of Economic Statistics*, May.

Kaldor N. (1960), *Essays on Economic Stability and Growth*, Duckworth & Co., London.

Knight F.H. (1930), "Statics and Dynamics: Some Queries Regarding the *Mechanical Analogy in Economics*" (first published in German Translation: Zeitschrift für Nazionalökonomie, August) in Idem (1956), *On the History and Method of Economics*, the University of Chicago Press, 179-201.

Kuznets S. (1940), "Schumpeter's Business Cycles", *American Economic Review*, June.

Lange O. (1941), "Schumpeter's Business Cycles: Book Review", *Review of Economic Statistics*, November.

______. (1965), *Teoria reprodukcji i akumulacji*, Panstwowe Wydawnictwo Naukowe, Warsaw.

---

[17] The anomaly is that "economics" is the only science to break the "law of Lavoiser", with regard to which it admits the existence of the surplus by hypothesis without explaining its nature, and considering every detection about this nature like a philosophical concession towards the "essences"

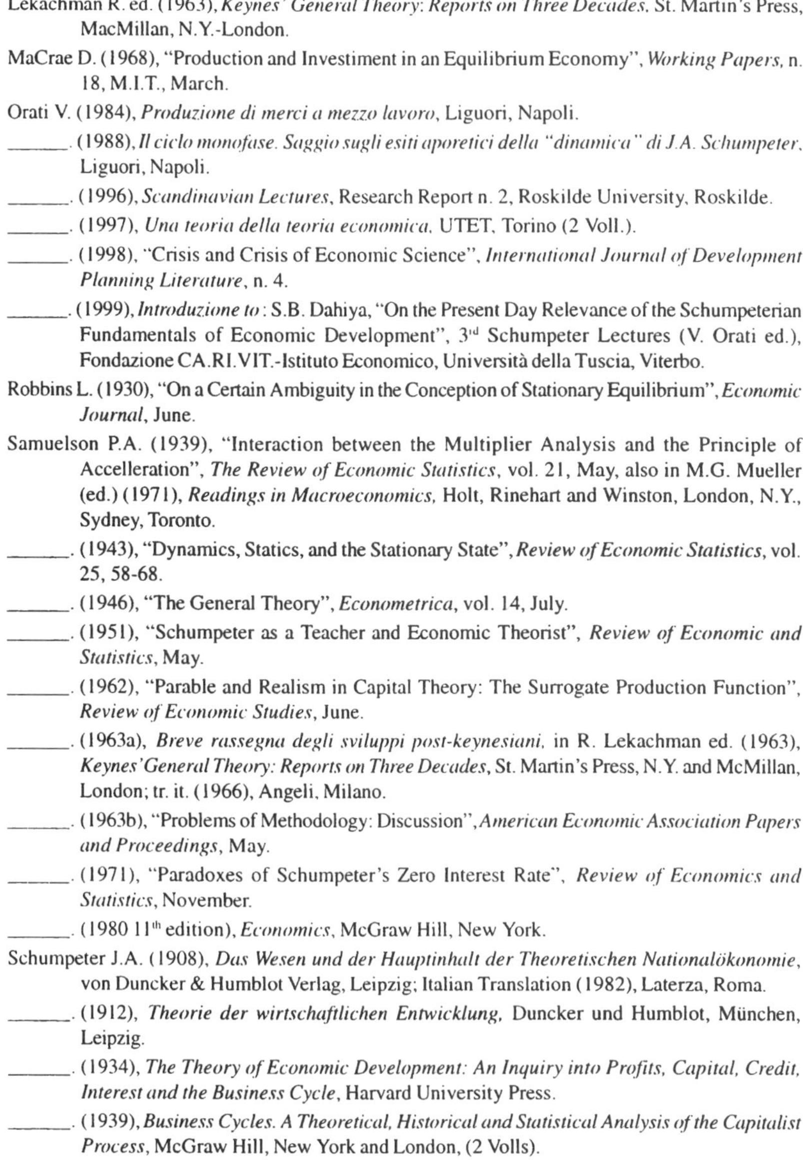

Lekachman R. ed. (1963), *Keynes' General Theory: Reports on Three Decades*, St. Martin's Press, MacMillan, N.Y.-London.

MaCrae D. (1968), "Production and Investiment in an Equilibrium Economy", *Working Papers*, n. 18, M.I.T., March.

Orati V. (1984), *Produzione di merci a mezzo lavoro*, Liguori, Napoli.

______. (1988), *Il ciclo monofase. Saggio sugli esiti aporetici della "dinamica" di J.A. Schumpeter*, Liguori, Napoli.

______. (1996), *Scandinavian Lectures*, Research Report n. 2, Roskilde University, Roskilde.

______. (1997), *Una teoria della teoria economica*, UTET, Torino (2 Voll.).

______. (1998), "Crisis and Crisis of Economic Science", *International Journal of Development Planning Literature*, n. 4.

______. (1999), *Introduzione to*: S.B. Dahiya, "On the Present Day Relevance of the Schumpeterian Fundamentals of Economic Development", 3rd Schumpeter Lectures (V. Orati ed.), Fondazione CA.RI.VIT.-Istituto Economico, Università della Tuscia, Viterbo.

Robbins L. (1930), "On a Certain Ambiguity in the Conception of Stationary Equilibrium", *Economic Journal*, June.

Samuelson P.A. (1939), "Interaction between the Multiplier Analysis and the Principle of Accelleration", *The Review of Economic Statistics*, vol. 21, May, also in M.G. Mueller (ed.) (1971), *Readings in Macroeconomics*, Holt, Rinehart and Winston, London, N.Y., Sydney, Toronto.

______. (1943), "Dynamics, Statics, and the Stationary State", *Review of Economic Statistics*, vol. 25, 58-68.

______. (1946), "The General Theory", *Econometrica*, vol. 14, July.

______. (1951), "Schumpeter as a Teacher and Economic Theorist", *Review of Economic and Statistics*, May.

______. (1962), "Parable and Realism in Capital Theory: The Surrogate Production Function", *Review of Economic Studies*, June.

______. (1963a), *Breve rassegna degli sviluppi post-keynesiani*, in R. Lekachman ed. (1963), *Keynes'General Theory: Reports on Three Decades*, St. Martin's Press, N.Y. and McMillan, London; tr. it. (1966), Angeli, Milano.

______. (1963b), "Problems of Methodology: Discussion", *American Economic Association Papers and Proceedings*, May.

______. (1971), "Paradoxes of Schumpeter's Zero Interest Rate", *Review of Economics and Statistics*, November.

______. (1980 11th edition), *Economics*, McGraw Hill, New York.

Schumpeter J.A. (1908), *Das Wesen und der Hauptinhalt der Theoretischen Nationalökonomie*, von Duncker & Humblot Verlag, Leipzig; Italian Translation (1982), Laterza, Roma.

______. (1912), *Theorie der wirtschaftlichen Entwicklung*, Duncker und Humblot, München, Leipzig.

______. (1934), *The Theory of Economic Development: An Inquiry into Profits, Capital, Credit, Interest and the Business Cycle*, Harvard University Press.

______. (1939), *Business Cycles. A Theoretical, Historical and Statistical Analysis of the Capitalist Process*, McGraw Hill, New York and London, (2 Volls).

______. (1950), *Capitalism, Socialism and Democracy*, Harper, New York.

______. (1951a), *Preface* to the Japanese Edition of *The Theory of Economic Development* in R.V. Clemence ed., *Essays of J.A. Schumpeter*, Addison-Wesley, Reading, MA., 158-163.

______. (1951b), *Ten Great Economists from Marx to Keynes*, Oxford University Press, New York.

______. (1954), *History of Economic Analysis*, Oxford University Press-Allen & Unwin, Oxford-New York.

Sievers A. (1962), *Revolution, Evolution and the Economic Order*, Prentice-Hall, Englewood Cliff, N.J..

Silk L. (1978), *The Economists*, Avon Books, New York.

Swedberg R. (1991), *Schumpeter. A Biography*, Princeton University Press, Princeton N.J..

Sweezy P.M. (1972), *Modern Capitalism*, Monthly Review Press, New York.

GENERALISING THE *TABLEAU ÉCONOMIQUE*; ISNARD'S *SYSTÈME DES RICHESSES*[1]

Albert E. Steenge* and ***Richard van den Berg*****

ABSTRACT

In the literature we see an ongoing debate about the position in the history of economic thought, of François Quesnay's *Tableau économique*. According to some, the development of the *Tableau* has made Quesnay one of the greatest economists of all time. Others, on the other hand, view the *Tableau* rather in terms of an interesting effort which lacks any real significance. Professor Samuelson, in his work, seems to occupy an intermediate position.

In this paper we hope to show that by looking at Quesnay's work in connection with that of Achylle-Nicolas Isnard, a direct successor and critic, the greatness and novelty of Quesnay will become apparent. Isnard employed Quesnay's views on circularity, but as opposed to Quesnay he emphasised the productivity of all sectors of the economy. By presenting a novel mathematical presentation of Isnard's work, we will show that his work is extremely relevant in order to interpret and unify present-day efforts regarding circular-flow types of models, including today's input-output models. In this sense, we aim to provide a direct link from the *Tableau* to modern theory.

---

* Faculty of Public Administration and Public Policy, University of Twente, AE Enschede, The Netherlands.

** Holborn College, Greyhound Road, London, UK.

[1] Many people have contributed to the ideas formulated in this paper. The authors thank Roberto Scazzieri and other participants of recent meetings of the Wealth of Nations Research Group, for valuable comments and assistance.

They are particularly grateful to Paul A. Samuelson for discussions with the first author while he was Visiting Scholar at the Massachusetts Institute of Technology during the academic year 1997-98.

1. INTRODUCTION

In recent decades there has been a renewed interest in François Quesnay's *Tableau économique*. Since this construction was the first formal depiction of the economy as a reproductive system, it attracted attention especially from writers familiar with modern theories in which circularity in production was a fundamental feature. One of the first to be involved in this reinterpretation of the *Tableau* in the light of modern theory was Phillips (1955), who depicted Quesnay's model as a closed Leontief model.[2] Other writers who followed this line — more or less true to the spirit of modern Leontief modelling — were Maital (1972) or Barna (1975). Yet other writers explored the similarities between Quesnay's theory and that of Sraffa (Cartelier 1977, following a suggestion of Sraffa himself), while others again expressed doubts about various aspects of these comparisons (Meek 1962; Vaggi 1983,1985,1987; Pressman 1994), or put forward formal restatements of the analysis of the *Tableaux*, intended as alternatives to modern theories (esp. Eltis 1975a, 1975b).

In a very well-known contribution, Samuelson (1986) offered a number of highly illuminating thoughts on the ongoing discussion in the light of modern developments. He captured the spirit of the debate by starting with a reference to the teachings of Schumpeter who "shocked" his Harvard audience by declaring that of the four great economists, three were French. François Quesnay was one of them, "presumably because he was a precursor of general equilibrium and circular flow", Samuelson added.[3] He then proceeded to ask himself if Quesnay was actually that great a precursor of modern thought. Samuelson seems a bit sceptical, stating that (*ibid.* p. 47): [4]

> Hume and Cantillon, Quesnay's predecessors, and Turgot, Quesnay's successor, are more to my personal taste than Mirabeau and Quesnay.

After having presented Schumpeter's views, Samuelson went on to observe that contemporaneous comments were often of a very sceptical nature, to say

---

[2] Leontief repeatedly referred to the great inspiration of Quesnay's work regarding his own views. An example here is Leontief (1941), but also in his earlier work Leontief acknowledged Quesnay's inspiration. Interestingly, though, Leontief never commented on the specifics of the *Tableau*.

[3] The other economists were Cournot and Walras.

[4] The same spirit seems to be present already in much earlier work, see (e.g. Samuelson 1962: 4).

the least. Mirabeau is put in his place in a quote by Adam Smith. Also Linguet is mentioned in passing, followed by Gray (1931), who referred to the *Tableau* in terms of 'an embarrassing footnote'. Indeed, in comparison with the modern upsurge in interest in Quesnay's contribution to formal economic theory, the early reception of his *Tableau* was surprisingly negative and limited. One explanation for this relative lack of acceptance of the auspicious new approach of *le Docteur* is simply to be found in the highly abstract nature of the reasoning employed in the *Tableau* which posed a kind of 'barrier to entry' even to enlightened contemporaries (Argemi, Cardoso, Lluch 1995:477). Another explanation is the fact that in the views of both the physiocrats and their critics the analysis of the *Tableau* was inextricably linked to the doctrine of the exclusive productivity of agriculture, *i.e.*, the opinion that only the agricultural sector is capable of producing a *produit net* or surplus. Many contemporary economists would have felt that rejection of this doctrine, and the associated policy prescriptions, would bring with it a rejection of the apparatus of the *Tableau* itself.

In this paper we shall discuss a notable exception to the initial general failure of Quesnay's theory to inspire further developments in the formal analysis of economic reproduction and circulation. This exception is A.N. Isnard's *Traitè des richesses* which was published anonymously in 1781 without arousing much immediate interest. Isnard's modern reputation is in the first place based on the claim that he influenced Leon Walras in several important respects, a claim made most fully and quite convincingly by Jaffé (1969).[5]

Isnard was critical of several of Quesnay's ideas, but this did not lead him to reject the formal apparatus developed by the founder of the physiocratic school. On the contrary, Isnard presents a number of mathematical examples called *systémes des richesses* which can be seen as generalisations of the *Tableau économique*. His analysis highlights several important points. First, Isnard alleges that Quesnay only achieves the desired distributive outcome (i.e., he whole *produit net* being appropriated by the landowning class) by assuming specific relative prices in the *Tableau*. To illustrate this point he

[5] The connection between Isnard and Walras was made earlier, see esp. Schumpeter 1954; a recent re-examination of Jaffé's evidence has been made by Klotz (1995). Here it was argued, however, that Isnard's theory was not only historically but also analytically closer to Quesnay (a view also taken by Gilibert 1987).

rigorously distinguishes between production and circulation in real terms and in terms of value. Second, following Quesnay he suggests that on the one hand reproduction, or the exchange of inputs, and on the other hand the distribution of the surplus, or the allocation of final goods, should be treated as two separate issues. This starting point differs substantially from the interpretation of the *Tableau* as a closed Leontief model. Third, it can be argued that in relation to various modern writers, Isnard's theory provides a general framework within which different rules for the distribution of the surplus can be accommodated.

Returning for a moment to Professor Samuelson, we should add that he concluded his 1986 contribution with the observation that the *Tableau* was 'an interesting footnote' in the history of economic thought. This observation was followed by the remark "Where early pioneers are concerned, posterity must be grateful for what they accomplished and must not scold over mere imperfections". Below we hope to show that Schumpeter's view - as mentioned above — may be more acceptable if we view Quesnay's work in relation to Isnard's. Together they can be seen as having laid the foundation for work with a very modern flavour. In this sense we may certainly say that Quesnay has contributed 'an interesting *chapter*' to economic thought.

This paper has the following structure. Section two discusses Isnard's criticism of physiocratic theory which inspired his alternative views. In section three the manner in which Isnard generalises the *Tableau* is examined by means of a new way of treating separately the issues of reproduction and the distribution of the surplus. In section four Isnard's approach is compared to the theories of Leontief and Sraffa.

2. ISNARD'S CRITICISM OF PHYSIOCRACY

Achylle-Nicolas Isnard (1749-1802) was trained as an engineer at the *Ecole des Ponts et Chaussés* in his native city of Paris.[6] Early on, however, he developed an interest in the then wide discipline of political economy. 'Since my earliest youth I heard reasoning about politics, trade, and finance, and I much desired to reason about it too' (Isnard 1781, I:xii). It is likely that it was during his studies he was first exposed to the theories of physiocrats. At

[6] Renevier (1909:5-23) provides the fullest biographical sketch. Jaffé (1969) and Klotz (1994) give summaries.

the end of the 1760s the *économistes*, as the physiocrats were called at the time, exercised a considerable influence both on enlightened opinion and on government policies. They edited their own journal, organised regular discussion meetings and received famous foreign visitors like Adam Smith. In 1766, the year that Isnard commenced his training at the school of civil engineering Quesnay published the final version of the *Tableau économique* in the *Journal d'agriculture* (June). Judging by references in his *Traité des richesses* the young Isnard carefully read this and other important physiocratic publications.[7] There is even some evidence that he entertained personal contacts with the circle around Quesnay.[8]

The clearest indication of the influence Quesnay exercised on Isnard is the fundamental agreement between their theories. Both men share the same basic conception of the economic system as a whole. This basic conception is expressed in several places in the *Traité*. Isnard writes, for example:

> While one part of the goods of the land is destined to the maintenance and renewal of the funds of a new production [*fonds d'une nouvelle reproduction*], or to establish a new productive fund, there is another part which is absolutely free and destined to the needs and enjoyments of the people [...]. Of those two parts of wealth, one fulfills the end of production [i.e., consumption], and the other represents the means of production [*moyens de la production*] (Isnard 1781, I:92-3; cf. I:60).

The physiocratic character of this passage is evident. As with Quesnay, in Isnard's theory total production [*la somme total des richesses*] divides into on the one hand inputs required in the next round of production, (what Quesnay calls *avances* and Isnard 'the means of production or the goods which form the productive fund' [I:30]) and a surplus, (which Quesnay denotes by the term *produit net*, and Isnard calls the 'disposable wealth', *richesses*

---

[7] The *Tableau* is indirectly discussed in many places in the *Traité*. Direct comments on specific features of the *Tableau* can be found in volume I, page 40 and 52 in footnotes and in volume II, page 8. It seems likely, but not certain, that Isnard referred to the final version of the *Tableau* of 1766, also known as the 'Formula'. Other works of Quesnay, quoted by Isnard , are the *Encyclopédie* articles '*Fermiers*' and '*Grains*' (1781, I:65) and the *General Maxims* (1781, II:8).

[8] One letter survives of an apparently larger correspondence between Dupont and Isnard dated 28 October 1773 (Letter W 2-27 of the correspondence of Dupont de Nemours in the Eleutherian Mills Historical Library). Dupont addresses the 24 year old with '*mon trés cher et trés aimable Isnard*' and refers to 'our dispute', suggesting a friendly and ongoing contact.

disponibles, or consumption goods, *jouissances*). This distinction is a fundamental aspect of the theories of Quesnay and Isnard. It has important consequences for their conception of the allocation of products within the economic system. In particular, it implies that the question of the distribution of the surplus is for them an issue that is analytically distinct from that of 'simple reproduction'. As will be argued in section 3, a modern reformulation that wants to remain faithful to their theories has to maintain this analytical distinction.

While Isnard adopts Quesnay's distinctions between 'total production', 'advances' and 'net product', a crucial difference between the two men is that the former extends this analysis to *all* sectors producing goods and services. This involves a radical rejection of Quesnay's opinion that agriculture is the only sector capable of producing a surplus. Indeed, most of Isnard's criticism of physiocracy is aimed at their famous doctrine of the exclusive productivity of agriculture (see Isnard 1781, I:xiii). It is useful to distinguish between two aspects of the doctrine, both of which are contested by Isnard. The first is that agriculture is the only productive sector of the economy that is capable of producing a net product. The second is that the whole net product is appropriated by a single class, the *propriétaires*, or land-owning class.

The idea that the very nature of agricultural production sets it apart from other kinds of production is expressed by Quesnay by juxtaposing the 'multiplication' of wealth which takes place in agriculture with the 'addition' of 'pre-existing' wealth occurring in industrial activities (Quesnay 1766b:207).[9] Only in agriculture 'new wealth' could be created, an event made possible by the involvement of a 'productive' input, namely the soil. Thus, Quesnay and his closest followers ascribed the possibility of the existence of a surplus in agriculture to a free gift (*don gratuit*) of nature.[10]

Isnard's criticism of this first aspect of the physiocratic doctrine of the exclusive surplus generating capacity of agriculture is exceptionally lucid.

---

[9] Isnard (1781, I:40 n.g) rejects this juxtaposition out of hand.

[10] The term 'free' did not imply that it would not be necessary to incur expenditures before a harvest could be obtained. On the contrary, from his earliest economic writings Quesnay stressed the importance of prior expenditures in agriculture (see Vaggi 1987: 217). Rather, it meant that, provided proper agricultural techniques were used and appropriate advances made and provided that the harvest could be sold in a liberalised market, the value of the total product would be in excess of all items of cost.

While the physiocratic doctrine was regularly attacked during the last decades of the 18th century, objections were often based on ill-defined opinions of what it means to call an activity 'productive' or 'stérile' (see Delmas and Demals 1990). In comparison Isnard's discussion is a model of clarity. His analysis starts with a criticism of the distinction drawn in physiocratic theory between the nature of agricultural and industrial processes of production. With respect to agricultural production he accuses the *économistes* of confusing production with creation (Isnard 1781, I:15n), that is a mysterious process whereby 'something is made out of nothing'. Instead, Isnard argues that all processes of production are formally the same. Production in general is any process whereby 'the form [of inputs] changes in such a manner that [they] give new pleasures' (*ibid.* 14).[11]

This conception of production is closely related to Isnard's ideas with respect to the notion of productivity, *i.e.*, the capacity to produce a surplus. Importantly, in Isnard's theory productivity is not a property of one specific sector (or input, like land) but a property of the system of production as a whole. In order to illustrate his ideas he presents different versions of a new economic model, probably inspired by Quesnay's *Tableau*, which he calls *systéme des richesses* (*ibid.* 39) The simplest example given by Isnard reads as follows:[12]

10 M	+	10 M'	produce	40 M
5 M	+	10 M'	produce	60 M'

where M and M' stand for physical units of two different kinds of products. The surplus, or 'disposable wealth' is easily determined. Isnard notes: 'Thus, to produce *the total of the two products* a consumption of 15 M and 20 M' is

[11] In a later pamphlet he criticises the arbitrariness of the 'line of demarcation' (Isnard 1789:24) drawn by the physiocrats between 'productive' and 'unproductive' activities in slightly different words: 'why distinguish between a field which has the capacity to give a first form to a sum of elements by means of the labour of men, and a craft [*métier*] which has the capacity to give a second form to that sum of elements of nature by means of the labour of men? (*ibid.* 25).

[12] This example appears on page 36 of volume I. Other examples on pages 40-41 of vol. I and pages 4-5 of vol. II involve five and eight commodities/sectors respectively. Isnard seems to assume that the number of commodities assumed does not alter the logic of the analysis, and criticises the physiocrats for always assuming the existence of only two types of products and three classes (1781, II:8).

required, and the value of the disposable wealth is 25 M + 40 M'.' (*ibid.* 36; emphasis added.)

In comparison with the final version of Quesnay's *Tableau* two things are important to note. First, in contrast to Quesnay, Isnard expressly formulates his example in terms of physical quantities. Although some commentators (Jaffé 1969:21; Klotz 1994:36) have signalled difficulties with Isnard's notation, it is important to emphasise that M and M' in the above example stand for physical units of two different types of commodities. Thus, the inputs of each sector as well as the surplus of the economy as a whole are heterogeneous bundles of physical quantities.[13] When Isnard wants to emphasise the physical nature of the surplus he speaks of the 'real mass of disposable wealth' [*la masse réelle de richesses disponibles*] (Isnard 1781:42).

If we transcribe the final version of the *Tableau* in Isnard's manner it reads

2 A + 1 M   produce 5 A (agricultural sector)

2 A   produce 2 M (industrial sector)

The quantities in the *Tableau* are not any longer expressed in monetary terms (*milliards* of *livres*) but directly in terms of two kinds of physical inputs (agricultural products A and industrial products M respectively). Using Isnard's notation, it is immediately clear that the physical composition of the net product in the *Tableau* is 1 A + 1 M, which is indeed conform the structure of the final demand of the class of landowners assumed by Quesnay.

However, and this is a second important difference with Quesnay's theory, Isnard's manner of identifying the surplus differs from his forerunner. For Isnard the contribution to the surplus of each sector is its total production less its own reproductive requirements *and* that of the other sectors. Hereby he avoids the idea underlying the *Tableau* that first the whole surplus of the

[13] In a passage written some years later he shows a keen awareness of the fact that addition of heterogeneous inputs is only possible if they are given monetary values: 'Since commodities or products of different kinds enter into the costs of production, a relation of homogeneity has to be given to those products which allows them to be compared to one another [.] [T]his relation is obtained from the values which those commodities or products obtain in exchange, or from the comparison made between all commodities or products to one commodity which serves as common measure.' (Isnard, 1789:7-8).

economy is produced in agriculture, which only subsequently allows industrial production to take place (through the expenditure by the farmers and landowners of 1 *milliard* each on industrial products, used by the artisans to purchase agricultural goods).

A further feature of the Isnard's example (and of the *Tableau* written à la Isnard) is that the net product is not immediately allocated to a particular sector or class. This must be seen as a deliberate choice of Isnard. He bases on this his criticism of the second aspect of the physiocratic doctrine of the exclusive productivity of agriculture, as distinguished above. Quesnay and his followers argued that, since the net product was due to the fertility of the soil, the owners of the land, the *classe des propriétaires*, would under normal circumstances appropriate this net product in the form of rent. Without offering a plausible *economic* explanation of the persistence of rent under competitive circumstances, the physiocrats maintained that the farmers would hand over the whole difference between the proceeds from the sale of their harvest minus their costs of production to the landlords (see Van den Berg 2000).

It should be pointed out that the handing over of the net product was *not* seen as a payment of the farmers for the services of the landlords. Within the general picture of the *Tableau*, the payment of rent was not considered a cost or payment of a service, but rather the transfer of an unearned income or the payment for the use of a right.[14] The reason to emphasise this point is that in the original transcription by Phillips (1955) of the *Tableau* in the form of a closed Leontief model, rent payments were treated as a payment for a service. This way of accounting for rent obscures the very point on which the physiocrats insist repeatedly, namely that it embodies that part of the social product that is *in excess* of the advances necessary to continue reproduction.

While Isnard, like Quesnay, does recognise rent as a surplus income, he rejects the idea that only the owners of land could normally share in the surplus. He criticises the physiocrats for maintaining '[...] that in the general

[14] In this sense the appropriation of rent by the landlords is conceptually not unlike the extraction of surplus labour by the capitalists in Marx. In Marx's theory the capitalists pay for the right to use the labourers' time and manage to let them produce in that time a value which is in excess of what is paid in wages. The sale of labour time is an (or even the only) unequal exchange. In Quesnay's theory, farmers manage to extract from the land a value that is in excess of the advances spent on the land. This 'exploitation' of the land then takes the form of an unequal transfer to the landlords whose property would not have yielded any income without the spending of the farmers.

distribution of wealth labour and capital only receive the salaries due to that labour and to that capital' (Isnard 1781, I:40 n.g). In order to contest this opinion, Isnard attempts to demonstrate that the distributive outcome whereby the whole surplus is appropriated by a single class depends on a specific assumption with respect to relative prices. It is for this reason that his *système des richesses* is expressed in strictly physical terms, which, without further assumptions, makes it is impossible to say which sector or class will appropriate the surplus. The further assumption required, according to Isnard, are relative prices. Commenting on his example he notes: 'To know what each producer receives of that disposable wealth, one has to suppose values to those two products' (*ibid.* 36).

As opposed to Quesnay, who assumes that the whole surplus is appropriated by a single sector, Isnard maintains that such a distribution is merely one of the many possibilities. If one supposes in his example that the exchange rate between a unit of M and a unit of M' is 3:1 then '[...] the disposable revenue of the proprietors or of the producers of 40 M will be equal to zero, and that of the producers of 60 M' will be equal to the total mass of disposable wealth, 25 M + 40 M', or 48 1/3 M' [...]' (*ibid.*). However, this distributive outcome is only the result of the relative price that is assumed. For this reason, according to Isnard,

> M. Quesnai and the *Economists* were mistaken when they stated as a general fact that industry is not productive. It is possible that the works are not productive [*i.e.* returning a surplus income] to the [industrial] workers [...]. But industry really produces useful qualities, and increases wealth by increasing the total mass of disposable wealth. When the value of works surpasses the value necessary to the existence of the workers, industry is productive both relative to the [industrial] workers and relative to other owners (I:39).

In effect Isnard thus says that the distributive outcome of the *Tableau économique* is the result of an implicit assumption with respect to relative prices. (Or, conversely, that relative prices are the result of a desired distributive outcome that is imposed). Quesnay presumes that only the prices of agricultural products exceed the costs of their advances (or 'fundamental price'), and the whole of this difference is handed over to the class of landowners, so that the incomes of both the farmers and the artisans only just cover their costs of production. It is interesting that Isnard already suggests this interpretation of the *Tableau* since, largely due to the implicit character of Quesnay's assumption the role of relative prices within the *Tableau* is still disputed by modern commentators.[15]

Isnard's model can be seen as a generalisation of that of Quesnay, specifically with respect to the idea of distribution. Very much in accordance with physiocratic analysis Isnard argues that relative prices will in the first place have to guarantee reproduction:

> [producers] will not produce useful things if they do not expect to have the costs returned to them, that is to say, the value of the advances necessary to the existence of that commodity. One has to assume therefore that the value of a commodity is *at least equal* to the costs of production (*ibid.* I:35; emphasis added).

The words 'at least equal' in this passage are crucial. The analytical complication in (and at the same time richness of) the models of Quesnay and Isnard consists in the fact that there is a surplus to be distributed and spent which requires further assumptions. Some commentators seem to deny the need for such further assumptions in the theories of Quesnay and Isnard, when it is argued that these writers see '[...] the economic behaviour of every individual as completely determined by the reproductive requirements of the system' (Gilibert 1987:424; cf. 1981:151). This is an oversimplification. In Quesnay's case the fact that the whole surplus is appropriated by the landowning class is not dictated by the reproductive requirements of the system. Nor is the spending pattern of the landowners dictated by need for inputs required for the reproduction of their service. Similarly in Isnard's model a whole range of different distributions are possible without endangering the reproduction of the system. Also it can be said that all classes which obtain some of the disposable wealth of the system have some discretionary spending power.

While Quesnay can be said to employ a simple rule for the distribution of the surplus ("the whole *produit net* is handed over to the landlords"), Isnard does not commit himself. Instead he argues that a whole range of

---

[15] On the one hand, Pressman (1994:181), for example, maintains that Quesnay 'virtually ignored' the issue of relative prices, and only had 'a definite theory of output' but 'no theory of value'. On the other hand, Gilibert (1989:93) argues that Quesnay implicitly assumed the 'one set of prices [which] allows the *Tableau* to reproduce itself and to guarantee the desired outcome (a net revenue appearing only in agriculture).

prices is possible, as he says in one place 'an infinite number' (1781,I:41), which result in as many different distributions of the surplus. The only definite thing that can be said is that '[...] the real mass of disposable wealth, [...], will always be divided among those [producers] for whom the value of their products exceeds the value of the costs'. This lack of a determinate opinion with respect to the 'normal' distribution of the surplus can be either considered as a strength or as a weakness of Isnard's analysis. As will be argued in the next section, it is a strength in the sense that it suggest a general framework within which different assumptions with respect to the distribution of the surplus can be accommodated.

The fact that Isnard does not adopt a simple rule for the distribution of the surplus may also explain why the relation in his work between his analysis of production and that of the determination of market prices is somewhat difficult. The latter contribution, appearing on pages 16 to 21 of volume I of the *Traité*, is in fact the most well-known part of his theory. The reason for this is that a number of commentators has likened Isnard discussion of market equilibrium to that of Léon Walras (see especially Schumpeter 1954:217, 307, 954-5; Jaffé 1969). In these sections Isnard argues that the (exchange) value of products is determined through a process whereby the marketed quantities of the various products balance out against one another.

This conception is not completely strange to physiocratic thought, something Isnard acknowledges when pointing out that '[...] according to their own [*i.e.*, the physiocrats] principles about the freedom of trade [...] it is in exchange that values are determined' (Isnard 1781, I:41 n.g). In the physiocratic literature one does indeed repeatedly find the observation that prior to being exchanged products are merely useful physical objects (*biens*) which only become wealth (*richesses*) and obtain a value when exchanged. This idea informs Isnard's observation that strictly speaking '[...] useful things stop being wealth when their relation [of exchange] is annulled' (*ibid.* I:16).

While the basic notion that goods only acquire value in exchange is also found in the physiocrats, the mathematics Isnard applies to the idea constitutes a highly original contribution. He states that if given quantities of only two kinds of products were traded, for example the respective quantities a and b of commodities M and M', then one can formulate the exchange equation aM = bM (*ibid.* I:18). However, as soon as more than two kinds of commodities are traded things become more complicated:

> Since the offers are composed of several heterogeneous commodities it is not possible to deduce from the equality, or from the equation which we have just discussed, the relation between two particular commodities. To find the relation between commodities taken two by two, one would have to formulate as many equations as there are commodities (*ibid.* I:19).

Isnard then demonstrates this important insight algebraically by calculating the relative prices for given quantities of three commodities (*ibid.* I:20). This analysis is remarkable and has been rightly praised. It is also true that the idea to use a system of simultaneous equations for the determination of prices anticipates (and as Jaffé [1969] argues may actually have inspired) Léon Walras. However, this is where the similarity with Walrasian general equilibrium theory stops.

It is important to note that Isnard's analysis of market equilibrium is not much more than the description of a formal mechanism. As several commentators have observed, in the section where Isnard presents his analysis of exchange he simply assumes exchanged quantities as given. Some commentators have concluded from this that Isnard does not have any views to offer at all with respect to the question how marketed quantities are determined. Baumol and Goldfeld (1968:253) comment rather curtly that '[t]he use of fixed and unexplained quantities offered in exchange for other items [...] [is] typical for the crudity of the early works in mathematical economics'.

However, more than casual reading of Isnard's work learns that he does not intend to leave the determination of quantities to be exchanged in the market unexplained. He clearly states: 'We will later determine the quantities of commodities produced and brought to the market' (Isnard 1781,I:19). He returns to this remark in section 6 of chapter 2 which commences with the following remark:

> As we have seen [*i.e.*, on the pages 16 to 21], the values of products are established in the market without the costs or expenditures of producers being considered: but they will not produce useful things if they do not expect to have the costs returned to them [...] (*ibid.*34-5)

This passage shows that in Isnard's opinion there certainly exists a connection between his analyses of exchange and of production. However, the fact that he gives a distinct treatment to the issue of the determination of market prices may be explained by his insight that within a surplus producing economy there is not a single set of prices consistent with reproduction.[16] The existence of range of price sets and corresponding distributions of the surplus thus also explains the somewhat loose connection between his discussions of exchange and of production.

3. MODELLING ISNARD'S APPROACH

Concerning Isnard's approach, we may ask ourselves what the significance is of his attempt to develop Quesnay's model for modern theory. Does his work provide a closer link to modern input-output theory than that of Quesnay? Or does it perhaps suggest a different approach to certain economic problems? To help us find an answer to these questions, let us begin by writing down Isnard's simplest example in the now familiar input-output mode. We have:

Table 1:

	M	M'	Disp	Tot
M	10	5	25	40
M'	10	10	40	60

The symbols M and M' here denote sectors of the economy producing, respectively, goods M and M'. 'Disp' denotes the surplus (*richesses disponibles*) and 'Tot' stands for total output. Isnard starts his analysis with the economy having reached consensus on the composition of the physical surplus. This is reflected by the fact that column D is given. Given that, it has to find a procedure for the distribution of the surplus.

We recall that all entries are in real terms. No prices are yet assumed. Isnard points out that 'The total sum of disposable products depends absolutely

[16] Obviously, if Isnard had assumed that 10 M + 10 M' produce only 15 M and 5 M + 10 M' produce 20 M' then the marketed quantities would have been (15-10) M and (20-10) M'. The exchange equation would then have been 5M=10M', which would give the only relative price ensuring continued production.

[i.e., in *physical terms*] upon the needs of nature; she requires a certain portion of the general mass of wealth; she leaves the rest to the enjoyment and the needs of man' (I:37; emphasis added). Also: 'The industry that diminishes the costs of production, increases the total of disposable wealth, regardless of the variation in values' (I:37). In this passage the term 'nature' stands for the requirements imposed by the specifics of the relevant technologies. Isnard thus shows a keen awareness of the fact that technology should be analysed in terms of the quantitative proportions as occurring in production. In our view, this legitimises us to interpret the entries in the intersectoral part of Table 1 (*i.e.*, the part describing the exchange of inputs between sectors M and M') in terms of fixed input proportions per unit of output.[17] This allows us to derive the following implied input coefficients matrix A_I:

$$A_I = \begin{bmatrix} 1/4 & 1/12 \\ \\ 1/4 & 1/6 \end{bmatrix}$$

Isnard has seen sharply that relative prices play a central role in the mechanism underlying distribution. Indeed, in his view prices will determine the ultimate distribution of the surplus. Isnard also seems to have realised that actual market prices depend on a great many factors of an accidental nature.

We may formulate his conception as follows. We have at hands a quantitative description of a productive economy, *i.e.* an economy that is able to produce a surplus. The composition of the surplus may vary. Given our knowledge of the needed inputs for reproduction, we can calculate how large the surplus will be, given total output. Hereafter, the economy has to decide on the distribution of the surplus — over the sectors.

Let us first consider the concept of 'productivity'. The literature on multi-sectoral models contains several methods for measuring what may be called an economy's 'productivity'. As was noted in the previous section, Isnard, in contrast to Quesnay, considers productivity as a property of the economic system as a whole. It can therefore be argued that for our purposes

---

[17] As observed later on, the straightforward derivation of such technical input coefficients for the *Tableau*, as proposed by Phillips (1955), is much more problematic. Isnard, in any case, is much clearer on this point than Quesnay.

a measure based on the matrix of input coefficients A_I is most appropriate. The reason is clear: the columns of this matrix give us, for each sector, the inputs required per unit of output. For all sectors combined, *i.e.* for the economy as a whole, we have a measure for quantifying the relation between inputs and outputs, taking into account the existing sectoral interconnectedness. This measure is the Perron-Frobenius eigenvalue of A, to be denoted below by the symbol $\lambda(A_I)$. A well-know theorem tells us that the economy is productive if and only if

$$\lambda(A_I) < 1$$

In that case, we may write

$$x = (A_I)x + f$$

where f stands for the surplus and x for total outputs.[18] It can be shown that now for each positive x there exists a positive f (and *vice versa*).

Now let us devote a few words to the problem of how to look upon the relation between relative prices and the distribution of the surplus. When the surplus is being distributed, the proprietors in a particular sector succeed in 'appropriating' a part of the surplus. This means, in terms of prices, as already observed in the previous section, that this sector's products must command a price not only covering the value of the inputs but also the value of that part of the surplus that is being appropriated. Evidently, addition of the surplus parts of all sectors will equal the economy's total surplus. Thus, we see here that there is only one way in which a sector can appropriate a part of the surplus, namely by having a market price higher than what has to be paid in terms of inputs. In general, we may expect that the larger the share of the surplus that a sector is able to appropriate, the higher its (relative) price will have to be.

Now let us see if we can make the above more precise. As was discussed in section 2, Isnard analysed the establishment of market prices separately from his analysis of production and in this latter analysis simply imposed those prices. From the above, we have that we may view the distribution

[18] For Isnard's input coefficients matrix we have $\lambda(A_I) = 0.359$.

problem, from the points of view of the two sectors, as a problem of appropriation of (scalar) multiples of the bundle D. We now may write down the equation which gives us the possibilities that exist in the economy. We know that market prices p must cover both the outlays on inputs and the value of the share of the surplus appropriated by each sector. Let us denote the multiple (of D) that sector M receives by α and the multiple that M' receives by β. Prices p must then satisfy the following equation:

$$p = p[A^{I}(\alpha,\beta)] \qquad \alpha,\beta \geq 0$$

where

$$\{A^{I}(\alpha,\beta)\} = \left[\begin{bmatrix} 1/4 & 1/12 \\ 1/4 & 1/6 \end{bmatrix} + \left[\alpha\begin{bmatrix} 5 \\ 8 \end{bmatrix} \beta\begin{bmatrix} 5 \\ 8 \end{bmatrix}\right]\right]$$

Thus, matrix $A^{I}(\alpha,\beta)$ is the sum of two other matrices, *i.e.* A_{I} and a matrix which tells us, via the parameters α and β, the multiples of D that, at the unit level, each sector appropriates. Corresponding to the above equation for market prices, we have the following equation which describes real outputs:

$$[A^{I}(\alpha,\beta)]x = x \qquad \alpha,\beta \geq 0$$

We may approach this equation in several ways. If we consider the determination of prices and distribution as a simultaneous process, we are confronted with an equation system consisting of two equations in (2 + 2) = 4 unknowns. One way to proceed will be to assume a particular distribution of the surplus, *i.e.* to assume specific values for α and β and then to calculate corresponding market prices. Another one will be to assume specific prices and then to calculate the corresponding values of α and β. (This latter procedure being the procedure suggested by Isnard). The method of assuming a particular distribution of the surplus, naturally, may reflect economic reasoning with respect to the normal outcome effected by competitive forces. For example, one may assume, with Quesnay, that in a fully liberalised economy one sector will normally appropriate the whole surplus (see Gilibert 1981,1989). Or, following Ricardo, we may assume that normally the surplus will be distributed as a uniform proportion over the capital advanced in each sector. The opposite method of assuming a set of market prices and consecutively calculating the distribution may not evince any specific economic reasoning. Isnard, for one, only uses the method to demonstrate that variations in relative prices give rise to as many distributions of the surplus. Clearly, the parameters α and β should be interdependent in the sense that, provided proper standardisation, if one increases, the other one must decrease. (For additional remarks on the methodology employed, see Steenge 2000).

Let us see now which values of α and β are allowed. (Note that because we are working at the unit level, we have introduced already a specific standardisation). From the above price and real output equations we know, of course, that the determinant of matrix $[I - A^{I}(\alpha,\beta)]$ must be zero:

$$|I - A^{I}(\alpha,\beta)| = 0 \qquad \alpha,\beta \geq 0$$

The allowed values of α and β now can be straightforwardly obtained. Some manipulation tells us that:

$$1/12 - 2/3\ \alpha - \beta = 0 \qquad \alpha,\beta \geq 0$$

Graphically we have:

Figure 1:

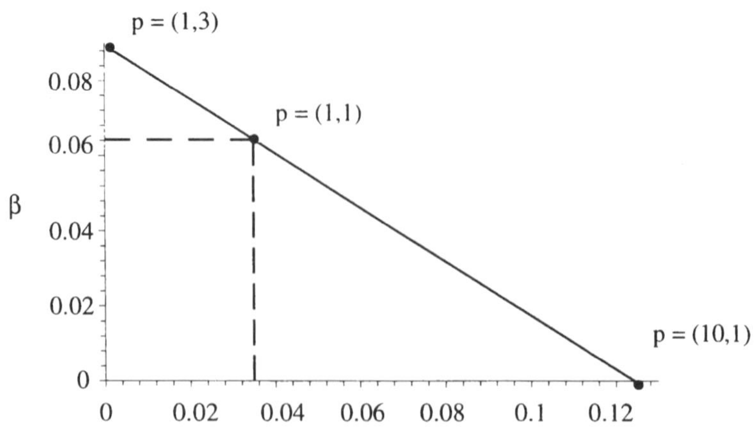

Each combination of α and β corresponds to a different distribution of the surplus. For example, if we have α = 1/26 and β = 3/52, we have

$$A^1(1/26, 3/52) = \begin{bmatrix} 5/26 & 15/52 \\ 8/26 & 24/52 \end{bmatrix}$$

In this case, sector M receives 100(9/13) percent of the surplus and sector M' the remaining 100(4/13) percent. If $\alpha = 0$, we have β = 1/12. This corresponds to the case where sector M' appropriates the entire surplus. *Vice versa*, if $\beta = 0$, we have that a = 1/8, and sector M receives the whole surplus, *i.e.*, the distributive outcome given as an example by Isnard (see section 2).

In our model, to each admitted point on $L = |I-A^1(\alpha,\beta)| = 0$ corresponds a different set of market prices p. For example, to the point (1/26,3/52) correspond unit prices for both M and M'. To the extreme points we mentioned, correspond prices 1 and 3, and 10 and 1, for units of goods M and M', respectively. (Outside these two price ratios the economy is not viable; anywhere between them it is). It is not difficult to show that, starting from one of the extremes, say from the point α = 1/8, β = 0, the price of M will decrease while simultaneously the price of M' will increase, both in relative terms, naturally. Similarly, to each set of prices in the range given by Figure 1, a unique set of values of α and βcorresponds. That is, a uniquely determined distribution of the surplus. Thus, we observe that each point on L represents an equilibrium point in Isnard's sense. To each set of prices p, a pair of values (α,β) corresponds, standing for a different distribution of incomes.

Comparison with the structure of Quesnay's Tableau économique and Leontief's input-output table

The above restatement of Isnard's theory has the advantage of allowing a formal comparison both with the *Tableau économique* and with modern theory. The comparison with Quesnay's *Tableau* is interesting because, as we have seen, Isnard was substantially influenced by this model. An obvious modern candidate for comparison is Leontief. Not only has his system become the leading multi-sectoral system based on circularity, Leontief himself repeatedly alluded to the similarity between his own system and the 18th century precursors. In a well-known paper Phillips (1955) took this allusion serious by rewriting the *Tableau* in the closed Leontief format. He presented the following table:

Table 2 :

	F	A	P	T
F	2000	2000	1000	5000
A	1000	0	1000	2000
P	2000	0	0	2000
T	5000	2000	2000	

where F stands for Farmers, A for Artisans, P for Proprietors and T for Totals. If we would consider (only) the first two rows (corresponding to sales by farmers and artisans, respectively, we would have a table rather similar to Table 1. There is a difference though. As we recall, Table 1 was in physical units. Phillips table, following Quesnay, is in monetary units. However, by *supposing* that the units in the Phillips table have been measured in physical units worth, say, one pound each, we may interpret the table in real units. (See also Pressman 1994:110-113). We now easily derive an input coefficients matrix from the table. We obtain:

$$A_Q = \begin{bmatrix} 2/5 & 1 \\ 1/5 & 0 \end{bmatrix}$$

where straightforward calculation gives $\lambda(A_Q) = 0.690$. We have a surplus consisting of 1000 units of agricultural products and 1000 of manufactured ones, respectively. Now let us approach the problem of the distribution of the surplus following Isnard. We then would have two sectors each of which tries to obtain his share of the surplus. The relevant system matrix would be

$$A^Q(\alpha,\beta) = \left[\begin{bmatrix} 2/5 & 1 \\ 1/5 & 0 \end{bmatrix} + \left[\alpha\begin{bmatrix} 1 \\ 1 \end{bmatrix} \beta\begin{bmatrix} 1 \\ 1 \end{bmatrix}\right]\right] \qquad \alpha,\beta \geq 0$$

As we have seen, distribution of the surplus implies that the Perron-Frobenius eigenvalue $\lambda[A^Q(\alpha,\beta)]$ must be equal to unity. This in turn implies that the determinant of matrix $[(I - A^Q(\alpha,\beta)]$ must be zero. So,

$$\left| I - A^Q(\alpha,\beta) \right| = 0 \qquad \alpha,\beta \geq 0$$

This gives us the following functional relation between α and β:

$$\alpha + (2/5)\beta - 1/5 = 0, \qquad \alpha_1,\beta \geq 0$$

see Figure 2. Similarly to the Isnard case, we have that each admissible combination of α and β corresponds to a particular set of prices, and *vice versa*. Following Quesnay, only agriculture is able to appropriate the surplus. This means, in terms of Figure 2, that *only* the combination $\alpha = 1/5$, $\beta = 0$ is admissible. That is, the extreme point A of L_2 represents the only admissible point. To A, as is easily verifiable, correspond *unit prices* for the products of agriculture and manufacture. Thus, the physiocratic distribution implies the existence of a particular and well-defined set of market prices. This is precisely the point made by Isnard!

Figure 2 :

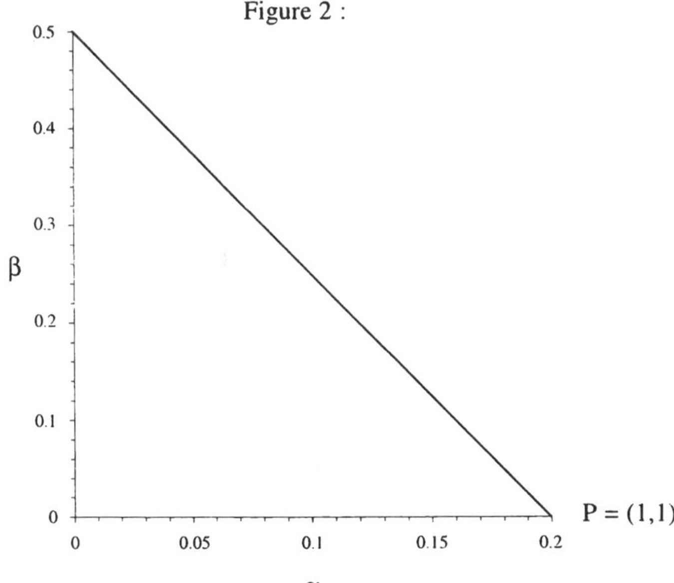

Let us, as a final exercise, compare the above two models with today's input-output model. We shall employ a numerical example of a hypothetical economy that has been repeatedly employed in the literature (see *e.g.* Leontief 1970).[19] Leontief models are built around the concept of a production function. These functions give us, for each of the distinguished 'sectors' of the economy, the required inputs to produce a unit of, say, grain or steel. Two kinds of inputs are distinguished, intermediate and primary ones. Intermediate inputs are those inputs whose production is explained in terms of the model, here: grain or steel. Primary inputs are those inputs the production of which is not explained, such as labour or capital. The quantity available of these is a datum for the model. Here we shall, because of limited space, confine ourselves to the standard case where only one primary factor, homogeneous labour, is distinguished.

The model's prime purpose is to determine which outputs are necessary to satisfy a certain exogenously determined 'final demand'. This final demand constitutes, in real terms, the remuneration of the primary production factor, labour. The quantity of this real wage is, for each sector, given by its production function. (Thus, the notion of 'a surplus', as used in the physiocratic sense, is absent!) So, in a Leontief-type formulation we would have a table consisting of three rows, instead of two as above. Borrowing Leontief's example we have:

Table 3 :

	G	S	F	T
G	25	20	55	100
S	14	6	30	50
L	80	180	-	260

Here G and S stand for grain and steel, F for final demand, L for labour, and T for totals. All entries are in real terms. The corresponding matrix of intermediate input coefficients reads:

[19] We shall distinguish an agricultural sector producing 'grain' and an industrial sector producing 'steel'.

$$A_L = \begin{bmatrix} 0.25 & 0.40 \\ 0.14 & 0.12 \end{bmatrix}$$

(with $\lambda(AL) < 1$). Besides matrix A_L we need additional information on the sectoral labour inputs to fully describe the economy's technology. We have:

$$l = [0.80 \quad 3.60]$$

The real output model now can be written in the familiar Leontief form:

$$x = Ax + f$$

(where we have adopted the convention to denote final demand by the symbol f and the required total output by x). Prices have to satisfy the relation:

$$p = pA + wl$$

where w denotes the wage rate (in money terms). Now let us first determine the possibilities this Leontief economy has for distributing the produced final demand. We have, employing a similar notation as before, that:

$$\left| I - A_L(\alpha,\beta) \right| = 0 \qquad \alpha,\beta \geq 0$$

where

$$A_L(\alpha,\beta) = \left[\begin{bmatrix} 0.25 & 0.40 \\ 0.14 & 0.12 \end{bmatrix} + \left[\alpha \begin{bmatrix} 11 \\ 6 \end{bmatrix} \beta \begin{bmatrix} 11 \\ 6 \end{bmatrix} \right] \right]$$

After some manipulation we obtain the following relation between α and β:

$$12.08\alpha + 6.04\beta - 0.604 = 0 \qquad \alpha,\beta \geq 0$$

Graphically we have:

Figure 3 :

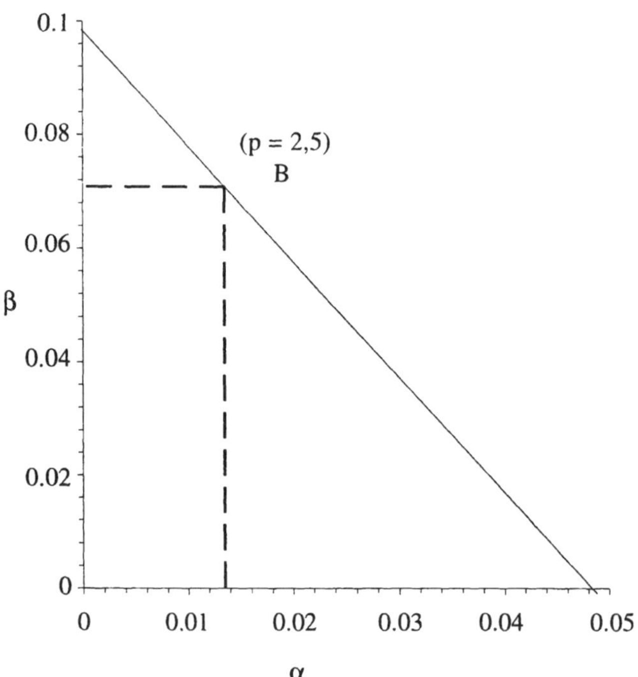

Given the interpretation of labour's remuneration in terms of requirements as dictated by sectoral production functions, the only prices consistent with the model are 2 and 5, for a unit of 'grain' and 'steel', respectively. We observe (again) that compared with Isnard's conception of the economic process we do not really have 'a distribution problem'.

4. CONCLUDING REMARKS

In this paper we have discussed the work of Achylle-Nicolas Isnard. We have seen that Isnard proposes a strict distinction between the issues of (re)production and distribution. Regarding the distribution of the surplus, Isnard very decidedly states that this can take an infinite number of forms: to account for actual distribution as found in reality, one requires, in addition to technical coefficients and the pricing of inputs, a great deal of additional information of a socio-economic nature. In this sense Isnard's work is of a much more general nature than that of Quesnay. He justly points to the fact that the distribution of the surplus in Quesnay's *Tableau* reflects a very specific assumption regarding market prices. And this is not all: in seeing distribution of the surplus as being determined by a multitude of factors, Isnard's work can also be seen as more general than much of today's work. We have briefly discussed the case of Leontief's standard model. Out of an infinite number of possibilities, Leontief has imposed that market prices should reflect embodied labour. From the perspective of Isnard's *système*, therefore, Quesnay's *Tableau* and Leontief's modern input-output *Tableaux* are two of a kind: in both types of *Tableaux*, the distribution of the surplus is determined by the imposition of *specific prices*.

However, we should recall in all of this that Quesnay's *Tableau économique* was always Isnard's main source of inspiration. Indeed, we may say that Isnard's work has enabled us to see a new correspondence between the *Tableau* and work done by present-day authors. In this sense we hope to have shown — as a comment on Professor Samuelson's view — that Quesnay's work does not merely constitute a curious 'footnote' in the history of the discipline, but that it initiated a whole 'chapter' of economic thought which is still relevant today.

REFERENCES

Argemi, L., J-L Cardoso and E. Lluch, 1995. 'La diffusion internationale de la physiocratie: quelques problèmes ouverts', *Economies et Sociétés*, 22-23, 473-80.

Barna, T., 1975. 'Quesnay's "*Tableau*" in Modern Guise', *Economic Journal*, vol. 85, 485-496.

Baumol, W.J. and Goldfeld, S.M., 1968. *Precursors in Mathematical Economics: An Anthology*. London School of Economics and Political Sciences.

Delmas, B. and Demals, T., 1990. 'Du Pont et les "éclectiques": La controverse sur la stérilite pendant la période révolutionaire', *Economies et Sociétés*, 13, 123-139.

Eltis, W.A.,. 1975a. 'Francois Quesnay: A Reinterpretation 1: The *Tableau* Economique', *Oxford Economic Papers*, vol. 27, 167-200.

_____ 1975b. 'Francois Quesnay: A Reinterpretation 2: The Theory of Economic Growth', *Oxford Economic Papers*, vol. 27, 327-351.

Gilibert, G., 1981. *'Isnard, Cournot, Walras, Leontief. Evoluzione di un modello', Annali della Fondazione Luigi Einaudi*, vol. XV, 129-53.

_____ 1987. 'Circular Flow' in *The New Palgrave: a dictionary of economics*, eds. J.Eatwell, M. Milgate and P. Newman. London: Macmillan. Vol. 1, 424-26.

_____ 1989. 'Review of *The economics of François Quesnay* by G. Vaggi', *Contributions to Political Economy*, 8:91-96.

Gray, A., 1931. *The Development of Economic Doctrine*. London: Longman.

Isnard, Achylle Nicolas, 1781. *Traité des Richesses contenant l'analyse de l'usage des richesses en général et de leurs valeurs; les principes et les loix naturelles de la circulation des richesses, de leur distribution, du commerce, de la circulation des monnoies et de l'impôt et des recherches historiques sur les révolutions que les droits de propriété public et particulier ont éprouvées en France depuis l'origine de la monarchie*, Londres (et se vend à Lausanne chez François Grasset et Comp.) 2 vols.

______ 1789. *Réponses aux principales objections à faire contre l'impôt unique* (n.p., March).

Jaffé, W., 1969. 'A.N. Isnard, Progenitor of the Walrasian General Equilibrium Model', *History of Political Economy*, 1, 19-43.

Klotz, G., 1994. 'Achylle Nicolas Isnard, précurseur de Léon Walras?', *Economies et Sociétés*, 29-52.

Leontief, W.W., 1941. *The Structure of American Economy, 1919-1929*. Cambridge, Mass., Harvard University Press.

______ 1970. 'Environmental Repercussions and the Economic Structure: An Input-Output Approach', *Review of Economics and Statistics*, 52, 262-271.

Maital, S., 1972. 'The Tableau Economique as a Simple Leontief Model: An Amendment', *Quarterly Journal of Economics*, 86, 504-507.

Meek, R. L., 1962. *The Economics of Physiocracy. Essays and Translations*. Reprint 1993, Fairfield NJ: A.M. Kelley.

Phillips, A., 1955. 'The Tableau Économique as a Simple Leontief Model', *Quarterly Journal of Economics*, 69, 137-144.

Pressman, S., 1994. *Quesnay's Tableau Économique. A critique and reassessment*. Fairfield: A.M. Kelley.

Quesnay, François, 1766a. '*Analyse de la formule arithmétique du Tableau économique*', translated in Meek (1962:150-167).

______ 1766b. '*Dialogue entre Mr. H. et Mr. N.*' ('Dialogue on the Work of Artisans'), translated in Meek (1962:203-230).

Renevier, L., 1909. *Les théories économiques d'Achylle-Nicolas Isnard d'après son ouvrage "Le Traité des richesses"*. Poitiers.

Samuelson, P.A. (1962). 'Economists and the History of Ideas', *American Economic Review*, Vol. II, 1-18.

______ 'Quesnay's "Tableau Economique" as a Theorist Would Formulate It Today', *The Collected Scientific Papers of Paul A. Samuelson*. Kate Crowley ed. Cambridge Mass. and London: MIT Press, vol. 5, 630-663.

Schumpeter, J.A., 1954. *History of Economic Analysis*. Reprint 1994. London: Routledge.

Steenge, A.E., 2000. 'The Rents Problem in the Tableau Economique; Revisiting the Phillips Model', *Economic Systems Research*, forthcoming.

Van den Berg, R., 1998. *Dissident Physiocrats. Value, surplus and distribution in the economic writings of Le Trosne, Turgot, Morellet and Isnard*. Ph.D. Thesis, De Montfort University.

______ 2000. 'Differential Rent in the 1760s. Two Neglected French Contributions', *The European Journal for the History of Economic Thought*, forthcoming.

Vaggi, G., 1983. 'The Physiocratic Theory of Prices', *Contributions to Political Economy*, 2, 1-22.

______ 1985, 'A Physiocratic Model of Relative Prices and Income Distribution', *Economic Journal*, 95, 928-947.

______ 1987. *The Economics of François Quesnay*. Basingstoke: Macmillan.

THE NEOCLASSICAL CLASSICAL FALLACY

*O.F. Hamouda**

ABSTRACT

"The Classical Classical Fallacy" (1994) exemplifies Samuelson's vigourously sustained interest both in the capital controversies and in his conviction in the persuasive role of mathematics. Although in the article Samuelson has attempted to tackle the issue of capital from the perspective of Marxists, neo-Ricardians, Sraffa, Stigler, Wicksell, Schumpeter and Bohm Bawerk, and Hicks, the present consideration of it restricts itself to his treatment of the "fallacy" of Ricardo and Hicks and its misunderstanding. It is an in-depth discussion of three numerically comparable examples from Ricardo, Hicks and Samuelson. Since Samuelson's main goal was to establish that it is fallacious to hold that 1) fixed capitals are prejudicial to wages and the demand for labour and 2) circulating capitals are favourable to the real wage rate and the demand for labour, it is argued that Samuelson's approach to the topic is much more general than that intended by either Ricardo or Hicks. The present contribution sheds light on the tremendous difficulties connected with the concept of capital and the issue of machinery's effect.

There are many unresolved issues which have kept economists debating for centuries. The concept of physical capital is one of them, whether in its relation to the income distribution discussion or to its combination to the other factors of production, or simply in terms of its measurement. These issues have generated tremendous controversy over the centuries, and there remain many unsettled questions. A satisfactory general theory of both circulating and fixed capital has yet to be provided. Capital theory has occupied a great deal of the time of Paul Samuelson, among the many topics in economics treated by his prolific work.

* Dept. of Economics, Glendon College, York University, Toronto, Canada.

Samuelson's article, "The Classical Classical Fallacy" of 1994[1] exemplifies its author's vigourously sustained interest both in the capital controversies and in his conviction in the persuasive role of mathematics. More than any of his predecessors, Samuelson should be credited for his extensive methodology of mathematics, both in exploiting mathematical language as a powerful tool in debates as well as in providing the guidelines for others to quantify economic analysis. He came to believe that, better than any well-written prose, the ultimate means of persuasion in argumentation is the language of mathematics.[2] He was also persuaded of the capacity of mathematics to reveal the underlying truth (or falsity) of an economic proposition. This has given him tremendous perspectives that often his predecessors and contemporary non-mathematical economists do not have.

A lengthy seven-page appendix to "The Classical Classical Fallacy", not to mention the mathematized discussion of Section I, demonstrates Samuelson's dedication to mathematics as a tool of persuasion within this article. The Appendix, a "quasi-mathematical" explication, is represented by Samuelson as "a convenient springboard for economists who want to pursue further the presumptions, *possibilities, and impossibilities* involved in comparisons of fixed and circulating capitals". (emphasis added, Samuelson, p. 630) Instances of the "great [mathematical] simplicity" for which Samuelson continues to strive abound in the article. Exponential depreciation, "where the rate of depreciation of the durable input is a constant, independent of intensity of its use and of the instrument's age" (p. 622) is but one, for which he specifically notes his conviction that its mathematical formulation will cost him little in "loss of realism".

In the classical fallacy article as a whole, Samuelson has attempted to tackle the issue of capital from the perspective of Marxists[3], neo-Ricardians[4], Srafa[5], Stigler, Wicksell, Schumpeter and Bohm Bawerk,[6] and Hicks. In this

[1] *Journal of Economic Literature*, Vol. XXXII (June 1994): 620-39.

[2] He is so mathematically skilled that, whatever economic problem is presented to him, his instinct is to provide immediately a mathematical model for it.

[3] whom he thinks got Marx all wrong ...

[4] whom he seems to see as pathetically pale replicas of the original.

[5] whom with Marx, he co-opted, by identifying each independently of his followers (with good reason!). In the case of the Wicksellian-Srafian perspective, he carefully avoided the capital controversies and reswitching.

[6] Grouping them all together as authors either who were not sufficiently skilled in mathematics or who did not have enough mathematics to do justice to the problem ...

context, he makes a very strong statement which if indeed he has proven is correct, would be extremely "damning" to more than one generation of his predecessors all together. In the article's first and fourth sections, entitled respectively "Manageable Models of Fixed Capital" (pp. 622-24) and "Why We Succumb: Wage Fund Notions" (pp. 627-30), he plunges into the challenges of the comparative analysis of fixed and circulating capitals. In Section IV he notes his suspicion that "muddled ... notions about circulating capital as a species of 'the wage fund' " are at the root of the classical conception of capital" (p. 627). Land as a rival to capital is addressed by Samuelson at intervals throughout.[7]

As there is just too much to address in Samuelson's article, even to do justice to its main point which derives from the classic issue in Ricardo, 'does capital do possible harm to labour?', I shall restrict myself to Samuelson's tracing it in his treatment of Ricardo and Hicks. I shall leave to others, if it has not already been undertaken[8], to accept the challenge to revisit or rebuff the charges in the case of the other authors Samuelson addressed. My modest contribution is to just that in the case of Hicks and, by extension backward, in the case of Ricardo. As my narrow focus will revolve around the technical interpretation of the "fallacy" in these authors and Samuelson, I shall restrict myself to Ricardo's "On Machinery" in his *On the principles of political economy and taxation*, chapter 32 in the Third Edition (1821)[9], and to Hicks' Chapter 9, "The Industrial Revolution" and its Appendix in his *A theory of economic history* (1969)[10], in light of Samuelson's article of 1994. I shall restrict myself even further only to the effect of machinery on the demand for labour, leaving aside the issues of the impact of machinery on changes in prices, rent, and wages, to argue that Samuelson has misinterpreted both Ricardo and Hicks and moreover, that his model does establish the so-called classical fallacy.

---

[7] With the issue seen to be resolved by p. 630.

[8] No article of Paul Samuelson ever goes unnoticed, and "The Classical Classical Fallacy" is no exception in having generated its share of debate. As, however, I am restricting the focus of my concerns to Ricardo and Hicks, I am returning straight to their original writings and leaving other responses to Samuelson aside here.

[9] David Ricardo, *On the principles of political economy and taxation* Third Edition London: John Murray, 1821 in The works and correspondence of David Ricardo, Eds, Piero Sraffa and Maurice H. Dobb, Cambridge: Cambridge University Press, 1951, Volume I, pp. 386-97; see also the chapter, "On Wages", op. cit., ed. cit. pp. 93-109.

[10] John R. Hicks, *A theory of economic history* Oxford: Oxford University Press, 1969, Chapter 9, pp. 141-59 and Appendix, pp. 168-71.

I. WHAT IS THE ISSUE AND WHAT IS THE "FALLACY"?

While Ricardo and Hicks are very clear as to the specific issue each addresses, the impact of machinery on labour in a real-world or historical context, Samuelson approaches the topic in a more general way. For his part, he broadened the issue by differentiating capital, raw materials, machinery and labour, and by including the impact of capital and raw materials on land (and labour) and the competition between capital and raw materials, and land and labour. He rendered the discussion thereby, on the one hand, much more complex and problematic than intended by others, such as Ricardo and Hicks, and, on the other hand, as will be shown below, much less relevant to their concerns and strengths. Further, Samuelson's approach to the particular issue of a "fallacy" is so broad as to render its source illusive, its substance perhaps even ambiguous.

In his relatively short paper of 12 pages, Samuelson refers to what he calls "the classical classical fallacy" many times, each time with a different scope. He proceeds in his article to give what he considers to be counter-examples to some of them. One phrasing of the "fallacy" which focuses on the Ricardian issue of the machinery effect and the demand for labour addresses specifically fixed capital:

- **"*Fixed capitals* are prejudicial to wages** and **the demand for labour."** (Samuelson, p. 620)

- "... inventing a viable technique that involves machinery and displaces a previous technique that uses circulating capital only - such an invention ought demonstratably to be especially likely to lower W/P1 [the nominal wage rate] and raise R/P1 [the nominal rent rate] at any unchanged profit rate of r*." (Samuelson, p. 623) (i.e., fixed capitals lower nominal wages and raise nominal land rent)

- **"A technological change that made machinery newly viable"** was **"the kind of invention that could put people out of work temporarily,** reduce market-clearing wage rates, and in long-run equilibrium at an unchanged subsistence wage rate call for a significantly reduced population"[11]. (Samuelson, p. 620)

[11] The "equilibrium population size is precisely the resultant of the number of workers needed technologically to work with the specified number of land acres." (Samuelson, p. 621)

Another run at the "fallacy" by Samuelson addresses the apparent corollary, the effect of machinery on circulating capital and labour, and the shift from fixed to circulating capital:

- ***Circulating capitals***, distinguishable from wages paid to workers, are **"favourable** to the real wage rate and **to the demand for labour."** (Samuelson, p. 620)

- The shift from circulating to fixed capital lowers real wages.

- **"A new invention that displaced machinery in favor of various raw materials as** inputs, would supposedly raise the short-run real wage and **increase demand for labour."** (Samuelson, p. 620)

One way to develop the analysis of Samuelson's point about the classics' (and moderns') dedication to the ideas above is to take each one of the "fallacies" and any pertinent corollaries and to justapose them with the ideas of his key authors, guided by Samuelson's case analyses A-D (p. 631) to counter their or his assertions. For this to be fruitful, one must start with the assumption that Samuelson has presented cases which address the so-called fallacy and has proven, as he set out to, that the impact of capital can be positive or negative in relation to the demand for labour, and wages. This approach was not possible here since, as will be argued, the "fallacy" is no fallacy, at least in the instances of Ricardo and Hicks. Further, Samuelson's Cases A-D are not meet to the task of challenging the fallacies he proposes. Therefore, the tack taken here has been to analyse Ricardo and Hicks first in light of Samuelson's claims and then Samuelson's cases on their own merits.

II. CAPITAL AND MACHINERY AND LABOUR

1. Ricardo's model

The story of Ricardo's "recantation", including how he changed his views and under whose influence, is explicitly told by Ricardo himself. In a whole chapter on machinery which is one of the concluding chapters of the third edition of his book, *On the principles of political economy and taxation*, Ricardo discusses the effect of machinery on various factors with a particular interest in its impact on labour, in light of the raging concerns of his time, both academic and political, the poor laws, luxury taxes, war-based economies, and influx or flight of gold and technology. Amidst these complicated concerns, Ricardo provided a very clear model of how fixed capital affects the demand for labour: how initially it is harmful, as in his example (pp. 388-92), where at first, (in modern terminology, 'in the short run'[12]) it diminishes the demand for labour, but how, over time ('in the long run') it increases the demand for labour. In order to be able to grasp quickly what Ricardo is hoping to convey, Table 1, here below, encapsulates the essence of his argument on the machinery effect, using his numbers.

Table 1 exposes the process of the effect of machinery on labour under certain given conditions: prices are fixed for a sequence of periods, wages are fixed throughout, each worker costs one unit of output, each period the capitalist retains the same net produce "which he consumes himself, or disposes of as may best suit his pleasure and gratification" (pp. 388-89). Ricardo's numerical model is simple, which allowed for his calculations to be possible. All his units are corn. He uses nominal wages expressed in corn output units. The Table shows in a sequence of periods how Ricardo saw the introduction of a machine within a second period would lead in a third period to a decrease in labour. He assumed that the capitalist is not concerned with rate of profit but rather with a stable net product of 2,000l.

Period 1 begins with a total capital of 20,000l., 7,000l. in fixed capital, inherited from the past, and 13,000l. in the wagebill of L workers producing the value of 15,000l. of "food and necessaries". (Ricardo, p. 388) This leaves the capitalist with 2,000l. net output and will yield him a rate of return of 10%. In Period 2 Ricardo introduces a machine. To do so, L workforce is divided in half, one half to produce the machine worth 7,500l., the other half to continue to produce "food and necessaries" for a value of 7,500l. of gross produce. The total labour continues to cost 13,000l. Out of the 7,500l. of gross produce, the capitalist keeps 2,000l. for himself and 5,500 as the wagebill to be advanced at the beginning of the next period. The rate of return or profit in Period 2 is still 10%.

For Period 3 the capitalist disposes of only 5,500l. for the wagebill with which he can only employ L' < 1/2L workers. His fixed capital has, however, now been increased from 7,000l. to 14,500l. with the introduction

[12] Cf. O. Hamouda, "On the Notion of Short-run and Long-run: Marshall, Ricardo and Equilibrium Theories", *British Review of Economic Issues*, Volume 6, Number 14 (Spring 1984), pp. 55-82, esp. Section 4, pp. 72-77, for the meaning of short and long term in Ricardo.

of the new machine. For a wagebill of 5,500l., this machine, which renders labour more efficient, produces 7,500l. The capitalist's net income is still 2,000l.; his total capital, now 22,000l., yields a rate of return of 9%. This situation can, without alteration in the values of all the variables, go on forever, as an equilibrium. Why, however, would a capitalist integrate a technique without employing enough labour to utilize it fully? Ricardo assumes that in a subsequent period the capitalist would forego part or the whole of his net income of 2,000l. to re-employ more workers, since with the new machine they will produce more additional product value than the additional wagebill.

Between Period 3 and an ensuing Period n, the reinvestment of some portion or all of the net produce will lead to a situation in which "the improved means of production, in consequence of the use of the machinery, should increase the net produce ... in a degree so great as not to diminish the gross produce" (p. 392). Depending on the amount of net income reinvested, by Period n, 2L' workers, making better use of the fixed capital of 14,500l., employed with a wagebill of 11,000l., will produce 15,000l. in output. This will generate 4,000l. net produce from which the capitalist keeps at least 2,000l. and reinvests the balance. The rate of profit in Period n is reaching 16% (15.68%). With a reinvestment of 2,000l. in Period n+1, all the workers displaced in Period 2 can be re-employed and an output of 17,727l. generated, which itself generates 4,725l. net produce and a rate of profit of over 17%. It is easy to see how, from there on, capital accumulation will lead to further increase in labour, output, rate of return, etc.

The numerical example stops here in Ricardo. He was, however, aware of the implications of the pressure of the increase of the demand for labour on wages, the pressure of the increased output on prices, and the impact of the increase of prices on real wages. One can speculate what might happen by Period m by which time the increase of labour beyond L would have created pressure on the nominal wages to rise and the increase in production would have led to a decrease in prices and hence to a further increase in real wages and a decrease in rate of return. To address these situations, however, one has to turn to the body of Ricardo's work and take them up in the context of his general discussion of the market price, wage, and profit versus the natural price, wage and profit, and rent and his reference to depreciation and the impact of the repeated introduction of new machinery and discoveries. Ricardo's numerical example shows how at first the demand for labour and the rate of return diminish, then how later both labour and rate of return are benefited under the assumption, of course, of constant prices and wages. It is clear, however, from his example alone that the recantation, on which too much emphasis has been placed since in the overall process the "harm" to labour, while serious, is temporary and is overcome to the complete benefit of labour in the long run, applies only to the initial effect of machinery and is not to be confused with his general discussion of the productivity of land and population.

In his 1994 article Samuelson seems to have envisaged a Ricardian model, "the simplest imaginable version of Ricardo's own model", in which technological changes "do damage to labor and do that with no reference to any particular kinds of change in capitals" (p. 621). In brief, Samuelson has referred perhaps not directly to Ricardo but to a Ricardian model which is found in some misleading Ricardian literature and has become taken for granted as Ricardo's own. a) It is clear from Table 1 that Samuelson's assumption about Ricardo's model's having an unchanged rate of return is incorrect, since rate of return does change in Ricardo's numerical model. Perhaps that rate has been mistaken in Samuelson for the capitalist's contentment with keeping a constant net produce amount. b) Samuelson's claim that Ricardo does not make explicit "an invention's long run steady-state effect(s) and its likely effects on the transient adjustment path of the system" (p. 623) is curious. c) Samuelson's statement, "some of his [Ricardo's] 1821 exposition about a new machine's effects refer to the immediate process in which resources are diverted to producing enough of the newly profitable machinery item to move its stock up to the equilibrium level at which all transient (...) excess profits have been eliminated" (p. 623), does not concur with Ricardo's explanation of Period 1. d) Ricardo's dealing with 'the Net Product of Rent's having to be raised by a viable invention in the long run', is simply not a part of his numerical example here. The assertions concerning Net Product of Rent have to be considered in the larger context of Ricardo's *On the principles of political economy and taxation*, where many more variables are considered to be changing and the economy never settles into equilibrium.[13] e) Samuelson's claim that Ricardo's proof "did not involve directly any contrast between fixed and circulating capital" (p. 626) is also puzzling, given Table 1.

Of course, the issue Samuelson is addressing is Ricardo's depiction of

---

[13] Op.cit., pp. 74-75.

an initial deleterious impact on labour with the introduction of machines, the "fallacy". In Table 1 from Period 1 to Period 2 labour does indeed diminish from 13,000 to 5,500 which would seem to represent the decimation of the population by more than half. Had Samuelson stayed with this example of Ricardo, one might have conceded that these figures do reinforce his assertion of a Ricardian "fallacy". The devastating drop in Ricardo's numerical example was, however, clearly for illustration. Not two pages following the account (p. 395), despite the fact that Ricardo saw labour and capital in competition, he wrote,

> I have been supposing that improved machinery is *suddenly* discovered, and extensively used; but the truth is, that these discoveries are gradual, and rather operate in determining the employment of the capital which is saved and accumulated, than in diverting capital from its actual employment.

2. Hicks' Ricardo model

Much of Hicks' work, beginning with his *Theory of Wages* (1932) all the way to 1973, especially his *Capital and Time*, had to do with capital controversies: its theory, fixed vs circulating types, its measurement, etc. Of course, Ricardo on capital is mentioned in many places. Hicks devoted a great deal of attention to the issue of the introduction of machinery. The discussion that interests us here, which Samuelson singled out for narrow criticism, is the one in Hicks' Appendix to his *A Theory of Economic History* (1969). Samuelson (p. 631) sees Hicks' model there as but one case of his own more generalized model. While one might address Hicks' more detailed picture of the machinery effect with all the alternative scenarios he considered, many inferable from *Capital and Time*, since Samuelson's attribution of the fallacy to Hicks can be rebuffed with reference mainly to the discussion in *A Theory of Economic History*, that discussion will suffice here to see how Hicks understood Ricardo and where he stood in relation to him on the issue of machinery.

Hicks opened his 1969 "Appendix" with the curious assertion that Ricardo "did not work out an arithmetic example" and proceeded to produce one himself as to the impact of the introduction of machinery on labour (Hicks, p. 168). Table 1, described above, albeit a tabular presentation not found in Ricardo, does represent, however, the numbers and arithmetic relationships which can be found exactly as in the prose example of Ricardo (pp. 388-92).

It is therefore puzzling why Hicks made such an opening statement. Hicks proceeded to produce an arithmetic example with his own numbers, but with very similar relationships to those Ricardo had described.

To argue numerically the impact of the introduction of machinery on labour, Hicks defined the gross rate of profit as being the net output per unit of cost (in labour wage terms) per machine. Samuelson rightly pointed out that Hicks' definition of profit rate is questionable. Indeed defining the rate of profit in this manner renders the analysis of the process as a whole, which includes old and new machines, quite cumbersome, since one has to keep track of the rate of profit of the older, yet operational machines and the new machines. The rate of profit does not, however, affect the calculation of Hicks' numbers because reinvestment depends solely on the difference between the net income and a constant amount of that net income held as the capitalist's profit for his consumption (as in Ricardo). Nor does it change Hicks' numbers to redefine Hicks' rate of return as the total net output over the total cost, as in Ricardo, Table 1.

In order here to compare Hicks' model, Table 2, with that of Ricardo, Table 1, Hicks' notation is converted into that of Ricardo. Let there be two sectors, one devoted to the construction of machines and the other to the operating of the machines. Assume there are at any time 100 machines in operation, with a depreciation of 10 per period, hence a construction of 10 machines per period. In Period 0, it takes 100 workers to construct 10 machines and 1,000 workers to operate 100 machines. Each machine produces 100 units of output and the wage of each worker equals 8 units of output. Both units remain constant in terms of output throughout the model. In Column 1 of Table 2 the numbers are laid out in terms of totals. 1,000 + 100 workers, paid at 8 units of output, will cost 8,000 units in the wage-bill. The 10 machines produced per period will cost 800 units. This makes the total capital per period equal to 8,800 units. 100 machines producing 100 units each of output will produce 10,000 units of gross output. Net output is the 10,000 units of gross output minus the wage-bill, or 1,200 units. As in Ricardo, Hicks' assumption is that the capitalist is from period to period interested in withholding from reinvestment a constant net produce, in Hicks' case the initial "Surplus" of 1,200 units.

First of all, all these numbers derive directly from those found in Hicks' Appendix table (p. 169). [14] Second, as in Ricardo (Table 1), for all Hicks' variables to be commensurable, it is crucial that every one of them be defined in terms of the same unit, i.e. "corn"; thus, this is the case in Table 2. Hicks' model is therefore simple and primitive. Third, in order to proceed in the same vein as that of Ricardo, the profit rate has been redefined, as in Ricardo, as the total net output per total unit of capital (e.g. Column 1, 1,200/8,900 = 13.48%, which is different from the 25% Hicks derives from his definition of return per machine).

To analyze the impact of the introduction of machinery on labour, Hick's model can be interpreted as follows: In Period 1 the new viable technique, which will be labour-saving in the operating sector, is introduced into the construction sector. While the old machine required 10 workers to operate it, this new machine needs only 8 workers. The new machine demands, however, 15 workers, instead of 10, in its construction. Thus, in Period 1, the 100 workers who previously constructed 10 old machines, can produce only 6.67 new machines.

When the numbers are computed for n columns, we see that, with the introduction of new machines gradually replacing the old with every period, the over-all result is that in the short run, i.e. until the tenth period, employment and output decrease. Yet, by the time the new machines have replaced all the old machines and the process is comprised entirely of new machines (by Period 12), output is restored to the same level as Period 1 and will begin to soar. Employment begins to soar one period later. These increases are entirely the result of the increase in productivity within the operating sector whose technique is labour-saving. As in Ricardo, once a longer-run period is reached, the demand for labour and the output begin to increase dramatically; this will create pressure on both wages and prices to rise and on rate of return to decline. As in Ricardo, in the numerical model the discussion does not proceed that far. Hicks' model therefore concurs tightly with Ricardo's model in many important regards.[15]

[14] The actual numbers in Table 2 are different, but only slightly, from those in Hicks' own Appendix; this difference is due to Hicks' having rounded his numbers upward to avoid the cumbersomeness of decimals. Table 2 is generally more detailed than Hicks' Appendix table. Expressing more of the data from the variables he chose to omit, but with numbers internally generated, is to allow for a more complete description of the process.

[15] This is particularly of note when comparing Ricardo's and Hicks' models to Samuelson's Case D, Table 3 below.

Given Table 2, it can be seen, that Hicks' modelled quantification, with a slight alteration, reveals the same implications as Ricardo's model, in terms of the impact of machinery on labour, i.e. in the short run the introduction is harmful to labour, but over time it becomes beneficial, even though the fixed capital changes in every period in Hicks' model, while for Ricardo it changes only during the first period.

We now turn to Samuelson's attribution of the classical fallacy to Hicks. Just as Samuelson's interpretation of Ricardo is taken out of context, so too on the basis of a larger approach to Hicks' ideas has he misrepresented Hicks' different perspectives on the impact of labour on machinery. Hicks' own numerical example, from which Table 2 is generated, Samuelson considers in isolation and as Hicks' only understanding of the machinery effect. Seen in context, however, it is included by Hicks to support his interpretation of Ricardo in his analysis of economic history and is meant to be understood in that light. It is only one example of a particular, but very important, case of machinery introduction, used to rebuff the criticism of those who believed categorically that machinery is harmful to labour.

First, Samuelson's assessment of Hicks' account - "I do not find his exposition to be completely coherent" (Samuelson, p. 626) - is rather puzzling. It would appear that Samuelson based his criticism of Hicks on the analysis distilled into Table 2, deriving from Hicks' numerical example in the Appendix (1969). Thus, whether in light of Table 2 alone or in light of its relation to Table 1, it is difficult to see where Samuelson sees incoherence.

Second, unlike Samuelson Hicks does not hold the generalized view that most of Ricardo's successors had the same views on machinery. He clearly observed that there were divergent answers offered by economists to the question, "what would be the effect of the new opportunities for fixed capital investment on the demand for labour?" He even felt that differences of opinion among even the greatest economists was "not surprising (or disgraceful)". (Hicks 1969, 149)

Third, one might rightly surmise that Table 2 was not Hicks' only analysis of the machinery effect. What Ricardo had posed himself was according to Hicks "by no means a simple question", and Hicks clearly did not think that a simple answer would suffice. Hicks was aware of many alternatives. In fact the issue of the machinery effect was developed by Hicks in great detail through various scenarios and alternatives, particularly in *Capital and Time*. All the answers to the various possibilities raised by Samuelson can in fact be found in Hicks' analysis of the Traverse in *Capital and Time*, but there is no need to extend the discussion that far to respond to Samuelson's characterization of Hicks' approach.[16] Hicks even considered the instance in which

> So long as the proportion of fixed to circulating capital remains constant, ... the growth rate [or slow-down rate] of each will be the same, and will be the same as the growth rate [or slow-down rate] of the capital stock as a whole. (Hicks, 1969, 151)

As indicated above, it is, however, worthy of note that the numerical example of Table 2 is only one of Hicks' statements on the machinery effect, and one specifically designed to facilitate understanding of Ricardo, the Industrial Revolution, and the impact of the introduction of a succession of machines to counter the potentially negative effect of depreciation on net investment and to guarantee "a purely favourable effect upon the demand for labor" (Hicks, p. 154) On the other hand, in the same chapter, he explicitly refers to the "several forces at work; sometimes one is dominant, sometimes another", (Hicks 1969, 149) which might or might not affect, positively and/ or negatively, the demand for labour as a result of the introduction of machinery. The 'force' of obvious interest to Samuelson is, of course, capital, (fixed or circulating) and whether its increase (or decrease) can increase (or decrease) labour. From Hicks' perspective,

> It is not the whole capital employed in industry, but only the circulating capital part of it, which is strongly correlated with the demand for labour from industry (still at a constant level of real wages). (Hicks, 1969, 151)

Fourth, so does Hicks fall into the so-called classical fallacy? It may at first appear so, but ... as just one example reveals, Hicks felt "If there is a switch to fixed capital, and *as a result of that* the growth rate of the whole capital stock rises, there are two forces at work on the growth of circulating

[16] "Hicks specifies a viable invention that replaces (i) a machine which had been *built with little labor but required much ongoing labor to work with it*, by (ii) a new machine that requires more initial labor but *so much less ongoing operating labor* as to make the new equipment outcompete the old." (emphasis added , Samuelson, p. 626)

capital and they are pulling in opposite directions." (Hicks, 1969, 151) This is clearly an allusion to several possible scenarios, which in the terminology of *Capital and Time*,[17] would be called "strong" or "weak" switches to fixed capital, the former prejudicial to labour at least initially, but the later not necessarily so. In yet another instance in Hicks' *Theory of economic history*, he shows he believes that in the case of a constant labour-capital ratio, just as Samuelson does in his Case D (labour-land ratio), that, "It will then be true that anything which increases the growth rate of the capital stock as a whole will be inclined to increase the rate of growth of the demand for labour". (Hicks 1969, 151)

3. Samuelson's Ricardo ... Hicks model

Having just seen that in order to compare Hicks' numerical formulation of his specified case with the numerical formulation of Ricardo's numerical-prose model, we had to present Hicks' categories of variables (Table 2) in a way similar to Ricardo's (Table 1). Samuelson has presented the numerical examples, from which he then provided a generalization, in yet a different setting of the equations and with different definitions for the categories (Appendix, p. 631). Therefore, for the comparison of his model to those of Ricardo and Hicks, and for the subsequent assessment of the superiority of his theory over that of everybody else (being here Ricardo and Hicks), his table (Table 1, p. 631) has been rewritten here, as Table 3, without any changes to its values, to render it compatible with Tables 1 and 2.

From this presentation of Table 3, it seems that Samuelson's methods A, B, C, and D are snapshots of a sectorial economy (given the subscript $_{I}$)[18], completely unrelated to one another, where the coefficients of labour, land, raw materials, and depreciation of capital, respectively a_{LI}, a_{TI}, a_{II} and δ_{II}, are taken arbitrarily, although specified under the same set of assumptions. Thus, the distribution of output among factors, as well as the demand for labour, derives from the following relationships:

$$Q_I \quad - \delta_{II} a_{II} Q_I \quad = \quad C_I \quad = \quad wL \quad + \quad RT, \text{ i.e.}$$

Total Output - Used-up Input = Total Consumption = Wagebill + Total Rent.

[17] John R. Hicks, *Capital and Time* Oxford: Clarendon, 1973, Chapters VIII-IX.

[18] yet C_I is called "national income" and L, "population", which presumes that these snapshots are also those of an economy as a whole.

By assuming

i) land and wages constant in all four cases,

ii) the labour-land ratio given by the constant ratio of their respective coefficients:

$$L/T = a_{L1}/a_{T1}, \qquad T = 100, \qquad L = 100(a_{L1}/a_{T1}),$$

iii) output determined solely by the amount of land used and able to be increased only if the productivity of land changes,

from an accounting point of view, Samuelson can determine thus the distribution of who gets what of the ensuing output of 300, as well as the required labour, solely on the basis of the coefficients δ_{11}, a_{11}, and a_{L1}, for the same given a_{T1} in cases A, B, and C and for a different value of a_{T1} in case D.

This is very peculiar "corn model" in which:

- machines do not appear explicitly but implicitly, as fixed capital in the form of exponentially depreciating circulating capital,
- 'fixed capital' which depreciates in one period (where $\delta_{11} = 1$) is considered to be circulating capital,
- each Case has either all circulating or all fixed capital "involved"; while labour is a yet different category (Samuelson, p. 620) (!),
- the capitalist (the landlord, assumed to be the only means by which output might be increased, by bringing about an increase in the productivity of land) is introduced as "land", and yet rent is considered a component of total consumption,
- rent, as a consumption, is the only component out of which saving might come, but there is no allowing for saving out of rent, hence no generator for accumulation or any ensuing dynamics,
- wages are assumed to be advanced payment for labour and are considered a component of consumption,
- there can be no saving out of the only other component of consumption, wage, because wage is subsistence, and

- there is no concern for quantifying net output, and thus an explicit rate of return (distinguishable from the 'rate of discount')[19], in terms of the productivity of capital, is absent.

Samuelson's specification of his model is obviously very different from that of the standard corn model of Ricardo and of its adaptation by Hicks. The issue is not the fact that Samuelson's model is so different per se, but rather the confusion it engenders over which conclusions deriving from his model should be used to displace which conclusions of the rival ones. Before answering Samuelson's claim to have identified a fallacy among the classics, let's examine the interpretation of the various cases of Table 3 in the light of Tables 1 and 2. For the sake of comparasion, Samuelson's four cases are presented in the following way:

(The model leaves no room for any other assumption than that the landlord be taken to be the capitalist. Furthermore, it would not change the meaning of the model to consider its rent 'net income' and its gross output 'gross income'.)

Case A: Since "only circulating capital is involved" (Samuelson, p. 631), all capital is utilized in one period. That period is represented as Column A in Table 3. It seems that 100 workers and 100 capital produce 300, with the capitalist landlord's lending his land and receiving 100 as net output. The ratio of net return over the total capital, including land, yields a rate of return of 33%.[20] Under unchanged production coefficients, this situation can repeat itself forever.

Case B: "only a *fixed*-capital machine is involved" (Samuelson, p. 631). Fixed capital as the depreciation of δ_{11} = ¼ means that in this case the capital will last four periods, represented in four columns of B (Table 3). In each period the labour is ½ that of case A (a_{11} = 1/6), i.e. 50 workers. The capital is double that of Case A, but spread over 4 periods ($\delta_{11}a_{11}$ = (1/4) (2/3)), i.e. 50 per period. 50 workers and 50 capital per period produce 300,

[19] In fact profit does not appear in Samuelson's simple model(s) of his Table 1 (p. 631). When it does appear later (p. 622), it is called *r* (rate of interest). This is rate of discount, which he calls 'interest rate' as well as 'rate of profit'.

[20] Obviously this 'rate of return', not to be found in Samuelson, is specific to the reinterpretation of rent as net income and 'used-up input', land, and labour together as total capital.

with the capitalist landlord's again lending the same land and receiving 200 as net output. His rate of return per period is 100%. This situation can only continue beyond a fourth period, for another four periods, if capital of the same nature is introduced again without cost.

Case C: This case "involves circulating capital only" (Samuelson, p. 631). There is therefore only one period, represented as Column C. Labour is reduced to 33.3 workers ($a_{L1} = 1/9$). Capital ($\delta_{11}a_{11} = (1)(1/6)$) is one half of Case A, i.e. 50. 33.3 workers and 50 capital, and the same borrowed land, produce 300. Therefore the net return is 216.66, or a rate of return of 118%. Under unchanged production coefficients, this situation, like the one in Case A, can repeat itself forever.

Case D: The case, like case B, "involves only a [*fixed*-capital] machine" (Samuelson, p. 631). δ_{11} is now 1/6 which means that the fixed capital is used up in 6 periods, represented as the columns of Case D. The labour coefficient has returned to its level in Case A, i.e. $a_{L1} = 1/3$, but the efficiency of land is now doubled ($a_{T1} = 1/6$). Labour equals thus, given assumption (ii) above, 200. The fixed supply of land has previously produced 300 units of output; the same supply with twice the efficiency will therefore produce 600 units. Capital is $\delta_{11}a_{11}Q_1 = (1/6)(2/3)600 = 66.66$. The rate of return in this case is 91%. This situation can only continue beyond six periods for another six, if capital of the same nature is introduced again without cost.

What can be concluded from Samuelson's four cases? His main goal was to establish the (double) fallacy mentioned above that 1) fixed capitals are prejudicial to wages and the demand for labour (p. 620) and 2) circulating capitals are favourable to the real wage rate and the demand for labour (p. 620). Further he aimed to prove to Ricardo (and Hicks perhaps) "that a newly invented machine could ... be *rival* to land and *complementary* to labor", that "in the short run such machinery would lower land rent (i.e., would *lower* not raise Ricardo's Net Product) ... and either lower or raise the rate of profit". (Samuelson, p. 621) By looking at our presentation of Samuelson's table, Table 3, it can be seen that indeed Case D contradicts 1) and Case C, 2). From Samuelson's perspective, the existence of the fallacy (in Ricardo, Hicks, and others) is thereby established.

When, however, the two cases, D and C, are analysed closely, they reveal rather trivial, accounting-type correlations which are not addressing at all the rather serious impact of changing capital introduction that the context of Samuelson's discussion had set.

Case D: In order to compare Cases A and D, let's construct a Case D' which is half of D, i.e. half the land (50) produces 300 output, the same output as in Case A. This production requires 100 workers, also the same number as in Case A. The rate of return in Case D' is exactly the same as in Case D. The only variable which has changed between Cases A and D' seems thus to be the used-up imput (capital), which leads one to believe that the decrease of fixed capital between Cases A and D is the result of a tremendous increase in capital efficiency with labour constant, translating into an increase in net income. Samuelson's interpretation is, however, that the decrease in fixed capital has caused the increase in labour![21] Case D falls far short of proving that 'fixed capitals are prejudicial to the demand for labour' is a fallacy (1 above).

Case C: The misleading accounting-type correlations are even more obvious in Case C. Again, let us construct in Table 4 models of various other techniques, Cases C', C'' and C''', where labour and land coefficients, land and output (a_{L1}, a_{T1}, T, and Q_1) are held constant. Assume circulating capital only, i.e. $\delta_{11} = 1$, and let a_{11} vary in such a way that used-up imputs (circulating capital) are decreased (in C), decreased even more (in C'), are the same as Case A (in C''), and are increased (in C'''). What Table 4 reveals is that no matter what happens to circulating capital - whether it increases or decreases, even dramatically - labour remains constant. Capital's only effect is on net output. Therefore Case C also falls short of proving that circulating capitals are favourable to the demand for labour (2 above).

What seems the cause of the huge increase in labour in Case D, as a result of the increase in fixed capital, or its decrease in Case C, as a result of the decrease of circulating capital, has nothing in this peculiar model to do with the efficiency or inefficiency of capital (presumably the reason for its integration or not), but is rather linked to the efficiency of land, as defined in Samuelson's model. Due to Samuelson's assumption of a fixed land-labour

---

[21] The exact increase (or decrease) in the demand for labour is by definition. Since there is a proportional relationship between labour and land, any increase in the productivity of land (a_{T1}, equal to 1/3 in cases A, B, and C, becomes in case D 1/6) will necessarily lead to an exact increase in labour. For the doubling of the output of 300 to 600 and labour from 100 to 200, see Samuelson's table, Table 3..

ratio, any time there is a change in the efficiency of land ceteris paribus, labour will increase (or decrease) in the same proportion. This is exactly the case Hicks pointed out in his *A Theory of Economic History* in which when the labour-capital ratio is constant, the slow-down rate or "growth rate of each will be the same" (Hicks, 1969, 151). Not only has Samuelson not addressed the issue of machinery in its proper context in Ricardo and Hicks, the Cases of his model cannot prove what he set out to prove.

Many of Samuelson's predecessors have had tremendous difficulty with the concept of capital and the issue of machinery's effect. Sometimes, as in the case of "The Classical Classical Fallacy", the crux of the economic problem is not revealed nor resolved by attempts at translating or discussing it in the chosen mathematical terms. In conclusion, despite the ingenious intricacy and complexity of Samuelson's model, once again it shows how tackling capital is not easy! Thus, even if, like his predecessors, Samuelson has not been successful in resolving all its problems, he should at the very least be credited for keeping the discussion of capital vibrant and for tackling it in many ingenious ways.

Table I :
Ricardo (1821)

Periods	0	1	2	......	n	n+1	....	m
Lec (labour cc)	L	1/2L	L'		2L'	L		>L
Lfc (labour fc)		1/2L		....			....	
L (total labour)	L	L	1/2L		2L'	L		>L
FC Old	7000	7000	7000		14500	14500		7000
New			7500	....			....	
Total			14500					
W	1	1	1		1	1		**P**
P	-	-	-	....	-	-	....	**P**
Wagebill	**13000**	13000	5500		11000	**13000**		> 13000
Ycc Gross income	**15000**	7500	7500	....	**15000**	17727	....	>17727
Ycf fc output		7500		....			....	
Net income	2000	2000	2000		4000	4727		T 2000
Consumption	2000	2000	0	....	2000	2000	....	
Reinvestment	0	0	2000		2000	2500		
Total Capital	20000	20000	22000	....	25500	27500	....	20000
Rate of return	**10%**	10%	9%		15.68%	**17.1%**	....	< 10%

Table II :
Hicks (1969)

Periods	0	1	2	3	...	8	9	10	11	12	13	14	16
Lcc (labour cc)	1000	1000	953	906		726	703	691	689	800	926	1086	
Lfc (labour fc)	100	100	100	105		145	164	183	207	237	299	371	
L (total labour	**1100**	1100	1053	1011		871	868	874	897	1037	**1226**	1457	
FC Old	90	90	90	80		30	20	10	0				
New				6 67		44 21	53 28	62 96	73.94	86 16	**100**	115 84	
Add	10	10	6 67	6 67		9.07	9.68	10 98	12 22	13 84	15.84	19 84	
Total	**100**	100	96 67	93 34		83.28	82.96	83.94	86 16	**100**	115 84	135 83	
W	1	1	1	1		1	1	1	1	1	1	1	
P	-	-	-	-		-	-	-	-	-	-	-	
Wagebill	8800	8800	8426	8093		6971	6947	6998	7176	8302	9813	11663	
Ycc Gross inc.	**10000**	10000	9667	9334		8328	8296	8394	8616	**10000**	11584	13583	
Ycf fc output	10	6.67	6.67	7		9 68	10 98	12 22	13 84	15.84	19 94	24.7	
Net income	1200	1200	1240	1240		1356	1348	1395	1439	1697	1770	1919	
Consumption	1200	1200	1200	1200		1200	1200	1200	1200	1200	1200	1200	
Reinvestment			40	40		156	148	195	239	497	570	719	
Total Capital	8900	8900	8523	8107		7024	7010	7072	7262	8402	9929	11799	
Rate of return	**13.4%**	13.4%	14.54%	15 24%		19.31%	19.23%	19.72	19 82%	**20%**	17%	16%	

NB Decimal points are omitted except for the number of new machines produced

Table III :
Samuelson (1994)

	A	B			C	D			D'
Periods	1	1	...	4	1	1	....	6	1
A_{L1}	1/3	1/6		1/6	1/9	1/3		1/3	1/3
Lcc (labour cc)									
Lfc (labour fc)									
L (total labour	100	50		50	33 33	200		200	100
Capital a_{11}	1/3	2/3		2/3	1/6	2/3		2/3	2/3
δ_{11}	1	1/4		1/4	1	1/6		1/6	1/6
Total $\delta_{11}a_{11}Q_1$	100	50		50	50	66.6		66.6	33 3
w	1	1		1	1	1		1	1
P	-	-		-	-	-		-	-
Wagebill	100	50		50	33.3	200		200	100
Ycc Gross inc	300	300		300	300	600		600	300
Ycf fc output									
Net income	100	200		200	216.6	333 3		333.3	166.[illegible]
Consumption	100	200		200	216.6	333.3		333.3	166 [illegible]
Reinv.= land	100	100		100	100	100		100	50
a_{T1}	1/3	1/3		1/3	1/3	1/6		1/6	1/6
Total Capital	300	200		200	183.3	366.6		366.6	183 [illegible]
Rate of return	33%	100%		100%	118%	91%		91%	91%

Table IV :
Samuelson (1994)

	A	**C**	**C'**	**C''**	**C'''**
Periods	1				
A_{L1}	1/3	**1/9**	**1/9**	**1/9**	**1/9**
Lcc (Labour cc)					
Lfc (Labour fc)					
L (Total Labour)	100	**33.33**	**33.33**	**33.33**	**33.33**
Capital $\mathbf{a}_{11}$	1/3	□1/6	□□1/9	□1/3	□2/3
δ_{11}	**1**	**1**	**1**	**1**	**1**
Total $\delta_{11}a_{11}Q_1$	100	50	33.33	100	200
w	1	**1**	**1**	**1**	**1**
P	-	-	-	-	-
Wagebill	100	**33.33**	**33.33**	**33.33**	**33.33**
Ycc Gross inc	**300**	**300**	**300**	**300**	**300**
Ycf fc output					
Net income	100	□216.6	□233.3	□116.6	□66
Consumption	100	216.6	233.33	116.6	66
Reinv. = land	**100**	**100**	**100**	**100**	**100**
a_{T1}	**1/3**	**1/3**	**1/3**	**1/3**	**1/3**
Total Capital	300	300	300	300	300
Rate of return					

A "GENERAL" NON-SUBSTITUTION THEOREM ALONG SAMUELSONIAN LINES**

*Syed Ahmad**

ABSTRACT

The purpose of this note is to show that Professor Samuelson's path-breaking paper (1951) proving, what amounted to the 'simple' (i.e. with zero interest rate) non-substitution theorem can, with slight modification be generalized to prove the 'general' (i.e. with non-zero constant rate of interest) non-substitution theorem. The main result of the 'general' non-substitution theorem is that given the rate of interest and only one non-produced input, let us say labour, in the system, the equilibrium relative prices of the goods are determined solely by the conditions of production even if each good is produced under usually assumed neoclassical conditions using many produced inputs beside the non-produced labour. Thus demand plays no role in determining prices under quite commonly assumed conditions.

Professor Samuelson derived a theorem [Koopmans, 1951] which showed that given timeless production processes, and only one non-produced input (let us say, labour) in the system, together with the usual assumptions to be specified below, the equilibrium relative prices of the goods are determined solely by the conditions of production, even if the production conditions of each good is described by the traditional form of production function including many produced inputs. Thus demand plays no role in determining relative prices under these quite commonly assumed conditions.

---

* Department of Economics, McMaster University, Ontario, Canada.

** The author would like to thank Christopher Bliss, Leslie Robb, Oskar von dem Hagen and Atif Kubursi for their comments on earlier drafts of this paper. The participants in the Seminar at Bilkent University, Ankara also made useful comments. The responsibility for the views expressed are of course, entirely mine.

The symposium on the paper in which Arrow, Koopmans and Georgescu-Roegen participated,[1] and more recently the papers by Mirrlees [1969], Stiglitz [1970] and Bliss [1975] have generalised the original version to one in which time enters into the production structure. Two cases have been distinguished in this framework: one, in which the rate of interest is zero, the other in which it is positive. The theorem with a zero rate of interest (which has exactly the same results as in the timeless case) has been called the "Simple Non-Substitution Theorem" and the one with positive interest has been called the "General Non-Substitution Theorem". Both theorems can be summarised by the statement that, given the rate of interest, relative prices are completely determined by the conditions of production. Demand plays no role in price determination.

For proving this theorem, Samuelson used relatively simple calculus, which is more accessible to readers than the programming or similar approaches used by most subsequent writers. Moreover, the general non-substitution theorem has become closely tied to the growth literature, so much so that Mirrlees [1969] calls it the 'dynamic' non-substitution theorem. The purpose of this note is to show that Samuelson's simpler formulation can be relatively easily generalised to production processes which are not timeless, and can be modified to prove both the simple and general non-substitution theorems, without postulating any non-zero rate of growth for the economy. We now proceed with Samuelson's original formulation, modifying it wherever necessary, to suit our objectives.[2]

Besides the assumptions explicitly noted above, Samuelson also assumed that there was no joint production and the production functions were linear homogeneous. Following his approach, let the production function of good i be:

$$x_i = F_i(x_{i1}, x_{i2}, \dots x_{i,n+1}) \qquad (i = 1, \dots\dots, n) \qquad (1)$$

---

[1] See Koopmans, [1951].

[2] We should note the date of Samuelson's paper; it was published before Arrow-Debreu-McKenzie approach had highlighted the inadequacy of the counting of equations and unknowns for ensuring the existence of a solution (von Neumann's 1938 paper is not usually considered in this regard since it was not widely known at that time). Hence in what follows the equality of the number of equations and unknowns forms the basis of the analysis. A related geometrical approach which is, of course, less general but also less subject to this limitation, can be found in Ahmad (1991).

where (somewhat unusually) the first subscript designates *output* and the second *inputs* and, $x_{i,n+1}$ is the amount of non-produced input (labour) used for producing output i.

The amount available as final demand for the good, i, C_i, is:

$$C_i = x_i - \sum_{j=1}^{n} x_{ji} \tag{2}$$

which states that this amount is simply the total output of good i minus the use of this good as input in the production of all goods. For the non-produced input, an equation similar to (2) can be written. If one further assumes that none of this non-produced input (labour) is used as final product, then this equation will read:

$$0 = \bar{x}_{n+1} - \sum_{j=1}^{n} x_{j,n+1} \tag{3}$$

In (3), $\bar{x}_{n+1}$ is, of course, given.

Samuelson poses the problem as follows: given various amounts of $C_2, C_3, \ldots C_n$, find the maximum amount of C_1 which can be produced by the system. By using (2) and (1) this problem yields the following Lagrangian:

$$L = \lambda_1 \left[F_1(x_{11}, x_{12}, \ldots, x_{1,n+1}) - \sum_{j=1}^{n} \mathrm{xsubj1} \right]$$

$$+ \lambda_2 \left[F_2(x_{21}, x_{22}, \ldots, x_{2,n+1}) - \sum_{j=1}^{n} \mathrm{xsubj2} - C_2 \right]$$

$$\cdots\cdots\cdots\cdots\cdots\cdots\cdots\cdots\cdots\cdots\cdots$$

$$+ \lambda_n \left[F_n(x_{n1}, \ldots, x_{n,n+1}) - \sum_{j=1}^{n} x_{jn} - C_n \right]$$

$$+ \lambda_{n+1} \left[\bar{x}_{n+1} - \sum_{j}^{n} x_{j,n+1} \right] \tag{4}$$

where the λ's are Lagrange multipliers with $\lambda_1 = 1$.

Equating the partial derivatives of L with respect to the x_{ij}'s to zero, we get

$$\lambda_i \frac{\partial F_i}{\partial x_{ij}} - \lambda_j = 0 \qquad \left(\begin{matrix} i = 1, 2, ..., n \\ j = 1, 2, ..., n+1 \end{matrix} \right) \tag{5}$$

Set (5) contains n(n+1) equations while it contains n(n+1)+n number of unknowns, n(n+1) of x_{ij}'s and n of λ's.[3] The system, therefore, has n degrees of freedom.

However, since each of the F functions is homogeneous of degree one in the inputs, its partial derivatives are homogeneous of degree zero in those inputs. That is, they are functions of the *proportions* of the inputs. Thus if we choose the input $x_{i,n+1}$ as the denominator we can define these proportions as $b_{ij} = \frac{x_{ij}}{x_{i,n+1}}$. Now b_{ij}'s are the unknowns, which are n^2 in number (as $\frac{x_{i,n+1}}{x_{i,n+1}} = 1$, for $i = 1, ..., n$) and the number of λ's to be determined is n; this yields a total of $n^2 + n$ unknowns. We already know that the number of equations in (5) is n^2+n. These determine the b_{ij}'s, as well as the λ's, *without any reference to final demand* or to the quantity of x_{n+1}.

Now we can write (1) such that x_i is shown to be a function of b_{ij}'s and $x_{i,n+1}$, it becomes:

$$x_i = F_i (b_{i1}, b_{i2}, ..., b_{in}, 1) \_ x_{i,n+1} \qquad (i=1, ..., n) \tag{1N}$$

which can also be written as

$$M_i x_i = x_{i,n+1} \tag{6}$$

---

[3] There are n+1 number of λ's, but $\lambda_1 = 1$ is already known.

where $M_i = \dfrac{1}{F_i\ (b_{i1}, b_{i2}, ...)}$.

M_i can, of course, now be treated as a constant, because, given the conditions of production, all the arguments of M_i's together with all λ's are determined by the equations in (5) and therefore can be treated as constants.

From (6) we can write

$$M_1 x_1 + M_2 x_2 + ... + M_n x_n = \sum_{i=1}^{n} x_{i,n+1} = \bar{x}_{n+1} \quad (7)$$

or in vector form

$$Mx = \bar{x}_{n+1} \quad (7N)$$

where $x = [x_1, x_2, ..., x_n]'$ and $M = [M_1, M_2, ..., M_n]$.

Now define the input-output coefficients

$$a_{ij} = \frac{x_{ij}}{x_i} = b_{ij} \frac{x_{i,n+1}}{F_i(b_{i1}, \text{bsubi}\ 2, ...)\ \_\ x_{i,n+1}} = b_{ij} M_i . \quad (8)$$

(8) shows that all the input-output coefficients are constant. Hence we can apply the usual input-output transformation

$$[I - A]^{-1}\ C = x \quad (9)$$

where $C \equiv [C_1, C_2, ..., C_n]'$ and A is the matrix of input-output coefficients. Or, premultiplying both sides by M

$$M[I - A]^{-1} C = Mx = \bar{x}_{n+1} \quad \text{(from 7N)},$$

$$KC = \bar{x}_{n+1} \quad \text{where } K \equiv M[I - A]^{-1} \quad (10)$$

or

$$K_1 C_1 + K_2 C_2 + K_n C_n = \bar{x}_{n+1} \quad (10N)$$

as we find in Samuelson's solution.

(10) or (10N) thus represents the form of the transformation function of the final goods, C's. Its form is that of a hyperplane. Hence, whatever the form of the indifference hypersurface representing demand, the relative prices of various goods are completely determined by the production conditions.

The above is certainly one way of showing that the relative prices are determined by the system without any reference to demand. However, in fact, the relative prices were already determined before we reached this stage of the argument. We may recall that equations (5) determined all the λ's besides determining all the b's. It is well-known that these λ's are closely related to prices. The simplest way to see this, in the present context, is to treat good 1 as the numeraire. Recalling that $\lambda_1 = 1$, we can obtain the following, directly from (5):

$$\frac{\partial F_1}{\partial x_{1j}} = \lambda_j \quad (11)$$

In a competitive situation with timeless production, the marginal product of good (input) j in the numeraire industry must equal the price of good j; hence λ_j is the price of good j. This result will hold even if a particular good does not enter as an input into the production of good 1, and $\frac{\partial F_1}{\partial x_{11}}$ for good j thus remains undefined. Another equation in (5) would, in that case, yield price ratios for j in terms of goods other than good 1, which can then be translated in terms of good 1.

Thus, in the present case, the prices of the goods and of labour are determined, as the λ's are determined, and $P_j = \lambda_j$ for all j's.

[4] Many economists think that Samuelson proved the "Simple Non-Substitution Theorem", that is, for the situation when the rate of interest is zero. Since the result for this case is exactly the same as for Samuelson's timeless case, the belief has a solid basis.

II

The above is a slight deviation from Samuelson's proof of the timeless case in which the λ's are eliminated with the help of n equations instead of being explicitly determined, as we do here. This deviation helps us take the analysis to the next stage. In this section we examine the consequences for the above analysis if time is included in the production functions of the goods. This leads us to the so-called "Simple" and "General" non-substitution theorems.[4] To simplify the analysis, and also to eliminate the association which seems to have developed between the general non-substitution theorem and a positive growth rate, we shall assume that we are in a stationary state.

The production functions incorporating time can be simply written as:

$$X_i = F_i\left(x_{i1(ti1)}, x_{i2(ti2)}, \dots x_{in(tin)}, X_{i,n+1}\right)$$

where tij represents the period for which input j remains in the production process for producing output i.[5]

The way we have written $x_{i,n+1}$ implies that the direct labour input is assumed to be made only for the period in which the output is produced, while the indirect labour of earlier periods is already incorporated in other inputs.

We can then write the equation for the amount available as the final demand for good i as:

$$C_i = F_i\left(x_{i1(ti1)}, x_{i2(ti2)}, \dots, x_{in(tin)}, x_{i,n+1}\right) - \sum_{j=1}^{n} x_{ji(tji)} \qquad (2N)$$

and follow the same procedure[6] that we followed with (2), and obtain one λ for every good and labour. The λ's still represent the marginal products of

[5] In the above analysis we are essentially assuming a flow input-point output framework, with outputs defined in a "natural" way. However see footnote 8 below.

[6] The stationary state assumption allows us to ignore the tji subscript here, since the current use of xji is equal to its use tji periods earlier.

goods in the production of good 1 but, as these marginal products are available only some periods after the price of the input is paid, the price will be a discounted value of the marginal product. In fact, if t_{11}, the period for which good 1 remains in production for producing good 1, is positive then the price of good 1 itself in terms of its own marginal product will have to be discounted and will not equal 1, as λ_1, the undiscounted marginal product of good 1 in its own production equals 1.

To be specific, as good j remains in the production of good 1 for t1j periods its price in *terms of good* 1, will be $\frac{\lambda_j}{(1+r)^{t1j}}$, where r is the given rate of interest.[7] If good j does not directly enter into the production of good 1, but good k does, while good j enters into the production of good k, then

$$P_j = \frac{\lambda_j}{(1+r)^{tkj}} - \frac{\lambda_k}{(1+r)^{t1k}} = \frac{\lambda_j - \lambda_k}{(1+r)^{tkj+t1k}}.$$ [8]

As λ_j are determined and t_{ij}'s are given, in our approach, from conditions of production, the relative prices will be fully determined once the interest rate is given. Again, the demand for the goods plays no role in determining prices.

If the interest rate is zero, all r's disappear, t_{ij}'s become irrelevant, and $P_j = \lambda_j$ as in the case of timeless production functions.

---

[7] As is common in these models, it is assumed that a given and constant interest 'r' links any two successive periods. There is no money in the model and hence the implicit loan market must be denominated in terms of one or more of the goods in the model.

[8] The above relation holds even if the same input enters into the production process for different periods. If an input enters the production process of a good for, let us say, one period as well for two periods, its use as an input will be such that its marginal product as a two-period input will be exactly (1+r) times higher than its marginal product as a one period input.

The extension of the basic idea to a durable capital good case in a stationary state is more complicated, but conceptually probably not different. The price of a durable capital good will be its discounted marginal product over a period of time, which can itself be a discounted value, if the output itself is a durable good, and so on The production functions needed for carrying through this analysis will require both input and output time subscripts. This is not attempted here.

We have thus shown the validity of both the simple and general non-substitution theorems under the specified circumstances with the help of the relatively simple analytical technique used by Professor Samuelson in the original formulation of the problem.[9]

REFERENCES

Ahmad, S. (1991), *Capital in Economic Theory: Neoclassical, Cambridge and Chaos*, Aldershot, Edward Elgar.

Bliss, C.J. (1975), *Capital Theory and the Distribution of Income*, North Holland, Amsterdam-Oxford.

Koopmans, T.C. (ed) (1951), *Activity Analysis of Production and Allocation*, John Wiley & Sons, New York.

Mirrlees, J.A. (1969), "The Dynamic Non-Substitution Theorem", *Review of Economic Studies*.

Neumann, J. von (1938), "A Model of General Economic Equilibrium", Reprinted, *Review of Economic Studies*, 1945.

Stiglitz, J.E. (1970), "Non-Substitution Theorems with Durable Capital Goods", *Review of Economic Studies*.

[9] However see note 2 above.

SAMUELSON THE VAIN

*B.B. Price**

ABSTRACT

Any one who looks at Samuelson's collection of scientific papers realises the breadth and depth of his contribution to economics. His Principles of Economics and Economic Foundations laid a new groundwork and set the standards of post-war modern economics. There is no need to remind the profession that Samuelson is an icon. An unusual diversion from the impressive substantive content of his work is taken in this contribution, where of particular interest is a personal stylistic facet of Samelson's writing, his vain, provocative mannerisms. The paradox of the world-renown scholar indulging in gratuitous self-promotion is in fact quite curious, and the present short paper advances a possible explanation for Samuelson's persona's lifetime of overindulging in vanity. The exercise here of applying the astute 'intelligence-vanity' maxim of Cicero's Hortensius and Augustine's Confessions to Samuelson appears to affirm both that this very duality is also his driving force and that the vanity of Samuelson, tolerated, if not fostered by the profession, seems to be telling us more about the lacklustre state of the discipline he loves than about the man himself...

As anyone older than three years of age knows, one has to be one's own best promoter in this world. This sentiment has certainly flourished among the adult psyche in the years since Dale Carnegie and successors of his ilk. Nonetheless, there does still seem to be some notion of extremes in the realm of tooting one's own horn. Trademarks of old-fashioned vanity are still recognisable as such. Interestingly enough, the works of Paul Samuelson are redolent with such markers of apparently unbridled self-aggrandisement.[1] A

* Department of Economics, York University, Toronto, Canada.

[1] This reader has hoped initially to be able to make this assertion rapidly through an interesting and startling calculation which would show that over the course of an average yearly production of x articles from 1937 to the present the august economist's self-image was projected through x vain references ... The present note can, however, only allude to the initial desire for a method for measuring and recognising the elasticity of the vanity in question.

recent publication, "How *Foundations* Came To Be" (1998),[2] has brought into renewed prominence such stylistic flourishes, which, Cicero observed,[3] can even serve to distract from the age of the writer involved.

Paul Samuelson's work began to be collected, a few decades ago, into a series of his scientific papers, on every subject from the theory of consumer's behaviour and capital theory to current economics and policy issues.[4] Any one who looks at these volumes (with more to come) will realise the breath and depth of his contribution to economics. His *Principles of Economics* and *Economic Foundations* laid a new groundwork and set the standards of post-war modern economics worldwide. There is here no need to remind the profession that Samuelson is an icon. Much has been and will be written about all aspects of his scientific thought. A unusual diversion from the substantive content of his work is taken here, in this contribution to the special issue of the *Journal* in his honour, where of particular interest is a personal stylistic facet of the scholar, Samelson's vain, provocative mannerisms.

The issue here is the Samuelson *persona*, a vain economist.[5] At an early stage, he admittedly developed "ridiculous heights of self-confidence".[6] A bit later, as he came to economics by accident, he quickly understood that satisfaction through the maximisation principle was the focus in analytical economics which, with his mathematically gifted mind, he could exploit fully to his advantage.[7] As a very skilled theorist, it did not take him much to realise that subjecting vanity and conceit to the same principle underlying his economics produces self-satisfaction of a Paretian order.

---

[2] Paul A. Samuelson, "How *Foundations* Came To Be", *Journal of Economic Literature*, Vol. XXXVI (September 1998), pp. 1375-86.

[3] Cf. Cicero, *Hortensius*

[4] *The Collected Scientific Papers of Paul A. Samuelson*, ed. var., Cambridge, MA: The M.I.T. Press, 1966-, Vol. I-

[5] Publications are like children, not only for the life they have of their own, but also in that they end up defining their father or mother. The initial observation, the catalyst to this paper, is that the words of Samuelson's publications seem to define him, their father, in part as an arrogant and pretentious economist.

[6] Paul A. Samuelson, "How *Foundations* Came To Be", *Journal of Economic Literature*, Vol. XXXVI (September 1998), p. 1375.

[7] "Since at least the time of Adam Smith and Cournot, economic theory has been concerned with maximum and minimum problems. Modern 'neoclassical marginalism' represents the culmination of this interest." Paul Samuelson, "Market Mechanism and Maximization", in Samuelson, 1966, Vol. I, p. 425; citation originally published as the opening to Part I of research memorandum, dated March 28, 1949, by the RAND Corporation, Santa Monica, California.

Certain questions pose themselves. Why, might one ask, would such an intelligent scholar indulge in such self-promotion, when he seems far from needing a spotlight (he is the spotlight!)? How could he have for so long and how could he continue to get away with his self-glorification? How could his scholarly reputation survive it? What is the drive behind such an attitude? The present short paper is an attempt, not at providing psychoanalysis of the scholar, (that in itself would be arrogant and presumptuous), but at advancing a possible explanation as to why Samuelson's *persona*'s overindulging in vanity is benign. What might seem, in reading him quickly, as his having an 'attitude problem', is in fact more intricate.

The exercise of applying the astute 'intelligence-vanity' maxim of Cicero's *Hortensius*[8] and Augustine's *Confessions*[9] has been undertaken and appears to affirm that this same duality is the driving force for Samuelson. It seems to account for the personal strength and unabashed satisfaction he derives from his relentless and industrious production and from his sense of self-fulfilment. From a different perspective, this duality also represents the driving force behind his frustration with the way he feels his work is generally perceived by fellow economists, who misunderstand, misrepresent, or are unaware or simply critical of the particular brand of economics (or of its particulars) that he represents. With varying degrees and nuances of arrogance or pretence, Samuelson's rebuffs, sent in many directions toward many different individuals -- whether lay, illiterate literate, or knowledgeable economist, whether ally or adversary, whether member of a fringe school, a post-this, neo-that and trans-what have-you or of the orthodox core -- provide him with strength of a public kind.

I. SAMUELSON AS ECONOMICS: THE BIRTH OF AN ICON

Samuelson keeps reminding his readers how blessed is his luck in every respect. He was born in the right place, attended the right schools, at the right time. His most important book *Economic Foundations* came out at the right moment. These fortuitous circumstances were crucial to his success but not sufficient in themselves to make of him an outstanding economist as well as an icon.

---

[8] *Passim*

[9] Augustine, *Confessions*, passim, especially Book III, [IV] 7 and Book IV, [XIV] 28.

Samuelson tells us that he was blessed with the right training. He received just what was needed for the time. The economics discipline, in the hands of the new generation of economists, Tinbergen, Koopman, Frisch, Wald, and many, many others, was at its turning point toward mathematisation on the large scale. The newly emerging econometrics placed ever-higher demand on mathematical skills.[10] Indeed, the developments in mathematics and probability theory, and their potential adaptation and application to economics were ripe to be exploited by bright minds with the right preparation.[11]

As he acknowledges, Samuelson entered the discipline at a fortunate juncture. The twenties and the thirties were a period of vibrant debate about almost every unsolved issue that had divided economists since Ricardo:[12] the Pigou-Clampton empty-boxes exchange; the Sraffa-Robinson-Chamberlin imperfect competition discussion which brought new perspective to economics as well as sowing the seed of attacks on Marshall and equilibrium theory; the deliberations regarding constant and diminishing returns; the questions related to money, monetary theory and interest rates, the Hayek-Knight-Kaldor exchange regarding capital, the various aspects of business cycles; the vicious mutual Keynes-Hayek-Sraffa attacks which started with the publication of Keynes' *Treatise on Money* and Hayek's *Price and Production* and continued in a larger circle up to and after the publication of the *General Theory*. Whether the issues were theoretical, such as those surrounding Say's law, or whether, of policy concern, all were pursued while, on the one hand, the industrial world had hardly come out of the Depression and, on the other, the world was entering one of its harshest military episodes.[13] Since to the theoretical

---

[10] This does not mean that these new ways of doing economics were immediately accepted with no resistance.

[11] One of Samuelson's earliest published assessments of the "exciting" importance of mathematics on economics, regarding the first formulations of Wald's proof by Wald and Schlesinger and then by himself, stems from almost half a century ago: "Linear Programming and Economic Theory", a paper published as part of the Proceedings of the Second Symposium in Linear Programming, on the National Bureau of Standards and the United States Air Force, January 27-29, 1955; 2nd rpt. in Samuelson, 1966, Vol. I, pp. 493-504.

[12] This is not a complete account of the discussions raised in the twenties and thirties, nor does it do justice to all the participants in the noted exchanges. For one history of the period, see G.L.S. Shackle, *The Years of High Theory* (Cambridge: Cambridge University Press, 1967).

[13] Samuelson, among others, would acknowledge that many important theoretical developments derived precisely from this period's having been one of war, e.g., his comments on statistics in Paul A. Samuelson, "Exact Distribution of Continuous Variables in Sequential Analysis", *Econometrica*, Vol. 16, No. 2 (April 1948), p. 191; rpt. in Samuelson, 1966, Vol. I, p. 730.

richness of the time was added the unavoidable observation of real problems, in the guise of poverty, unemployment, and business struggles, there was no crying need to justify the usefulness of economics and economists.[14] Any astute young economist in any of the few centres where debates were raging at the time would have had no difficulty in lending his ideas.

When Samuelson came of age, most of the controversial debates of pure theory were fading away, just as before, with no definite resolution, which meant that many questions remained open and much work, still pending. Some positive developments, specifically important to Samuelson's mathematical interests and thus worth mentioning in this present context, were Hicks' rehabilitation of Walrasian general economics which culminated in his *Value and Capital,* together with his work with Allan on demand theory, the independent work of Slutsky, and to some extent, Pigou's welfare economics and its implications for microeconomics. They all laid the fertile ground for the 'takeoff' of the ensuing mathematical microeconomics of which, with some few years' delay, Samuelson was a part.

Indeed, Samuelson was lucky enough to have entered economics at this rich moment of high controversies, cross-fertilisation, lack of resolutions and agreement, and with some areas of application which looked virgin to mathematical tools. Even if one could say that the research agenda was handed to him on a silver platter, it required nonetheless from his part a great intelligence to see through all this amazing abundance of problems and issues and to be able to enter the arena and leave his mark. Certainly, the truism, that from the top of a hill, regardless of its local topography, all movements are downward, held at that time no fearful implications for Samuelson. During the vibrant period of the thirties and the forties, in a disciple that had its share of super-stars, Samuelson was to come to stand out from even this crowd. But, how?

---

[14] As Samuelson tells it:

The Great Depression stimulated an interest in the problems of governmental fiscal policy culminating in the development of the doctrine of the Multiplier by Clark, Kahn and Keynes. Similarly the Recession of 1937 has once again brought to the fore the pressing problem of the effects of governmental expenditure upon the level of the national income and business activity.

Paul A. Samuelson, "The Theory of Pump-Priming Reexamined", *The American Economic Review*, Vol. XXX, No. 3 (September 1940), p. 492; rpt. in Samuelson, 1966, Vol. II, p.1125.

1) What has made Samuelson special among his contemporary mathematical economists, who have almost all chosen to focus on one or a few areas, was that he took the eclectic route. Most of his peers became embroiled in the technical aspects of their work, pushing at the limits and evolving within that neighbourhood. While Samuelson, too was working and contributing at the discipline's frontier, to his credit, however, he also truly tackled at their root the most controversial economic issues of his time and of the past, (often with a 'plus ça change, plus c'est la même chose' attitude[15]).[16] It has been the broad range of his foci which has made him a complete economist[17] and has given him an edge over his contemporaries.

2) As a theorist and economic model builder, Samuelson has exploited his mathematical expertise to great advantage to advance the discipline inherited from his predecessors. He defined it in terms of mathematics as distinct even from its immediate antecedents, the neo-classicals; its analysis, he has said, with its heavy dependency on "the tools of linear and more general programing", might best be called "neo-neo-classical".[18] "It was a case of mathematics not as Queen of the Sciences but as the Handmaiden of the Sciences."[19] Being extremely talented in mathematics and being persuaded that everything of interest and relevance in a theory can be expressed in purely mathematical terms,[20]

---

[15] "Modern economic analysis can throw light on the ancient problems of Ricardo and Marx." Paul Samuelson, "Wages and Interest: A Modern Dissection of Marxian Economic Models", *The American Economic Review*, Vol. XLVII, No. 6 (December 1957), pp. 884, rpt. in Samuelson, 1966, Vol. I, p. 341.

[16] He was among but a few, including Hicks and to a lesser extent Kaldor.

[17] The Tables of Contents of his volume of *Collected Scientific Papers* suffice to reveal his sustained interest in so many different aspects of economics.

[18] Paul A. Samuelson, "Parable and Realism in Capital Theory: The Surrogate Production Function", *The Review of Economic Studies*, Vol. XXIX, No. 3 (June 1962), p. 193; rpt. In Samuelson, 1966, Vol. I, p. 325.

[19] Paul A. Samuelson, "Alvin Hansen and the Interactions Between the Multiplier Analysis and the Principle of Acceleration". *The Review of Economics and Statistics*, Vol. XLI, No. 2, Part I (May 1959), p. 183; rpt. In Samuelson, 1966, Vol. II, p. 1123.

[20] E.g.,

> In a recent paper the thesis was advanced that while it is not possible to demonstrate rigorously that *free* trade is better (in some sense) for a country than *all* other kinds of trade, it nevertheless can be shown conclusively that (in a sense to be defined later) free trade or some trade is to be preferred to *no* trade at all.

Paul A. Samuelson, "The Gains from International Trade", *Canadian Journal of Economics and Political Science*, Vol. 5, No. 2 (May 1939), p. 195; rpt. in Samuelson, 1966, Vol. II, p. 781.

Samuelson has had the ability to transform any economic issue into a simple mathematical proposition, with its multitude of relevant and irrelevant scenarios. The appeal to the new type of mathematical approach helped him to place virtually any controversy in a more general context than had his predecessors or contemporaries[21] and to see where the economics of others was incomplete.[22] This also allowed him to elevate and distinguish himself within the narrow circle of the economic Olympians.

3) Over the span of six decades, Samuelson's contribution has overall been positive and constructive. Whatever controversial debate he entered, whatever difficult theoretical problems he discussed, whatever policy issues he addressed, his primary goal has almost always been to provide a functional solution and perhaps more importantly, to mend the gaps, in the core of evolving economic theory, as inherited from Smith, Marshall, and Walras. Although he has enjoyed this challenge, Samuelson has, however, never stopped at the core. It seems that he

---

[21] E.g.,

> It was only at this point that I entered the scene. ... I took Hansen's model, recognized its identity to a second-order difference equation with constant coefficients, and proceeded to analyze its algebraic structure. At once I made the inference that the drop in income which had so struck Hansen was not the end of the story. ...if he continued his numerical example far enough, his downturn too would have come to an end; and he would have been able to generate a succession of never-ending expansions and contractions.

Paul A. Samuelson, "Alvin Hansen and the Interactions Between the Multiplier Analysis and the Principle of Acceleration", *The Review of Economics and Statistics*, Vol. XLI, No. 2, Part I (May 1959), pp. 183-184; rpt. in Samuelson, 1966, Vol. II, pp. 1123-24.

[22] Examples abound:

> Simple minded people often say that raising wage rates will cause machines or 'capital' to be substituted for labor. More sophisticated folk have wondered a little about this argument ... The acceptable answer to a question like this must, of course, depend upon the economic model that is envisaged.

Paul A. Samuelson, "A New Theorem on Nonsubstitution", in Samuelson, 1966, Vol. I, p. 520. Or Samuelson's replacing discrete time by flows in continuous time in his "Efficient Paths of Capital Accumulation in Terms of the Calculus of Variations", in Kenneth J. Arrow, Samuel Karlin, and Patrick Suppes, eds., *Mathematical Methods in the Social Sciences*, 1959 (Stanford: Stanford University Press, 1960), pp. 77-88; rpt. In Samuelson, 1966, Vol. I, pp. 287-98. Or his surprise at the contentment of early twentieth-century economists "with what was after all only preliminary [mathematical] spade work" (p. 92) in his "The Stability of Equilibrium: Comparative Statics and Dynamics", *Econometrica*, Vol. 9, No. 2 (April 1941), pp. 92-120; rpt. in Samuelson, 1966, Vol. I, pp. 539-64.

has taken just as much joy in writing on Bernoulli expected utility[23] or on the economics of Marx-Bortkiewicz as on the stability of the demand function or revealed preference. Unlike Marx, Keynes, Sraffa, or others who wanted to revolutionise economics by shifting it off course,[24] Samuelson's goal, by contrast, in choosing the technical approach, i.e. the mathematical method, was to reinforce its course. He chose to ground his contribution in its core and solidify its foundations, building on a rich inheritance, as, for example, in the case of his contribution on revealed preference, to give more strength to demand theory.

4) Even when Samuelson writes that Marshall, Wicksell, and Walras became economists because they wanted "to do good for the world", whereas he became an economist "because the analysis was so interesting and easy",[25] he belies his real concern for an economics engagé. His liberalism was appropriate from the start, and also its sincerity, a blessing in terms of allowing him to stand up as an economist on social issues.[26] Here again, for him the issue is no less straightforward and technical;[27] he speaks as it were in mathematical parables when referring to the "reality" in which, for example, virtually everything but taxes and government expenditure decisions can be ignored[28]. One can be compassionate without having to worry about charity; the government through taxes and transfers can alleviate economic disparities, poverty, discrimination and their evil social consequences, etc. For an economist, therefore, to be helpful (whether out of compassion or not) in providing the means of maintaining the stability of the social fabric is to appeal to using mathematical

---

[23] See Paul Samuelson, Paper for the conference, "Les fondements et applications de la théorie du risque en économetrie", May 1952, (abstracted as "Utility, Preference and Probability" in Samuelson, 1966, Vol. I, p. 127) for his early definition of this theory.

[24] Samuelson might not agree with this, believing that his *Economic Foundations* has provided a revolution, that of shifting the debate from a general discussion to one of proofs, theorems, etc.

[25] Paul A. Samuelson, "My Life Philosophy", *The American Economist*, Vol. 27, No. 2 (Fall 1983), p. 5; rpt. in Samuelson, 1986, Vol. V, p. 789.

[26] Samuelson has long been an adherent of some aspects of Keynesianism and welfare state economics, both post-war social phenomena.

[27] By making the social economic problems, such as differences, poverties, disparities, (issues not under discussion in terms of morality, guilt, etc. on a personal level) a public concern which should be dealt with through fiscal taxes and fiscal policies and transfers, the issue becomes a matter of technicality, of who in society should pay what and how, and who should receive the transfers. The resolution can then derive from optimality and cost-benefit analysis through mathematical skills and not from philosophy.

techniques in the cost-benefit analysis of fiscal policies. By this method it is possible to arrive at all kinds of 'optimal' scenarios. The implementable ones are admittedly second-best solutions from any purist's perspective, but for other reasons, Samuelson occasionally advances an equally distancing remove from the dictates of mathematical abstraction. When conclusions come too close to implying the advantageous pursuit of right or left extremist policies, Samuelson shows himself ready to introduce a different notion of 'feasible optimum' with counter-balancing variables deriving from specific interventionist steps.[29] He would write that "... the Pareto-Lerner necessary conditions for an optimum must be supplemented by distributional considerations if a sufficient set of conditions for an optimum and for policy prescriptions is to be given."[30] The whole remains nonetheless at the level of calculations, and any discussion of morality and ethics is left to the less-mathematically-blessed to indulge in philosophical discussion. For Samuelson, economics ends at its mathematical boundaries.

It is these conditions, 1-4, which have made Samuelson both an outstanding economist and an icon. The eclectic model-builder, he has cleverly found a way to show how powerful mathematical skills can envelope under one umbrella as many areas in economics as possible to exploit as many scenarios as a theory can conceive, whether the issues are ideological or practical or theoretical. "Contrary to the impression commonly held, mathematical methods properly employed, far from making economic theory more abstract, actually serve as a powerful liberating device enabling the

---

[28] He has repeated affirmed that economists must neglect neither taxes nor government expenditure and spend some energy on considering both: e.g., Paul A. Samuelson, "Aspects of Public Expenditure Theories, *The Review of Economics and Statistics*, Vol. XL, No. 4 (November 1958), p. 332ff; rpt. in Samuelson, 1966, Vol. II, p. 1233ff. and "The Pure Theory of Public Expenditure", *The Review of Economics and Statistics*, Vol. XXXVI, No. 4 (November 1964), p. 387ff.; rpt. in Samuelson, 1966, Vol. II, p. 1223ff.

[29] E.g.,

> We are anxious to point out that even in the two factor case our argument provides no political ammunition for the protectionist. ... It is always possible to bribe the suffering factor by subsidy or other redistributive devices so as to leave all factors better off as a result of trade.

Wolfgang F. Stolper and Paul A. Samuelson, "Protection and Real Wages", *The Review of Economic Studies*, Vol. IX, No. 1 (November 1941), p. 73; rpt. in Samuelson, 1966, Vol. II, p. 846.

[30] Paul A. Samuelson, "Comment on Welfare Economics", in Samuelson, 1966, Vol. II, p. 1102.

entertainment and analysis of ever more realistic and complicated hypotheses."[31]

It must, however, also be noted that Samuelson has taken the 'sure-thing' route, in that the mathematical method of tackling economic problems (in theory) is one that can yield precise, definite answers. Owing to the elements of good training and good perception of the issues and problems, Samuelson has cleverly built an enormous corpus of recognisable contributions.[32] His economics is canonical, that of the majority, and is quite understandably perceived to be non-critical, non-destructive and not anti-economics.[33] While perhaps not seeming to treat the *status quo* of economics as sacred, Samuelson certainly has never been about abandoning its premises for any doctrine favouring an extreme, and generally unpopular, departure from their prevailing dominance. It is therefore also not surprising that his contributions are always well received by the driving core and accepted by its adherents for their strengthening intention and worth in their technical and theoretical aspects. They are almost always taken for granted upon publication with very little resistance within the intellectually sheltered environment.

Samuelson's publications have earned him a lot of praise in a discipline where, when it takes someone as a target, it is vicious and potentially devastating.[34] Criticism of Samuelson from within has turned usually on insignificant technicalities, which he handles with ease. Faced with virtually any mathematical opposition, given a confidence deriving from his technical

---

[31] Paul A. Samuelson, Interactions between the Multiplier Analysis and the Principle of Acceleration", *The Review of Economics and Statistics*, Vol. XXI, No. 2 (May 1939), p. 78; rpt. in Samuelson, 1966, Vol. II, p. 1110.

[32] Though condition 1 refers to his eclecticism, Samuelson does not claim to be doing everything. See his comments on his treatment of Marx, attached to n. 50 below.

[33] While mostly this has gone without saying, occasionally Samuelson has felt the need to indicate his canonical posture, e.g.,

> These results do not - and were not intended to -demolish the orthodox doctrine of a presumption that unilateral transfer payments will tend to deteriorate the terms of trade of the paying country. But they do suggest that the orthodox doctrine is still in need of vindication and further examination.

Paul A. Samuelson, "The Transfer Problem and Transport Costs, II: Analysis of Effects of Trade Impediments", *Economic Journal*, Vol. LXIV, No. 254 (June 1954), pp. 264; rpt. Samuelson, Vol. II, p. 1012.

[34] Witness the harsh treatment of Hayek and his retreat from the discipline. At the time that his economics was labelled fascist, non-compassionate, etc., there was, regardless of his libertarian ideas, not enough acceptance of his unfashionable and unorthodox methods to support his arguments.

skill, Samuelson cleverly translates the other's position into mathematical terms and thereby defends his own stance. Any serious attack on him has become synonymous with an attack on economics. In these instances, Samuelson considers most often that it is not the logic of a particular theory of his which is put in question, but the premises upon which or the means by which he has built it. He thus also dismisses such criticisms easily, but in these cases as their being irrelevant to his offering. Even when forced to recognise the limited scope of his conclusions, he can brush the critique under the rug into a footnote.

Notwithstanding his contributions, given a remarkable lack of devastating criticism, from within the discipline, Samuelson has been allowed to become "puffed-up". A certain self-satisfaction has undoubtedly come from his success; like Ali, "he is the greatest".[35] For someone who likes challenges, however, his being taking for granted with little serious resistance might explain Samuelson's vanity, as being the consequence of his intelligent frustration. More than an observation about Samuelson himself, it speaks to the changing state of the economics discipline, more and more focused on lemmas and theorems. Although it can be recognised that as a group, post-war economists, like Samuelson, have succeeded in developing a highly sophisticated technical economics. It must, however, also be seen that, as individuals, they reflect a loss of the vitality and compassion with regard to theoretical economic issues, as compared to economists of the pre-war period.

II. DUALITY 'INTELLIGENCE-VANITY': SOURCE OF SATISFACTION, CAUSED BY FRUSTRATION

There are boundless manifestations of Samuelson's intelligence in the quantity and quality of his writings, as well as in their importance as contributions. There is also an abundance of vain outbursts expressed continuously from the beginning of his writing career through to his current production. The following diagram, which interweaves the dual characteristics of vanity and intelligence, is intended to schematise the colourful variety of Samuelson's vain stylistic interjections: from the most self-absorbedly elevating to the most viciously opponent-denigrating; from the pretentious to the dismissive. The object in this section is to consider the relationship between displays of vanity and the reactions deriving from intelligence. Against the diagram, a

[35] Also, like Ali, he seems to believe that simple truth needs constant repetition.

'literary' theory about vanity and intelligence will be presented.[36] The exact meaning, and therefore the significance, of this relationship are not easy to determine. For brevity, we give the name 'Samuelson vanity theory' to the notion that a rational individual, confronted with two different types of demands on his intelligence, potentially eliciting self-satisfaction and frustration, chooses between them, neither being however mutually exclusive, as if tailoring his vanity response -- arrogance or pretence -- as to which is the more suitably maximising.

In good quantitative economist fashion, let us suppose a case of strong correlation, here between Vanity and Intelligence. Let us also assume that *Vanity* can manifest itself both as Arrogance and as Pretence, where *Arrogance* (A) is both the self-conscious appreciation of one's greatness as well as a capacity for the dismissive treatment of others, and *Pretence* (P), both the self-conscious appreciation of one's productivity as well as the capacity for affirmation of one's achievements vis-à-vis others. Let us suppose that *Intelligence* (the ability to act quickly, with precision and accuracy) leads through either Satisfaction or Frustration to one or the other form of vanity. *Satisfaction* (S) is taken here to be the self awareness of one's intelligence and the pleasure taken in one's production; *Frustration* (F), the feeling of not being understood and the desire to surpass, relative to others, the limits of one's own intelligence[37].

Both Cicero in his *Hortensius* and Augustine of Hippo in his *Confessions* pointed out what they perceived as the existence of an intimate yet publicly perceptible relationship between vanity and intelligence. The consistent manifestations of the intelligence of Samuelson in his writings and his simultaneous, vain concerns for recognition remind us that these ancients' observations about humanity are not totally passé in circles similar to theirs. It can be argued that, as in the case of Cicero and Augustine, most of Samuelson's vain reactions in the various circumstances throughout his writing can not only be described, but even explained, within this schema. Until now, much of the vanity analysis has not been directly concerned with its dynamics. The statisticians' assumption, that various relations can be

[36] Both are, of course, only heuristic devices for which a rigour useful to predict the qualitative effects of the causes they describe is not asserted.

[37] Note that this last condition precludes the application of his own "principle of duality" to this model.

approximated within a given range of observable data, must be taken very generously here where the relations are as follows.

Just as Samuelson acquires personal self-fulfilment (Quadrant AS) from the enjoyment he derives from his relentless and industrious production (Quadrant PS), as an Olympian he also requires an audience with which to share, of course, the products of his intelligence as well as his sense of success. The listeners the economics profession affords him are, however, an uneven distribution of followers and competitors, supporters and detractors. When Samuelson's contributions, with his technical subtleties, are understood and/ or represented differently, from the way in which he would like them to be, by the large average majority, whether they are followers who hold him up as an icon, or worse, anti-neo-classicals, his frustration with that audience comes out as arrogant disdain (Quadrant AF).

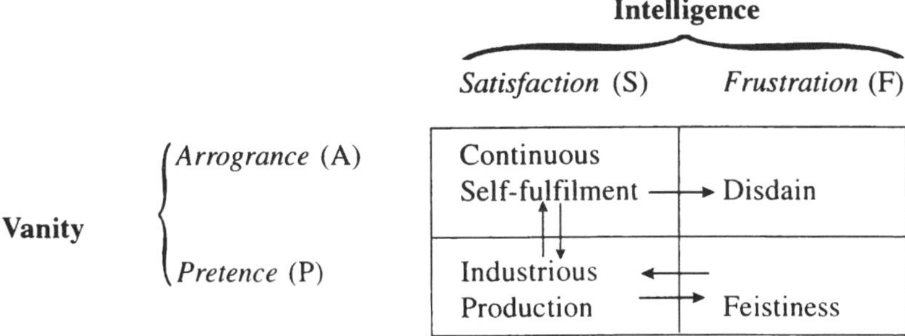

A second type of audience for Samuelson, the group comprised of both allies and adversaries, is the source of a different type frustration for him (Quadrant PF). As a scientist, Samuelson is aware that competition, which leads to progress, is carried out within a small circle of the decidedly above-average. His frustration with the fact that they do not all necessarily agree on the fundamentals, the methodology, or the goals and purposes of economics manifests itself, with varying degrees and nuances, in feisty attacks in many directions, sometimes personally targeted. Even vis-à-vis his allies Samuelson has always wanted to be first in any domain; as for his adversaries, he has had an incredible way of by bringing them to his perspective, salvaging anything of value for his economics and framing them as special cases within his much more general one.

Of course these descriptions and assertions have to be illustrated and supported with specific cases. It is beyond the scope of this paper to scrutinise every writing of Paul A. Samuelson. As a result, many of the conclusions derived might be deemed to be of restricted validity. Further, contradicting examples of expressions of outright humility,[38] which could undoubtedly be supplied by Samuelson's family and friends, might emerge to counter the far-from-innocent assumptions here about Samuelson's vanity. Indeed the common methodological situation, whereby refutation of a hypothesis must be conceded at a finite number of counter observations, while 'confirmation' thereof can never be strictly possible by a similar means of adding on the examples, exists here. Nonetheless, only concrete written statements, no suspected thoughts,[39] have been taken from throughout Samuelson's career and will be asked to suffice.

What is clear from the start is that it is neither 'error' nor 'failure' which caused Samuelson to spice up his prose with vanity. It would appear that from his very beginnings he has marched steadily through successful achievement towards greater self-fulfilment, sloughing off at successive stages unnecessary restrictive conditions. Samuelson's self-fulfilment (Quadrant AS) derives seemingly from his early arrogance and his satisfaction in its fruits. A sense of self-fulfilment was instilled well before any obvious manifestation of frustration. "My first published paper has come of age, and

---

[38] The closest Samuelson can be found to reflecting a humble *persona* himself derives from a passing comment in "Economics in a Golden Age: A Personal Memoir", in *The Twentieth Century Sciences: Studies in the Biography of Ideas*, G. Holton, ed. (New York: W.W. Norton & Co., Inc. 1972) p. 158; rpt. in Samuelson, 1977, Vol. 4, p. 884: "... one is a fool to take great pride in the chance circumstance that one's chemistry happens to be a favorable one."

[39] For which he has at least once been brought to task:

> Some years ago at the Boston Christmas meetings I gave a rather innocuous talk on the uses of mathematics in economics. When it was over, my friend Robert Bishop met an old teacher of mine and asked him how he liked the talk. 'I didn't like it,' was the reply. When interrogated as to what it was he did not like about it, he stated: 'Well, it wasn't so much what Samuelson said as what I knew he was thinking'. I suspect that most of the very interesting criticisms of my consumption-loan paper stem more from an extrapolation of what was alleged to have been in my mind than from a literal reading of my logical and mathematical theorems.

Paul A. Samuelson, "Infinity, Unanimity, and Singularity: A Reply", *The Journal of Political Economy*, Vol. LXVIII, No. 1 (February 1960), p. 76; rpt. In Samuelson, 1966, Vol. I, p. 240.

[40] Paul A. Samuelson, "An Exact Consumption-Loan Model of Interest with or without the Social Contrivance of Money", *The Journal of Political Economy*, Vol. LXVI, No. 6 (December 1958), p. 467; rpt. In Samuelson, 1966, Vol. I, p. 219.

at a time when the subjects it dealt with have come back into fashion."[40] In contrast to others, such as Hla Myint, who was privileged enough to study under two great teachers, Hayek and Hicks,[41] Samuelson's teachers are recounted as having been lucky to have been at the right place when he entered their classroom! Samuelson has written that, in presumably as early as 1938, he "shocked at least one" of his teachers, "by saying that the theory of comparative advantage does not guarantee a country against balance-of-payments difficulties, nor does it keep a country from being undersold in terms of every good."[42]

Samuelson's relentless and industrious production is already legendary. Equally obvious should be the unabashed self-fulfilment he receives from it (Quadrant PS). "One of the great pleasures of my life has been preparing for various Seymor Harris symposia, and I should like nothing better than to spend the next hundred years doing the same at five-year intervals."[43] It will be argued that of the duality, vanity-intelligence, pretence and satisfaction combined are the driving force that provides the strength for his flow of publications.

In the cases of Quadrants AF and PF, it is assumed that the individual guinea-pig, by his being the brunt of a vain outburst, reveals a Samuelson *persona* behaviour pattern - if there is such a consistent pattern. Samuelson seems to make distinctions among the individuals targeted by his vanity: some are treated with arrogance, others with a dose of his pretence. A lashing with the latter barb is, however, tantamount to receiving Samuelson's praise. For example, in assessing a book, he writes, "I shall pay it the compliment of judging it in the unsparing fashion appropriate to an important contribution to modern thought".[44]

From the perspective of Quadrant AF, Samuelson's vanity can be seen as an outcome of his frustration with most anyone, including the fellow economist, who ignorantly misunderstands or misrepresents his ideas. Perhaps

---

[41] Paul A. Samuelson, Review of *Theories of Welfare Economics, Economica*, Vol. XVI (November 1949), p. 371; rpt. in Samuelson, 1966, Vol. II, p. 1095.

[42] Paul A. Samuelson, "Theoretical Notes on Trade Problems", *The Review of Economics and Statistics*, Vol. XLVI, No. 2 (May 1964), p. 145; rpt. in Samuelson, 1966, Vol. II, p. 821.

[43] Ibid.

[44] Paul A. Samuelson, Review of *Theories of Welfare Economics, Economica*, Vol. XVI (November 1949), p. 371; rpt. in Samuelson, 1966, Vol. II, p. 1095.

the saying, "one fool can ask more questions than twelve wise men can answer", which he was wont to quip, represents the frustrating predicament into which Samuelson, as but one wise man alone, felt placed by them. He would refrain from stepping into overly "confused discussions"[45], but at the same time he often felt obliged to reply to the "simple-minded" folk,[46] displaying therein no dearth of arrogance. In virtually every article he assumes comprehension of many a *pons asinorum*,[47] thankfully instilled by others into the budding theorist.[48] This is not to suggest that, if Nature has silted harbours elsewhere, Samuelson should think it necessary to ruin his own, but rather to convey why it is particularly for this group of the wayward that Samuelson serves as the icon of economics and from whom he frequently acknowledges receipt of "a flattering amount of notice".49

In discussing determination of the source/s of frustration in a purely competitive environment, it is convenient to divide the analysis (of Quadrant PF) into the two groups to which Samuelson has been reacting with pretence: the ideological Antagonists and the Allies. By the 1950's at the latest Samuelson had come to realise that the postulates of earlier economic theorists could be dispensed with in favour of his own ideas by dealing with them more or less directly. In relation to certain ideological antagonists -- thinkers of classical and pre-classical economics who have made a worthwhile go of playing the game of dogma -- Samuelson seems to have an almost secret

---

[45] E.g., the one with respect to the volume of dissavings he dodged in his article "A Statistical Analysis of the Consumption Function", Appendix in A.H. Hansen, *Fiscal Policy and Business Cycles* (New York: W.W. Norton, 1941) p. 255, n. 8; rpt. in Samuelson, 1966, Vol. II, p. 1176.

[46] Cf. Note 22 for one reference to the "simple-minded".

[47] While, Samuelson assumed, many an economist had stumbled attempting to get over these preliminary 'bridges', he was equally persuaded that for many more, would-be economists, they provoked not just a slip, but the proverbial elefuga, or flight of the miserable ones, who at this point abandoned their mathematical pretensions entirely!

[48] E.g., acknowledgement of a proficiency of calculating a large variety of different "income multipliers" instilled by Professor Hansen and his associates into advanced students in business cycle theory, Paul A. Samuelson, "The Simple Mathematics of Income Determination", in *Income, Employment and Public Policy: Essays in Honor of Alvin Hansen*, L.A. Metzler et al., eds. (New York: W.W. Norton, 1948), first page; rpt. in Samuelson, 1966, Vol. II, p. 1197.

[49] Paul A. Samuelson, "The Gains from International Trade Once Again", *The Economic Journal*, Vol. LXXII (December 1962), p. 820; rpt. in Samuelson, 1966, Vol. II, p. 792. Such accolades are set by him counter-distinct to the serious discussion a publication might receive from serious economists world-wide, as, for example, from Erling Olsen and Murray C. Kemp, on his article "The Gains from International Trade", *Canadian Journal of Economics and Political Science*, Vol. 5, No. 2 (May 1939), pp. 195-205; rpt. in Samuelson, Vol. II, 1966, pp. 781-91.

admiration for their doctrinal approach, in its unabashed use of strong or extreme cases as the route to theoretical insight.[50] He has repeatedly advanced arguments whose effect, occasionally without purporting to be such, is to resurrect their theories in a modified form. He firmly felt and openly stated that modern, i.e. his, economic analysis could shed light on problems addressed by, for example, Ricardo and Marx, if not on the authors and their contributions per se.[51]

> I must assert agreement with the view that my paper on Marxian economic models did not do justice to Marx's own formulations of the issues treated. Nor was it ever intended to undertake such a task, whose extreme difficulty can be illustrated...
> ... I claim no competence or interest in such doctrinal history.
>
> Of the many uses we can make of the past, one - but certainly not the only one - is to reask some of the questions older writers posed and to provide them with answers in terms of modern analytical methods and terminology. The Marx-like or Ricardo-like model I described could be stripped of all proper names and could as well be described thus: a simple model involving ...[52]

Occasionally Samuelson acknowledged that the reverse could also be true, i.e., that the analysis of others of ideologically different positions might possess descriptive validity for his 'present-day economy'.[53]

As for his contemporary antagonists, Samuelson has developed a different strategy: identifying the position of his opponents as ideologically bound. E.g.,

---

[50] Although the reference author is the quite orthodox Walras, Samuelson states his abstract admiration for analysis via extremes in "Diagrammatic Exposition of a Theory of Public Expenditure", *The Review of Economics and Statistics*, Vol. XXXVII, No. 4 (November 1955), p. 350; rpt. in Samuelson, 1966, Vol. II, p. 1226.

[51] Paul A. Samuelson, "Wages and Interest: A Modern Dissection of Marxian Economic Models", *The American Economic Review*, Vol. XLVII, No. 6 (December 1957), pp. 884-912; rpt. in Samuelson, 1966, Vol. I, pp. 341-369.

[52] Paul A. Samuelson, "Wages and Interest -- A Modern Dissection of Marxian Economic Models: Reply", *The American Economic Review*, Vol. L, No. 4 (September 1960), p. 719-20; rpt. in Samuelson, 1966, Vol. I, pp. 370-71.

[53] Paul A. Samuelson, "Principles and Rules In Modern Fiscal Policy: A Neo-Classical Reformulation", in *Money, Trade and Economic Growth: Essays in Honor of John Henry Williams* (New York: Macmillan, 1951), p. 157; rpt. in Samuelson, 1966, Vol. II, p. 1271.

> I am concerned lest some of the homely truths expressed in the last part of Professor Stigler's recent sermon on welfare economics come under discredit because of some loose statements in the earlier parts. ... Speaking as but one of the authors cited, I must emphatically state that the 'new welfare economics' is not intended as a *substitute* for the 'old,' all pretensions notwithstanding. It is an attempt to derive *necessary* conditions whose validity is independent of value judgments as between individuals, or more accurately, whose validity depends only upon less restrictive, and less well-defined value judgments than had previously been assumed.[54]

A Samuelson ally is one of judicious, analytical and articulate intelligence,[55] i.e. a worthy competitor in the best sense of the word. He or she is one on whose input he can praiseworthily turn his sharpened knives. Nonetheless, the very appearance of a serious competitive challenge from within his own discipline seems to bring out of Samuelson a frustrated pretentiousness or a pretentious frustration apparently designed to reduce or eliminate the competition. One of Samuelson's ways of expressing 'frustration' with his "allies", those meet to the task of understanding him, has been his assuming the posture of having already brought a close to any chapter in the history of economics by his discussion of them. This is one little gem:

> I remember a meeting with Tibor Scitovsky, in Washington just before the war, at which he told me he was writing a paper on 'community indifference curves'. I risked a new friendship by replying: "That's strange. Long ago I proved that community indifference curves are impossible - they don't exist".[56]

In connection with debates to which full closure, according to him, has not been given, his *persona* is either:

---

[54] Paul A. Samuelson, "Further Commentary on Welfare Economics", *The American Economic Review*, Vol. XXXIII, No. 3 (September 1943), p. 605; rpt. as "Commentary on Welfare Economics" in Samuelson, 1966, Vol. II, p. 1041.

[55] It is thus that he describes the gifts of Hla Myint: Paul A. Samuelson, Review of *Theories of Welfare Economics*, *Economica*, Vol. XVI (November 1949), p. 371; rpt. in Samuelson, 1966, Vol. II, p. 1095.

[56] Paul A. Samuelson, "Social indifference Curves", *The Quarterly Journal of Economics*, Vol. LXX, No. 1 (February 1956), p. 1; rpt. In Samuelson, 1966, Vol. II, p. 1073.

a) the one who can treat the problem as exhaustively as, if not more exhaustively than, anyone else,

b) the one who, already carrying the flag, welcomes his allies upon their *belated* arrival, or

c) the one who can see now what others in the past could not.

An example of (a) can be found in the larger discussion of real national income, within which Samuelson publishes one "careful survey" in 1950.[57] In an article which is "not easy reading even to the author" (p. 1), he sets out to modify certain definitions and propositions in the theory of welfare economics, "many of them growing out of Hicks's own researches" (p. 2), to clear up initially at least one misunderstanding, to interpret Hicks (pp. 5-6) and Kuznets (pp. 9-10) generously, and in an appendix (pp. 21-29) "to appraise critically" Pigou on the subject.

As for (b), one might note Samuelson's overture to Abba Lerner, one of many august economists Samuelson welcomed to join a debate he had himself already catalysed:

> "Because Professor Lerner has made so many important contributions to modern economics, I am pleased to welcome his entrance into the discussion of some of the problems raised by my analysis of an exact consumption-loan interest model ... Such a dynamic problem ... is to me one of the most difficult in all economics, and I regard my own paper as a first tentative effort in a field that needs much cultivation."[58]

---

[57] Paul A. Samuelson, "Evaluation of Real National Income", Oxford Economic Papers (New Series), Vol. II, No. 1 (January) (Oxford: [Oxford] University Press, 1950), pp. 1-29; rpt. in Samuelson, 1966, Vol. II, pp. 1044-1072; pages cited are sequentially as follows in the reprinting: p. 1044, p. 1045, pp. 1048-49, pp. 1052-53, pp. 1064-72.

[58] Samuelson does go on in his reply to Abba Lerner's article on consumption-loan interest and money to write:

> For both these reasons I should not have felt too much chagrin if it were pointed out that I had made a boner in the course of my mathematical and logical discussion. It would not have been my first, and, considering the difficulties of the subject matter, I should have been able to find my consolations. But after reading Lerner's paper twice, I remain stubbornly convinced that my only plea to the crime he charges me with is 'Not guilty'.

Paul A. Samuelson, "Reply", *The Journal of Political Economy*, Vol. LXVII, No. 5 (October 1959), p. 518; rpt. in Samuelson, 1966, Vol. I, p. 235. For his inferring others' coming of age, see also, Paul A. Samuelson, "An Exact Consumption-Loan Model of Interest with or without the Social Contrivance of Money", *The Journal of Political Economy*, Vol. LXVI, No. 6 (December 1958), p. 467; rpt. in Samuelson, 1966, Vol. I, p. 219.

Persona (c) can be found in many a section entitled "Criticism of Existing Views" or such like.

> A comparison of the foregoing results [of our analysis] with Harrod's brilliant chapter ii will reveal many discrepancies. Upon rigorous analysis his exposition will be found to abound with *non sequiturs* and oversimplifications. On the whole Harrod's intuition surpasses his reasoned conclusions ...[59]

Samuelson is the one who, unlike Hicks, avoids assuming the role of the jackass and unlike Pigou, avoids becoming one![60]

The cause of the frustration Samuelson experiences with his allies is the challenge they pose to his pretence, to have already either solved or at least dealt well, to limits of the contemporary possibilities, with everything. The 'positive' aspect of his response is his turning to ever greater production on the subject in question, in order, then and there, "to settle the matter definitively"[61] Once provoked,[62] however, Samuelson's doubt is not necessarily easily or peacefully lulled. Thus, on the 'negative' side, these new writings,

---

[59] Samuelson does concede "of what investigator worth his salt is this not true?" "A Synthesis of the Principle of Acceleration and the Multiplier", *The Journal of Political Economy*, Vol. XLVII, No. 6 (December 1939), p. 795; rpt. in Samuelson, 1966, Vol. II, p. 1120.

[60] When Professor Hicks wished to discover what a 'classical' economist believed to be the determinants of the level of employment, he was very much in the position of the man who, having lost his donkey, had no recourse but to ask himself what he would do if he were a jackass, and then to do the same thing. But now the animal has come forward to speak for himself, and all economists will welcome Professor Pigou's new and stimulating book.

Paul A. Samuelson, "Professor Pigou's Employment and Equilibrium", *The American Economic Review*, Vol. XXXI, No. 3 (September 1941), p. 545; rpt. in Samuelson, 1966, Vol. II, p. 1183.

[61] As when he felt the need to amplify his own work on free commodity trade, upon having newly learned of a report by Lerner on international trade and equalisation of factor prices, which he found to be itself (emphasis added) "a masterly, **definitive** treatment", Paul A. Samuelson, "International Factor-Price Equalisation Once Again", *Economic Journal*, Vol. LIX, No. 234 (June 1949), p. 181, n. 1; rpt. in Samuelson, 1966, Vol. II, p. 869, n. 1.

[62] E.g., Samuelson's former student Professor Jagdish Bhagwati's opening, "I have a puzzle for you..." provoked his "Equalization by Trade of the Interest Rate along with the Real Wage", in *Trade, Growth and the Balance of Payments*, essays in honor of Gottfried Haberler (Chicago: Rand McNally & Co., 1965), p. 35; rpt. in Samuelson, 1966, Vol. II, p. 909. Samuelson had also identified "the classroom" as the locus "where the whole discussion originally started', with students, some of whom, presumably, like Bhagwati, once well-schooled, will have moved on to become Samuelson's allies: e.g. 1) "A Comment on Factor Price Equalisation", *The Review of Economic Studies*, Vol.

spurred on by the competitive ally, are frequently laced with the twinges of the frustrated, and perhaps even demasked, pretence of their author. Samuelson recognises his own difficulty in restraining himself from, what he calls, being "churlish" toward those who have responded to his "trumpet call for wisdom".[63]

III. CONCLUSION

For post-war economists Samuelson certainly has been the leading economist of his generation, notwithstanding the merit or demerit of his lasting contribution to economics, judgement of which has not been the purpose of this paper. Even the vanity of his *persona*, cultivated unscathed over such a long period, is certainly out of the ordinary. Historically, the development of economic theory has not been considered to owe much to the vanity of its economists.[64] The observations here are, however, presented not so much in the hope of furthering inductive investigations into these matters of vanity as of bringing out certain symbiotic relations among the players, given the variables under consideration. The intricacy remains, why has the profession tolerated Samuelson's vanity for so long? Any single note - whatever its accompaniment or ornamentation - if held a long time can become somewhat offensive to the ear. Perhaps, in the world of thick-skinned economists, one man's attack-camel is simply but another man's noisy gnat. On the other hand, undoubtedly Samuelson has found safety from personal criticism in numbers, in the number of illiterate literate economists and in the disproportionate number of economists of neo-classical mathematical inclination. Perhaps both possible scenarios are cases of nature's having clustered roots in such close array that it serves no useful purpose to try to unscramble them, but to be of interest the written word must have consequences, and the targeted vain words, presumably negative ones...

XIX, No. 49 (February 1952), p. 122; rpt. in Samuelson, 1966, Vol. II, p. 887; 2) "When recently a student challenged this result..." Samuelson found it "desirable to plug a gap in the theoretical literature", "International Trade and the Equalisation of Factor Prices", *Economic Journal*, Vol. LVIII, No. 230 (June 1948), p. 164; rpt. in Samuelson, 1966, Vol. II, p. 848; or 3) "... one of my students ... persuaded me to believe the stronger truncated theorem to be true ..." "A Fundamental Multiplier Identity", *Econometrica*, Vol. II, No. 3-4 (July-October 1943), p. 223, n. 2; rpt. in Samuelson, 1966, Vol. II, p. 1193, n. 2.

[63] Paul A. Samuelson, "The Turn of the Screw", *American Economic Review*, Vol. XXXV, No. 4 (September 1945), p. 674; rpt, in Samuelson, 1966, Vol. II, p. 1255.

[64] Samuelson has, however, fancied himself able to detect a pretentiousness in modern welfare economics; see his Review of *Theoretical Welfare Economics*, *The Economic Journal*, Vol. 68, No. 271 (September 1958), p. 539; rpt. in Samuelson, 1966, Vol. II, p. 1099. See, for a striking contrast, Walras' opening to *Pure Economics*.

Even the immortals he likes to cite, Einstein, Mozart, Gauss, Kepler, Coleridge, Newton, etc., suffered during their lifetimes a good deal of hardship, some of them having brought it upon themselves through their own vanity. In very few academic disciplines,[65] especially within the sciences, would such a sustained case be treated leniently. Analogous to the *homo economicus* (dear to 'scientific' economics), if the discipline of economics were to be blessed with many vain *doctori economici,* not necessarily all of the same stripe, but all like Samuelson in training, in breadth, and in the kind of striving to the level of excellence he has set for himself, then, in their facing each other, in the dynamic sum game, vanity would become a dead weight, and wane in importance for whatever reasons. With the stimuli from competition, a Darwinian process of ruthless natural selection of thoughts (not thinkers), severely punishing with oblivion any deviation however momentary from the intellectual optimum would produce and distil more robust results. It is still differences of opinion that make for horse races and horse markets. Thus, if to analyse a paradox is to dispel it, perhaps the vanity of Samuelson is paradoxically telling us more about the un-race-like, un-market-like state of the discipline he loves than about the man himself ...

[65] For Hollywood stars the case is of course quite different.

MONEY AND PRICE THEORY

Carlo Benetti * and *Jean Cartelier***

ABSTRACT

It is commonly admitted that the modern price theory fails in determining market prices out of equilibrium and in integrating the exchange activity at equilibrium prices. In this paper we show that these two difficulties have a common origin: the absence of a "market mechanism", *i.e.* an algorithm by which market prices and allocations resulting of a given set of individual actions are calculated. As a result of such a market mechanism, prices are determined directly as monetary prices, from which relative prices may be derived. In this way money and value theories are integrated. This problem is also examined on the ground of the history of economic analysis.

INTRODUCTION

Price theory and money theory should not develop separately. They are indeed the two faces of the same coin.

Modern price theory sums up in two central results, existence of general equilibrium prices and Pareto-optimality of competitive equilibria. It does not succeed however in demonstrating that these prices are market prices. This is the major failure of this approach. Introducing a market mechanism is necessary but is possible only through assuming the existence of money, as a general means of payment.

In the first section of this paper, relations between price determination and market mechanism are recalled. In the second section, a market mechanism - Cantillon's rule - is built in the basic pure exchange model and

* Université Paris X-Nanterre (FORUM-CAESAR carlo.benetti@u-paris10.fr)
** Université Paris X-Nanterre (FORUM-CAESAR jcartel@club-internet.fr)

some consequences of this introduction are drawn. A third section is devoted to interpretative remarks and to monetary control. Final section contains some remarks about the history of thought in this field.

1. PRICE DETERMINATION AND MARKET MECHANISM

In its more general meaning, market is a particular means of co-ordination between individual actions. The peculiarity is that individual actions are decentralised, *i.e.* the individuals do not know the state of the economy in which they are acting. Besides, such a state is the result of individual actions and it is commonly admitted that it can be different from what market participants expected.

A market mechanism is an algorithm by which prices and allocations resulting from a given set of individual actions can be calculated. In a competitive economy these actions concern quantities and not prices. The latter are supposed to be determined by the anonymous market competition. This conception is common to the general competitive equilibrium theory as well as to other price theories (production prices, labour theory of value, etc...). All this can be expressed by the fact that the agents, when they make decisions, take prices as parameters (such prices can be either expected prices or Marx's 'ideal prices' or they can be announced by an auctioneer).

In the most advanced price theory - the general competitive equilibrium theory - there does not exist any algorithm which could be interpreted as a market mechanism. It is impossible to calculate market prices and allocations which correspond to individual actions taken for a given vector of parametric prices. Market outcomes are determined only for very particular vectors of parametric prices, *i.e.* prices such as there does not exist any positive market excess demand. In other terms, in the general competitive equilibrium theory, the market mechanism is not defined except in equilibrium.

The existence of equilibrium positions are justified on the basis of the 'law of demand and supply', and it was believed for a long time that, in accordance with this law, disequilibrium positions were transitory: adjustment forces of demand and supply will push the economy towards an equilibrium. But this belief has no longer been justified since the well known failure of the stability theory (Fisher, 1983). Hence, it must be admitted for that reason that the general competitive equilibrium theory is not an acceptable theory of the competitive market.

This can be accounted for in the separation between the determination of equilibrium prices (by the system of simultaneous equations of market excess demand) and decentralised exchanges on markets. The exchange activity, which is an essential one in a market economy, is never considered; it is not even mentioned in the standard price theory. As a reaction against this paradoxical separation we could note the attention paid to transaction costs and the development of theories such as search theory and strategic market games.

Some conclusions of these different researches are:

- Even in a general equilibrium situation, it is not generally possible to complete the desired transactions in a decentralised way (Ostroy and Starr, 1974). As a consequence, the individual equilibrium allocations may not be obtained. Negative consequences on welfare properties are obvious.

- The non-tâtonnement processes without a general means of payment are arbitrary because the conditions of market efficiency are not fulfilled (Fisher, 1983).

- The theory of strategic market games shows that, without a unique means of payment, the prices which are obtained on different markets are incoherent (Sahi and Yao, 1989).

All these indications strongly suggest the necessity of introducing money in the general equilibrium theory. But this is a fruitless strategy. The existence of a generally accepted means of exchange, even if it were possible, could not modify the fundamental flaw of the general competitive equilibrium theory, *i.e.* the absence of a satisfactory market mechanism. The fact that the unique general means of exchange has a zero price at equilibrium, enables us to shorten the discussion on this point[1].

---

[1] On the in-achievements of modern monetary theory, see M. Hellwig (1993).

The central problem is that of the market mechanism. A simple principle can be found in the writings of some economists of the past, principle which we shall call 'Cantillon's rule' as a tribute to the first author who has presented it clearly. This rule (Cantillon, 1755) is as follows: "Prices are set by the proportion between commodities brought to the markets and the money which is offered in order to buy them". The same rule is adopted in many models of strategic market games (for a survey, see Shubik, 1990). It implies that money exists, and that individual actions concern quantities of goods as well as of money.

The adoption of this market mechanism deeply modifies the way of thinking the market theory. Market and money theories are one and the same theory. The question is not to show that a 'thing', which does not enter the utility functions and which is used as a general means of exchange, has a positive equilibrium price. In other words, contrary to a well-established tradition, the integration of money into value theory is an ill-formulated monetary problem, which would only makes sense if a price theory which excludes price formation by means of a market mechanism were acceptable. According to Cantillon's rule, money is the condition of the formation of a coherent system of market prices. It is important to note that this is true independently of the realisation of a general equilibrium of the markets. The relationship between money and commodities which is indicated by Cantillon's rule, is not an equivalence relationship, or an exchange relationship. The exchange is realised only by the selling and buying considered together, as shown by Marx. As a medium of exchange, money is a means and not an end. The relationship between money and goods is defined by the market mechanism.

The introduction of Cantillon's rule completely modifies the price theory. In this paper, we sketch a simple model of price formation, that is with a market mechanism and money in such a way that it can be compared with the standard Walrasian general competitive equilibrium theory[2].

2. A THEORY OF PRICES WITH A MARKET MECHANISM AND MONEY: A SIMPLE ILLUSTRATION

In order to transform the general equilibrium basic model into a theory of

[2] Another possible example is Marx's theory of value, C. Benetti and J. Cartelier (1994).

market price formation, it is necessary to combine it with a market mechanism and with a system of payment.

Let us consider a pure exchange competitive economy with L commodities $l = 1, \dots, L$, and H individuals, $h = 1, \dots, H$.

Individual h is described by: his/her initial endowment, $\underline{x}_h$, his/her utility function $U_h(x_h)$, assumed to have all the 'good' properties, with x_h being individual h's allocation after the market, the amount of a general means of payment (not a commodity) $\underline{\mu}_h$ which is available to him/her at the beginning of the market and which must be paid back at the end. Means of payment are nothing but pure intermediary of exchange and they do not enter utility functions. The total quantity of means of payment is $\Sigma\underline{\mu}_h = \underline{\mu}$.

The market mechanism

The market mechanism is made of the following rules:

1. There exists an organised market for each commodity - *i.e.* L markets - where individuals bring the quantities of commodities they wish to sell and spend the amount of means of payment corresponding to the expected value of the quantities of commodities they wish to buy m_{hl} under the constraint: $\Sigma m_{hl} \leq \underline{\mu}_h$

2. The L markets open and close simultaneously; they last a uniform discrete period of time (t)

3. Market prices $\pi_l(t)$ are determined according to Cantillon's rule :

$$\pi_l(t) = \frac{\sum_h m_{hl}(t)}{\sum_h \left| z_{hl}^-(t) \right|} \qquad \forall l \qquad (1)$$

   where $z_{hl}^-(t)$ is the excess-demand, if negative, of commodity l by individual h. Market prices are determined but as *monetary prices.*

4. Allocation of individual h of commodity l at the end of the market is:

$$x_{hl}(t) = \underline{x}_{hl}(t) + z_{hl}^-(t) + m_{hl}(t) / \pi_l(t) \qquad (2)$$

   and monetary balance of individual h is :

$$s_h(t) = \sum_l \pi_l(t) \left| z_{hl}^-(t) \right| - \sum_l m_{hl}(t) \qquad (3)$$

Money as payment system

The market mechanism described as Cantillon's ruled is very abstract. Means of payment are implied by this mechanism but they have not yet been defined. The market mechanism needs an institutional support. Here money enters the stage.

Money is not a 'commodity' which must have a positive price in order to become an 'economic thing'. It is rather a specific way of organising transactions.

There is a general agreement on the minimal properties of a market economy:

- individual decisions are decentralised, *i.e.* they depend on local and not on global conditions; as a consequence, prices generated by such decentralised transactions are generally not consistent; this prevents one from defining univocally individual budgetary constraints and deprives equivalence in exchange of any clear meaning

- the overall outcome results from a market mechanism co-ordinating these individual decisions

Money must be modelled in such a way that it allows the working of a market economy. To put it in a nutshell, it has to make transactions possible in disequilibrium as well as in equilibrium. This is the condition for transactions to be decentralised and for two individuals to conclude a transaction independently of other people. Money guarantees that market prices are consistent in contrast with barter.

To remind us that money is an institution, we shall use the term *payment system.*

Three elements are the minimal components of a system of payment.

1. A *nominal unit of account* is necessary to express prices in a monetary economy. Even if the unit of account is physically defined - e.g. by a

gold weight - such an economy will differ from one in which prices are expressed in gold. In barter, gold is not accepted as a means of payment by agents who do not demand gold. Acceptance of money is not ruled by the same principles as the demand for goods. In a gold currency system, gold coins and not gold itself are the commonly accepted means of payment. When minting and melting are not free this makes a great difference. It is not required that the unit of account should be physically defined. A dollar is a dollar. The unit of account is a language, the language used in the market.

2. A *minting process* is a necessary complement for the unit of account. The existence of a unit of account - say the dollar - only imposes that every means of payment has to be expressed in dollars. In order to transact economic agents must have means of payment. Any given individual may obtain means of payment by selling something to others. But the question is: how buyers may have means of payment? Clearly, if individuals may act in the market in a decentralised way, they must obtain means of payment without waiting for the sales of their commodities. The minting process is the process by which economic agents obtain means of payment independently of other people expenditures. Getting means of payment in that way allows one to act freely in the market, for instance to produce goods in view of selling them. Minting process and the so-called market division of labour are the one and same thing. Several kinds of minting processes can be found in history. Availability in the means of payment is not the same in a strict gold currency system and in a complex banking system with credit and a Central Bank. In modern theory, some examples of minting process can be found. The most familiar is the *cash-in-advance hypothesis*. Obviously, there is a need for further elaboration in this field. Since transactions take place in equilibrium as in disequilibrium, some individuals will experience at the end of the market that they spent more than they earned whereas others will discover that they earned more than they spent. In the aggregate, payments and receipts are necessarily equal but this is not true for individuals who have either monetary surpluses or monetary deficits. These monetary balances reveal that individual budgetary constraints and equivalence in exchange are not verified. Remember that a sale (or a purchase) is not an equivalence relationship.

3. Restoration of budgetary constraints requires a *principle of adjustment* (settlement of balances or postponement of payments through credit). As monetary surpluses and deficits are unavoidable, being inherent in market co-ordination where disequilibrium is the rule, it is not very sensible to think that high penalties for default would suffice to restore confidence. Neither individuals nor banks have sufficient knowledge to avoid disequilibrium situations. The problem is not to preclude beforehand occurrence of disequilibria but to make sure that disequilibria, if not too important: (i) do not put the entire economy in danger (ii) do not prevent economy from working as smoothly as possible so that confidence is self-enforcing (iii) do act as signals inducing appropriate adaptative behaviour from agents so that disequilibria are not cumulative.

A central Bank (or monetary authority) is the most common institutional device to get these outcomes.

Individual behaviour

Nothing has been said so far about the way individuals calculate their desired transactions. As a matter of fact, the market mechanism is compatible with any decentralised behaviour. The 'rules of the game' make up the framework in which individuals behave and it is to be defined logically prior to the behavioural assumptions. It is indeed possible here to adopt many different assumptions, be they founded on bounded or on Walrasian rationality hypothesis. To keep reasoning along general equilibrium tradition, we shall adopt the following assumptions:

1. The prices used by individuals to calculate their market plans are called *parametric prices*, p_{hl}. They are either announced by an auctioneer or expected by agents. We shall consider thereafter only the case where parametric prices are identical for all individuals (a special case is when expected prices are equal to market prices of the preceding period, $p_{hl}(t) = \pi_{hl}(t-1)$)

2. Individuals maximise utility functions respecting two constraints: (i) the value - at parametric prices - of desired purchases shall not exceed that of expected sales (ii) the value of desired purchases - $z_{hl}^{+}(t)$ is the excess-demand of individual h for commodity l if positive - shall not

exceed the amount of the means of payment available to individual h:

$$\sum_l p_l(t) z_{hl}(t) \leq 0 \qquad (4)$$

$$\sum_l p_l(t) z^+_{hl}(t) \leq \underline{\mu}_h(t) \qquad (5)$$

3. The quantity of the means of payment available to h is exogenous (it is also possible to assume a 'monetary authority' controlling the $\underline{\mu}_h(t)$'s according to the type of payment system which runs the market mechanism

4. Desired transactions are given by maximising individual utility functions under the constraints (4) and (5).

Under standard assumptions, desired transactions are thus continuous functions of parametric prices, initial endowments and amounts of available means of payment:

$$z_{hl}(t) = z_{hl}(p(t), \underline{x}_h(t), \underline{\mu}_h(t)) \qquad (6)$$

Market outcomes

Price formation

For given parametric prices, initial endowments and amounts of means of payment, individual h spends $m_{hl}(t) = p_l(t) z_{hl}^+(t)$ on market l. Cantillon's rule gives now:

$$\pi_l(t) = p_l(t) \frac{\sum_h z^+_{hl}(t)}{\sum_h z^-_{hl}(t)} \quad \forall\, l \qquad (7)$$

Market price for commodity l is defined if, for at least an individual, there is a negative excess-demand. This price is positive if, besides, there is also a positive excess-demand.

Relation (7) shows that formation of prices is decentralised market by market. General interdependence among markets is present however through some kind of Walras's law:

$$\sum_{l} (\pi_l(t) \sum_{h} \left| z^{-}_{hl}(t) \right|) \equiv \sum_{l} (p_l(t) \sum_{h} z^{+}_{hl}(t)) \qquad (8)$$

Which amounts to:

$$\sum_{h} (\sum_{l} \pi_l(t) \left| z^{-}_{hl}(t) \right| - \sum_{l} m_{hl}(t)) = \sum_{h} s_h(t) \equiv 0 \qquad \forall t \qquad (9)$$

Relation (9) is the specific form of Walras's law in a monetary economy. Let us call it the *monetary identity*. Monetary identity and Walras's law are expressions of equivalence in exchange but instead of putting emphasis on the interdependence among markets, relation (9) underlines interdependence among individuals.

The diagram below describes the working of Cantillon's rule. If S(p) and D(p) denote respectively market supply and demand for commodity *l*, market price is given by pD(p)/S(p). The relation between market price and parametric price is shown in the left part of the diagram. If ^p is the parametric price, market price is then ^π. All the quantities brought to the market for ^p are sold at ^π, determined by equality between area O^pAq_d and area O^π Dq_s (D and A are on the same branch of an hyperbola). If aggregate excess-demand market for commodity *l* is zero (D(p)=S(p)), market price of commodity *l* will be equal to the parametric price .

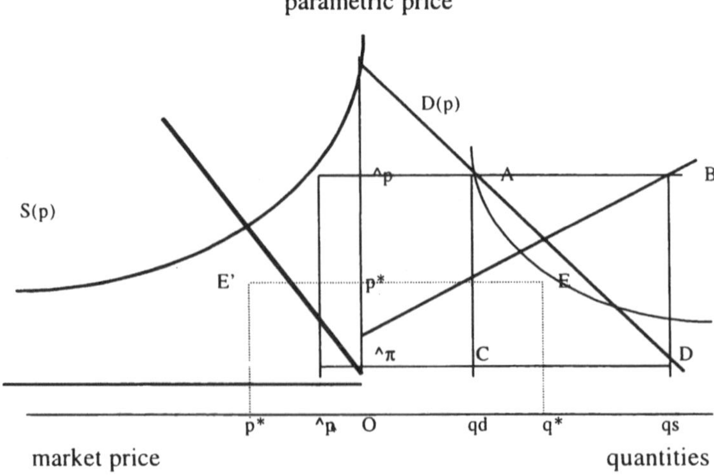

General equilibrium

If all aggregate excess-demand functions are simultaneously equal to zero, that is if:

$$\sum_h z_{hl}^+(t) = \sum_h z_{hl}^-(t) \quad \forall l \qquad (10)$$

market prices are general equilibrium prices.

It is also clear that if constraint (5) is not binding for any individual, such market prices will be also Walrasian equilibrium prices. If constraint (5) is binding for one individual at least, general equilibrium market prices differ from Walrasian prices[3].

General disequilibria

In general, however, condition (10) does not hold and market prices differ from parametric prices. This does not prevent prices from being determined and transactions from taking place. But as equation (3) makes it clear, individual non-zero monetary balances are the rule. Individuals are put away their budgetary constraints although their desired transactions do respect these constraints. In addition to the 'real' disequilibrium between desired and realised purchases, individuals face a 'monetary' disequilibrium.

There is a sharp difference between these disequilibria and those of different versions of the Walrasian theory.

In the traditional Walrasian model, individuals are always in equilibrium. Market disequilibrium is only virtual and can be known by a fictitious auctioneer only. In the so-called non-Walrasian price theory, individuals are always in constrained equilibrium, obtained by adding quantity signals to (fixed) price signals. Market disequilibrium prevents them from realising their desired constrained transactions. Actual exchanges are determined by the 'short side' of the market. *In every case, individuals are always in their budget set.*

---

[3] For a rigorous treatment of this point, see Dubey and Shapley (1994).

In our model, the economic rationale of exchange is very different. Transactions are not the way of modifying endowments at given known prices. They are conceived as a social process by which prices will emerge by means of the market mechanism. As a consequence of Cantillon's rule, markets work as a system by which commodities are reallocated among market participants. Thus, markets always clear, *i.e.* all commodities brought to the market are sold[4]. It follows that disequilibrium appears only in the individual accounts as a difference between expected (or parametric) and market price. Such individual disequilibria are both real and monetary. Therefore, there is a room for a monetary regulation of the economy.

3. INTRODUCTION TO THE MARKET DYNAMICS

Market dynamics is the product of individuals's reactions to their disequilibria, combined with a possible regulation by the monetary authority.

Individual disequilibria have two aspects:

(i) a *real* aspect which concerns the difference between the parametric and the market price. For commodities in positive excess-demand, quantities actually bought in the market and quantities desired may differ according to this real disequilibrium. No such thing can occur for commodities in negative excess-demand; Cantillon's rule ensures a strict equality between quantities sold and quantities brought to the market.

(ii) a *monetary* aspect which concerns the difference between the value of actual sales and that of actual purchases. This monetary disequilibrium is nothing but the individual balance $s_h(t)$ (3). Note that this monetary balance differs from the value of real disequilibria which is the difference at market prices of desired and actual purchases.

The twofold aspect of individual disequilibrium implies two individual reaction functions. The first one describes the reaction to the gap between expected prices and market prices. The second one - the reaction to the

[4] This implies that, in case of a negative market excess-demand, some individuals get quantities of commodity greater than desired. "It is a matter of letting one's stomach rather than one's purse absorb the fluctuations" (Shapley and Shubik, 1977, p. 947).

monetary disequilibrium - is less familiar. It expresses the way in which the reaction of the monetary authority modifies individual decisions.

(i) Starting from the observation of the market price at (t) agent h expects a new price at $(t+1)$ according to:

$$p_{hl}(t+1) = \Phi_{hl}(\pi_l(t), \gamma) \tag{11}$$

where γ is a parameter expressing the global reaction of the monetary authority.

(ii) The second function is the reaction of the monetary authority to individual disequilibrium:

$$\underline{\mu_h}(t+1) = \underline{\mu_h}(t) + \alpha_h(s_h(t), \gamma) \tag{12}$$

Both functions define individual reaction to the disequilibrium, hence the market dynamics.

From a general point of view, two remarks are important:

(a) The change of prices is endogenous to the model since it is induced by the change of individual decisions as a consequence of individual disequilibria. Prices change because individuals change their decisions. This is in sharp contrast with the Walrasian rule according to which one must introduce a fictitious agent, the well-known auctioneer, in order to change prices. We conclude that, contrary to a well-established tradition, the auctioneer is not a necessary consequence of the competitive hypothesis, *i.e.* the price-taker hypothesis. In ourmodel, the agents calculate their actions assuming that the prices they anticipate do not depend on their own actions. Nevertheless, the auctioneer is absent. His presence in the Walrasian general equilibrium theory must be related to the failure of this theory to explain the price formation.

(b) The market dynamics can *a priori* take any form, due to the variety of the reaction functions on which it depends. Accordingly, monetary regulation will play a crucial role. In general, it may shape arbitrarily individual reactions by modifying monetary constraints in an appropriate way.

This is an interesting property by comparison with general equilibrium. Sonnenschein has shown that, even if the utility functions are well-behaved, any relationship between prices and aggregate excess demand may be obtained. In our model, depending on the behaviour of the monetary authority, such an indetermination exists between prices and individual excess demand. It follows that one can find a particular behaviour of the monetary authority such that a well-behaved relationship between prices and the individual excess-demands can be derived. As a consequence, a well-behaved relationship between prices and the aggregate excess demand will exist.

4. HISTORICAL BACKGROUND

The theory of a market economy sketched above combines two main ideas:

- market prices result from individual decisions concerning *quantities* only (goods proposed for sale and means of payment spent for purchase),

- market adjustment is made of all modifications in actions of individual agents reacting to perceived disequilibria, namely to gaps between expected (parametric) prices and realised market prices.

Such a view about market is monetary in essence. The use of means of payment is a necessary condition for the economy to be effectively decentralised with coherent prices. Two kinds of adjustments seem *a priori* able to play the role of market forces: quantities or prices adjustment. But, under perfect competition only the first one makes sense since prices are beyond agents' control. A retrospective view on the history of the economic thought shows that the idea of an adjustment through quantities only belongs to Classical tradition as exemplified by Smith in the *Wealth of nations.*

Interestingly enough, a market mechanism very close to Cantillon's rule can be found in chapter 7:

"The market price of every particular commodity is regulated by the proportion between the quantity which is actually brought to market, and the demand of those who are willing to pay the natural price of the commodity, or the whole value of the rent, labour and profit, which must be paid in order to bring it thither." (Smith, 1976, p. 73)

Had Smith clearly defined *effectual demand* in money terms, he would have produced a full-fledged monetary theory of market. But it is obviously not the case and Smith favoured real prices (labour commanded) against money prices.

This does not however prevent his theory from being of special interest in our perspective. Equilibrium, and its corollary disequilibrium, appears to be very different of the modern one, built on Walrasian foundations. Smith's notion of equilibrium make sense for individuals - equality between realised and expected price - more than for markets. Accordingly, reactions to disequilibrium can be defined at the level of individual agents and not at the level of markets (thanks to the rule determining market prices, quantities brought to market are sold in any case). Agents modify the quantities they bring to the next market, maximising profit or revenues. Market mechanism described in the quotation above determine new market prices. Therefore, there is no need for an auctioneer. It is that very notion of equilibrium which is at the core of the model above.

A process of adjustment through quantities only is also to be found in Marshall's writings where disequilibrium is defines as the gap between two evaluations: that of the consumer (demand price) and that of the producer (supply price). Market price being equal to demand price, producers have to change the level of production according to the difference between the market and the normal rate of profit.

Such a process of adjustment is present in Walras's tâtonnement when production is considered. The difference between the selling price and the cost of production is responsible for the changes in composition and level of production. But this process is not the only one. It is combined with the price adjustment in which intervention of an auctioneer seems inescapable. Walras's market dynamics is composite. Morishima called it a "cross-dual adjustment of prices":

"(i) the price of a commodity (or factor) is raised or lowered whenever there is a positive or negative demand for that commodity (or factor) (ii) the output of a commodity is expanded or reduced whenever the excess of its price over its cost of production is positive or negative" (Morishima, 1977, p.59).

The "cross-dual adjustment of prices" is taken again by modern Classics who try to rehabilitate Classical tradition (see for example Duménil and Lévy). If adjustment in quantities can be easily accounted for in terms of individual economic calculus, it is not so for adjustment in prices. The only possibility to escape the non-desirable auctioneer seems to assume away perfect competition and to consider agents as price-makers. This amounts to leaving the battle field on which value theories traditionally confront each other, namely question of the working of the market as a decentralised and anonymous procedure of co-ordination between individuals determining prices and individual allocations. Instead, emphasis tends to be put on a problematic asymptotic global stability.

Whatever the interest of studying imperfect competition may be - it is great indeed - it prevents modern Classics from exhibiting general results, a feature common to general equilibrium theory as well. Imperfect competition has not yet proven to be an ideal place for general theorems.

The fact that such a state of affairs seems well accepted both by neoclassical and by classical economists comes from a sort of consensus inside the profession on the criticism Arrow addressed more than twenty-five years ago to general equilibrium under perfect competition.

Arrow's formulation is well-known:

"It is not explained whose decision it is to change prices (...) Each individual participant in the economy is suppose to take prices as given and determine his choice as to purchases and sales accordingly; there is no one left over whose job it is to make a decision on price" (Arrow, 1959, p.43).

This point is now a common place. Arrow suggested to explore the vast area of imperfect competition, a proposition perfectly sensible for many reasons. Realism is the first one: markets in the real world seem very far from perfect competition. The search for generality is a second one: perfect competition is a special case where there exists no strategic interactions between agents. A third one is, as Arrow himself indicated, that even under perfect competition, any agent in disequilibrium is in a situation where he has to anticipate reactions of other agents to his own behaviour.

Despite the general agreement on Arrow's position, it seems to be misleading. The traditional - ritual? - criticism about the auctioneer hides a more fundamental weakness of general equilibrium theory. It is not the perfect competition assumption which requires that prices have to be announced and changed by an auctioneer. It is rather the absence of a *market mechanism*, as we have seen above, which makes an auctioneer unavoidable.

The absence of a market mechanism in general equilibrium theory makes an auctioneer necessary but not sufficient. Without an auctioneer, it is true that prices could not be modified and equilibrium allocations could not be reached (the auctioneer besides moving prices must act as a clearing house equilibrium prices once determined). But, even with an auctioneer, it is still not possible to determine *market prices*. What general equilibrium theory deals with are only *parametric* prices which are arbitrary (because auctioneer's coefficients of reaction are undetermined) except for equilibrium prices which are those parametric prices for which aggregate excess-demand simultaneously vanish. Even in that special case, prices are not market prices properly speaking since they are not the direct outcome of individual actions, but only the indirect consequence of the rule followed by the auctioneer. Equilibrium prices are nothing but stationary parametric prices.

Confusion between market and parametric prices makes one believe that any change in prices must be accounted for by the auctioneer. Changes in market prices over time are due to anonymous forces of the market and not to any auctioneer. "Anonymous forces" are all individuals' actions in quantities which generate market prices through a market mechanism *à la Cantillon.*

Instead of criticising the perfect competition assumption as responsible for the auctioneer, it would have been better to verify whether general equilibrium theory, with or without auctioneer, is able or not to account for market prices.

The contemporary situation is the result of a complex historical evolution. The main stages are the following:

(i) separation by Ricardo of monetary theory from price theory;

(ii) the domination of the Currency school according to which the quantity of money is the independent variable and the monetary prices are the dependent ones;

(iii) acceptation by the profession of Walras' theory of price-adjustment (in the exchange economy); as a consequence every possible difference between expected and effective price disappears ;

(iv) acceptation by the modern Classics of the approach in terms of real wealth, *i.e.* of the classical tradition on the primacy of production relationships over market relationships.

We do not deal with all these points. Some of them are well known. It is more interesting to show some fundamental shortcomings in the modern treatment of the law of supply and demand. The elimination of money makes impossible to conceive of a decentralised price-adjustment market by market. As a matter of fact, the usual prices-adjustment is incompatible with a decentralisation of changes in market prices. Let briefly show this point.

To-day the law of supply and demand is identified with the variation of the price of a commodity according to the sign of the excess demand of this commodity. In order to act on the excess demands (determined in real terms) the prices must be real prices. That is the case, for instance, if they belong to the n-dimensional simplex, *i.e.* the real price of commodity $p_i/\Sigma p_i$. In the case of, say, an excess-demand in the market for *i* the law reads:

$$p_i(t+1)/\sum_i p_i(t+1) > p_i(t)/\sum_i p_i(t) \qquad (13)$$

The auctioneer cannot obtain such a result but if the decentralisation of price-adjustments is eliminated. If each price $p_i(t+1)$ (measured in abstract or monetary units of account) is modified independently from the other prices $\Sigma p_i(t+1)$ may not fulfil the condition (13). In order to avoid this, change of each particular price must be decided by taking into account the variations of all other prices, which is equivalent to a centralisation of the price-adjustment.

A real price is always defined in terms of a *numéraire*. If the *numéraire* is a commodity (or a linear combination of commodities) a change in a real price concerns several markets. Can the adoption of an external *numéraire* avoid this difficulty? The reply is negative if we accept the Currency school principles which is the case to-day in the modern theory of money. According to the quantity theory we have:

$$\sum_{l} p_l(t)q_l(t) = VM(t) \qquad (14)$$

where V is a constant and the $q_l(t)$ are given independently from $M(t)$ which is exogenous. This "constraint" imposes a centralisation: each $p_l(t)$ must be determined in order to fulfil (14) and consequently is not independent from the other $p_l(t)$'s.

Instead of the quantity theory we can accept the Banking school principle according to which the quantity of means of payment adjusts itself to prices expressed in money units. In this case, a formulation of the law of supply and demand in terms of money prices would be possible. It is obvious that the level of M must be controlled (the set of prices must be bounded). This implies a sort of centralisation. But, contrary to the centralisation of price changes, the money centralisation is legitimate as an external (and necessary) complement to the working of decentralised markets.

Even modified to take into account the role of money in decentralisation, the usual formulation of the law of supply and demand is not quite satisfactory. Market prices are an anonymous result of markets and not an effect an auctioneer's decision. In the model sketched above, changes in monetary prices are related to the individual adjustments of quantities. Such changes are a result and not a condition of the working of markets.

Historically the approach in terms of "market mechanism" is related to Marx's general approach. For him,

"The insufficiency of Ricardo's analysis of the magnitude of value - and his analysis is by far the best - [is the following:] classical political economy in fact nowhere distinguishes explicitly and with a great awareness between labour as it appears in the value of a product, and the same labour as it appears in the product's use value" (Marx, 1976, p. 173).

Starting from this distinction Marx analyses the "dual character of the labour embodied in commodities". He comments: "On the one hand, all labour is an expenditure of human labour-power, in the physiological sense, and it is in this quality of being equal, or abstract, human labour that it forms the value of commodities. On the other hand, all labour is an expenditure of human labour-power in a particular form and with a definite aim, and it is this quality of being concrete useful labour that it produces use-values" (Marx, 1976, p. 137). The first one is the "equal or abstract human labour ", the second is the "concrete useful labour ". As stressed by Marx, the basic difference between market society and primitive community or planned economy is that only in the first one, decision to produce or to work is taken privately. In such a case, the social evaluation of the commodities is obtained by means of their exchange on markets, *i. e.* through the formation of exchange values or fractions of social labour corresponding to each particular producer or private labour. This is what we have called a market mechanism. Ricardo does not distinguish these two kinds of labour. As a consequence, he calculates the exchange values according to quantities of labour which are to be interpreted either are technical data or as waged labour. Modern Classics have taken again such a view along with algebrist Marxists.

Marx does not provide any solution to this problem. He is however conscious of the deep difficulty which he expressed as a (non dialectical) contradiction.

Quantities of social labour do not appear as such but during the exchange process when individual labours loose their special features. Social labour is not given *a priori*. It is an outcome of exchange. As Marx put it: "on the one hand, commodities must enter the exchange process as materialised universal labour-time, on the other hand, the labour-time of individuals becomes materialised universal labour-time only as the result of the exchange process" (K. Marx, 1970, p. 45). Social labour is the condition and the result of the exchange.

As a matter of fact, in his analysis of the market economy, Marx adopts Ricardo's solution. An example is the marxian schemes of reproduction where the exchange values are dependent from technical conditions of production and independent from the quantities produced.

The concept of market mechanism provides a solution to Marx's problem (see Benetti and Cartelier, 1994). This solution is a development of a central aspect of Marx's theory, and also a basis for a possible alternative to the classical theory, Marx's positive theory and Walras's theory.

REFERENCES

Arrow, K. (1959), "Toward a theory of price adjustment" in *The Allocation of Economic Resources*, M. Abramovitz et al. (ed), Stanford University Press.

Benetti, C. and Cartelier, J., (1994), "Money, Form and Determination of Value", *International Conference in Bergamo, december 1994*, in R. Bellofiore (ed), *Marxian Economics: A Reappraisal*, vol. 1, London, Mac Millan, 1998.

Cantillon, R., (1755), *Essai sur la nature du commerce en général*, INED, Paris, 1952.

Dubey, P. and Shapley, L. (1994) "Noncooperative general exchange with a continuum of traders: Two models", *Journal of Mathematical Economics*, vol. 23, pp. 253-293.

Duménil, G. and Lévy, D. (1993) *The Economics of the Profit Rate*, Edward Elgar.

Fisher, F. M., (1983), *Disequilibrium foundations of equilibrium economics*, Cambridge University Press.

Hellwig, M., (1993) "The challenge of monetary theory", *European Economic Review*, vol. 37, 2/3, pp. 215-242.

K. Marx, *A Contribution to the Critique of Political Economy*, Progress Publishers, Moscow, 1970 [first edition 1859].

Marx, K., (1976), *Capital*, Penguin Books,[first edition 1867].

Morishima, M. (1977), *Walras's economics*, Cambridge University Press.

Ostroy, J. M. and Starr, R. M, (1974), "Money and the Decentralization of Exchange", *Econometrica*, vol. 42, 6, reprint in *General equilibrium models of monetary economies*, ed. by Starr, Academic Press, 1989, pp. 149-169.

Sahi, S. and Yao, S., (1989), "The noncooperative equilibria of a trading economy with complete markets and consistent prices", *Journal of Mathematical Economics*, vol. 18, pp. 325-346.

Shapley, L. and Shubik, M. (1977), "Trade Using One Commodity as a Means of Payment", *Journal of Political Economy*, 85, 5, pp. 937- 968.

Shubik, M. (1990) "A Game Theoretic Approach to the Theory of Money and Financial Institutions', chap. 5 of *Handbook of Monetary Economics*, vol. 1, ed. by Friedman, B.M. and Hahn, F. H., Elsevier Science Publishers, pp. 171-219.

Smith, A.(1976), *An Inquiry into the Nature and Causes of the Wealth of Nations*, Clarendon Press, Oxford, [first edition 1776].

SAMUELSON; A PERSONAL RECOLLECTION

*Frank Hahn**

ABSTRACT

Fortythree years association with Paul A. Samuelson as an economist of a very high order and a person of great sparklin and fine qualities is given in this paper briefly.

In 1956 I received an invitation to be visiting professor at MIT. I was delighted not only because I was rather young for this kind of invitation but even more because there was now a chance of getting to know Paul Samuelson. His fame in England after the war was very high and he dominated economic theory. I thought then and think now that this was a correct perception of his contribution.

I had seen him once before when, more or less just after the war, he gave a public lecture at the LSE. It elaborated on the welfare chapter in the "Foundations" and was delivered in a Socratic manner. For instance, he asked Ralph Turvey (then in his early twenties) whether Pareto efficiency was sufficient for a Welfare optimum and added "I ask the youngest here since they have no reputation to lose!." The interesting thing is that after the lapse of fifty years there are many professional economists who either could not answer this question correctly, or would never dream of asking it. This brief encounter had whetted my appetite and I was keen to have more.

* Churchill College, Cambridge, United Kingdom.

When I got to MIT I was not disappointed. Samuelson sparkled not only in seminars but at all times, especially at the departmental lunch table where he was totally dominant not only in an economics debate but in reminiscing about all sorts of famous people. As he had done in his LSE lecture he would suddenly swoop with a question and it was not always comfortable to be the victim, But he never seemed to take delight in catching one wanting and it was obvious that the style of debate had been developed by the sheer energy and joy of the chase.

However he was also following the rules of being American, that is, to be competitive well beyond what I had been used to in England. Unlike many young academics of today however this was purely intellectual competition, he never had any need to advertise! Yet there was an element of showmanship especially when it came to mathematics or physics. That showmanship was solidly based on knowledge and so justified, for it was almost always instructive. For instance I learned that a saddle point in phase space was characterised by "catenary" paths, a description which was new to me. However more important were the many connections which he made between economics and mathematical results, for example in the "Foundations" the use of the Le Chatelier Principle to study the effects of further constraints on the responsiveness of choice to changes in price. But there were very many others.

Looking back at these lunches during that and later visits I find it remarkable how little political and world events figured in our discussions. McCarthy was at his loudest during my first visit and Vietnam was occupying many of us in England during later visits. But neither were discussed. That naturally led me to wonder where Paul stood in these matters. (Notice that by this time the evident lack of standing on his dignity led me to think of him and address him as Paul). I questioned him on McCarthy on one occasion. It was clear that his heart and mind were in the right place. Vietnam I never discussed with him and his silence on that issue was attacked by Ed Kuh. I was told later that Paul argued that his usefulness to the anti-Vietnam side would be much reduced if he took a public stance. My own view is that public affairs just interested him only mildly if at all.

Paul did at a later stage write a column which alternated weekly between him and Milton Friedman. For a time he also contributed an article at the beginning of each year on the outlook for the US economy to the Financial Times. But all that was applied economics and not, as I recall, politics. Yet there was a political element since Paul was cast as the Keynesian. Although each piece was headed by a photograph of the author, readers began to mix up the two gurus. Once when Paul and I were waiting for our luggage after crossing the Atlantic, an excited gentleman rushed up to him crying "Aren't you Milton Friedman?" Paul repudiated this suggestion some what frostily.

In one respect he seemed "un-American". I had got used to the way American graduates were taught economics. First there was a close relation between textbook and lecture. Assignments were as likely as not to be taken from the author of the text. Second the teacher took whatever he taught very seriously as established knowledge and in general was a devotee of Friedman's "as if" methodology. I discovered that nothing of the sort was true of Paul with whom I was once told to give some theory seminars. Instead of teaching directly he thought aloud, and instead of systematic exposition he followed his thoughts irrespective of whether everyone was keeping up with him. I liked and enjoyed this, however I admit that the method reversed the usual procedure too much. Yet the latter also has a cost: American students seem to believe what they are taught which is not always a good thing in our subject.

For the forty three years that I have known him Paul never stopped writing and making important contributions. Some of these, like the overlapping generations model, have been of great and lasting significance and his late work on option pricing showed that his mind was as sharp as ever. But almost everything was grist for his mill: Pasinetti on savings and

Sraffa on the factor price frontier are just two examples. He also taught us the non-substitution theorem which made sense of a number of confused claims. He together with Solow and Dorfman quite early on squeezed what there was to be squeezed for economic theory out of linear programming. Notably the Turnpike theorem (which however needed some amendment). But this is not the place to list Paul's achievements which in any case must be well known. Rather I want to emphasise how exceptional he is and how lucky we are to have such a colleague.

All of this was combined with great kindness. On our first visit to MIT he and Marion, his then wife, entertained us and there was never any hint of condescension. (Of course most MIT colleagues were extremely kind and my wife and I formed lasting friendships especially with Bob and Bobby Solow). Later when England had exchange controls and I needed to go to Berkeley Paul provided me with dollars. In short he has been a great and admired friend.

MONOTONE PRICE MOVEMENTS: A NON-EUCLIDEAN APPROACH

Christian Bidard[1] and *Ian Steedman*[2]

ABSTRACT

It is shown that with an *appropriate* definition of the angle between the price vector at a generic rate of profit, $p(r)$, and that at the maximum rate of profit, $p(R)$, the angle always decreases as r rises towards R. However, the 'angle' required to obtain this nice result is the familiar Euclidean angle only in some special cases.

1. INTRODUCTION

An increase in the real wage lowers the rate of profit. It also has a differentiated effect according to the industry, since the costs in a labour-intensive industry are more affected than those in a capital-intensive industry. Therefore an adjustment of prices, with a higher relative price for the product of the labour-intensive industry, might seem to be required to reestablish a uniform profitability: relative prices change with distribution, apart from the exceptional case of a uniform organic composition of capital. But the laws governing prices are not as simple as just suggested: since the commodities enter into the production of other commodities, the inputs to a capital-intensive industry may themselves be labour intensive, etc. The classification of industries as « capital intensive » or « labour intensive » is itself relative and depends on distribution.

---

[1] University of Paris X-Nanterre, department of economics, Nanterre, France.

[2] Manchester Metropolitan University, department of economics, Manchester,Great Britain.

JEL Classification : C60, D40, D46, D57.

The movement of relative prices with distribution is indeed complicated. However we intend to show that, from a certain point of view, relative prices vary in a monotone way. Our calculations are reduced to a minimum, so that the difficulty lies only in the conceptualization of the proposed point of view (we do not pretend that it is uniquely correct: for a few other results, see Bidard and Krause, 1996, Bidard and Steedman, 1996, and Steedman, 1999). It implies an unexpected reference to a notion of non-Euclidean angle. This seemingly roundabout approach is the shortest way to obtain clear-cut results which can be interpreted in more conventional terms.

Our main result is that the « angle » between the vectors of relative prices at a given rate of profit r and at the maximum rate of profit R decreases monotonically when r increases. That statement only holds true, however, for an adequate notion of « angle ».

2. THE PROBLEM

Let there be n commodities which are reproduced by means of themselves and homogeneous labour. The ith method of production produces one unit of commodity i by means of quantities a_{ij} of input j ($i, j = 1,\ldots, n$) and l_i of labour. The inputs are therefore represented by a semipositive square matrix A and a semipositive labour vector l. For a given rate of profit r, the price-and-wage vector $(p(r),w)$ is the solution to

$$(1+r)Ap + wl = p. \tag{1}$$

It is unique up to a factor and semipositive if the rate of profit is smaller than the maximum rate of profit R. The maximum rate R is associated with a zero wage, and scalar $(1+R)^{-1}$ is the Perron-Frobenius root of matrix A:

$$(1+R)Ap(R) = p(R).$$

When r increases, the relative prices start from the labour vector l (for $r = -1$, which is formally possible), go through the vector of labour values $(I - A)^{-1}\,\ell$ (at $r = 0$) and, finally, reach position $p(R)$ which is independent of l. For $n = 2$ commodities, the relatives prices p_1 / p_2 vary monotonically; for $n \geq 3$ no such rule exists and monotonicity is even counter-intuitive in some numerical examples.

The Perron-Frobenius root has maximal modulus among all real and complex eigenvalues. In the complex plane, Figure 1 represents the dominant real eigenvalue I, other real (point B_i) and complex (point C_j) eigenvalues, and a point M, whose abscissa is $\lambda = (1+r)^{-1}$ with $(1+r)^{-1} > (1+R)^{-1}$. An immediate calculation shows that the ratios MI / MB_i and MI / MC_j decrease when M moves to the left, i.e. when the rate of profit increases. This is the only calculation required in the present paper, the remainder being a question of definitions and concepts.

Figure 1:

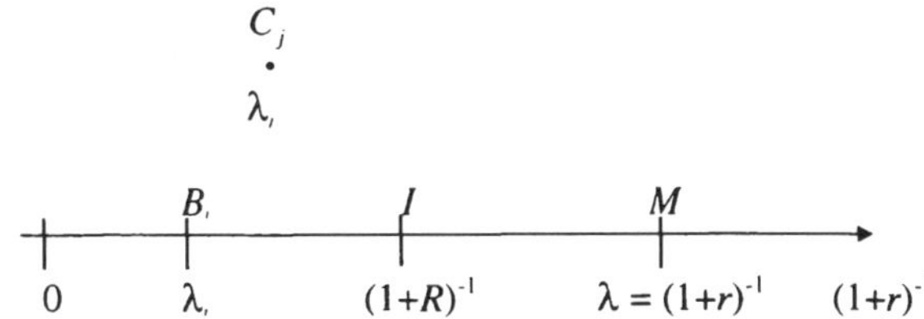

3. SIMPLE RESULTS ON EUCLIDEAN ANGLES

The origin of the difficulty in understanding the movement of prices is the interaction between industries. Let us first eliminate that phenomenon and examine what happens when every commodity is only produced by means of itself and labour. The input matrix is then diagonal: $A = \text{diag}\,(a_{11}, \ldots, a_{ii}, \ldots, a_{nn})$. For $r < R$ the price vector $p(r)$ solution to equation (1) is proportional to $\left(\ldots, p_i = l_i / \left[(1+r)^{-1} - a_{ii}\right], \ldots\right)$ or, using Figure 1 and since a_{ii} is an eigenvalue of A, to $\left(\ldots, \ p_i = l_i / MB_i, \ldots\right)$. Let a_{11} be the dominant eigenvalue. For the maximum rate of profit the price vector is proportional to $(1, 0, \ldots, 0)$. The angle between $p(r)$ and $p(R)$ is defined by means of the inner product (the inner product between vectors x and y is denoted $< x, y >$; therefore $< x, x > = \|x\|^2$):

$$\cos^2\left(p(r), p(R)\right) = \frac{< p(r), p(R) >^2}{\|p(r)\|^2 \|p(R)\|^2} = \frac{p_1^2(r)}{\sum_i p_i^2(r)}. \qquad (2)$$

Lemma 1. Let matrix A be diagonal. The Euclidean angle between $p(r)$ and $p(R)$ decreases as r increases ($r \leq R$).

Proof. According to formula (2)

$$\cos^{-2}\left(p(r), p(R)\right) = \sum_i \left(p_i^2 / p_1^2\right) = \sum_i \left(l_i / l_1\right)^2 \left(MI / MB_i\right)^2.$$

When r increases, ratio MI / MB_i decreases and, therefore, so does the angle. ◆

Lemma 2 reintroduces relationships between industries (A^T denotes the transpose of A).

Lemma 2. Lemma 1 also holds if A is symmetric ($A = A^T$).

Proof. A symmetric matrix is diagonalizable in a (real) orthonormal basis $\boldsymbol{B}$. When the labour vector and the prices are decomposed in that basis, the price vector is written $p(r) = \left[I - (1+r)D\right]^{-1} L$. Since basis B is orthonormal, the angle between vectors $p(r)$ and $p(R)$ can still be calculated by means of formula (2), the components being those obtained by the decomposition in $\boldsymbol{B}$. The calculation made in the proof of Lemma 1 is unchanged (a slight difference is that the labour vector might admit negative components L_i in $\boldsymbol{B}$, which does not affect the result). ◆

4. THE CONCEPT OF NON-EUCLIDEAN ANGLE

The results stated in Lemmas 1 and 2 are satisfactory... not the assumptions! There is no economic reason for the input matrix to be diagonal or otherwise symmetric. Nor may one hope to obtain significant extensions of the conclusion: counter-examples with locally increasing Euclidean angles between $p(r)$ and $p(R)$ are easily built. It is the very idea of Euclidean angle which is at stake. Assume a change in the physical unit of the ith commodity, say, the new unit is half of the previous one. The economic system itself is not affected. But the ith component of every price vector is halved and this affects the Euclidean angle between the vectors. The argument shows that the Euclidean angle, even if in common use, is not an absolute reference. It invites us to substitute a more adequate measure. The abstract procedure we follow avoids any additional calculation and is based on a reinterpretation of Lemma 2.

Here we meet two difficulties of different natures: one is conceptual and stems from the very the notion of angle; the other is technical and comes from the fact that real matrices may admit complex eigenvalues. In order to isolate the main problem, we delay the examination of the second difficulty until Section 6. In other words, our present aim is to find an adequate generalization of the monotonicity property to the family F of matrices which are diagonalizable and admit real eigenvalues only.

The basic principle is to reinterpret the proof of Lemma 2 by using the general, even if unusual, notion of positive quadratic form as a ground for the notion of angle. The idea is known in mathematics and physics, but rarely used in economics. The method we follow is rather roundabout and abstract but, after the detour, we will come back to simpler interpretations.

The 'naive' interpretation of the basic formula

$$< u, v > = \|u\| \, \|v\| \, cos(u, v) \qquad (3)$$

used in relationship (2) starts from the 'intuitive' notions of distance and angle. Then formula (3) is a definition of the inner product. The 'scholarly' construction proceeds the other way round. The very first notion is that of inner product; then the norm of a vector is defined as $\| u \| = < u, u >^{1/2}$ and, finally, formula (3) is used as a definition of the angle between two vectors. We follow this procedure. There exist two ways to extend it and, therefore, define non-Euclidean angles[3]. These ways are basically equivalent:

- The inner product of two vectors is usually defined as

$$< u, v > = \sum_{i=1}^{n} u_i v_i = u^T I \, v \qquad \text{(I = identity matrix)} \qquad (4)$$

Apart from linearity and symmetry, its important properties are:

[3] By non-Euclidean angles, we mean that the measure of the angles differs from the one commonly used from Euclid to P. A. Samuelson. The construction remains Euclidean in the generalized sense adopted by modern mathematicians.

$$< u, u > \geq 0 \quad < u, u > = 0 \Leftrightarrow u = 0 \qquad | < u, v > | \leq \| u \| \ \| v \| \tag{5}$$

The first two properties are used to define a norm as $\| u \| = < u, u >^{1/2}$; the third one (Cauchy's inequality) ensures the triangular inequality ($\| u + v \| \leq \| u \| + \|v\|$) and the existence of a scalar $\theta = (u, v)$ that satisfies equality (3). Now if, instead of (4), the inner product is defined as

$$< u, v > = u^T N v \tag{6}$$

where N is a given positive definite matrix, relations (5) still hold. Therefore, a scalar θ_N, different from θ, is defined in a similar way. We say that θ_N is the measure of a non-Euclidean angle between u and v.

- Alternatively, it is usually said that the standard formula (4) only holds if the basis in which vectors u and v are decomposed is orthonormal. But let us choose an *arbitrary* basis in R^n. After decomposition of the vectors in this basis, we define their inner product by means of formula (4). Then properties (5) hold and an angle θ_N is defined by means of equality (3). *Ex post*, since the inner product of two vectors of the basis is zero (Hint: apply formula (4) to these vectors), the basis appears as orthogonal *for that measure* and, even, orthonormal.

Let us apply this general construction to our problem. More precisely, we follow the second approach. Its successive steps are:

1. By assumption, there exists a basis $\boldsymbol{B}$ of R^n made of n real eigenvectors of matrix A. Say that the first vector of the basis is the Perron-Frobenius eigenvector of A.

2. Consider any vector in R^n, in particular the price-vector $p(r) = (I - (1+r)A)^{-1}l$ associated with the rate of profit r. This vector is decomposed in the basis $\boldsymbol{B}$, its components being $(p_1(r), ..., P_n(r))$ ($P_i(r)$ is not the price of the ith commodity).

3. Let the angle between $p(r)$ and $p(R)$ be defined by means of equality (3). Since the components of $p(R)$ are (1, 0, ..., 0) by construction, the simplified formula becomes

$$\cos^2 \left(p(r), p(R)\right)_N = p_1^2(r) / \left[\sum_i p_i^2(r)\right] \tag{7}$$

Then property:

Theorem 1. The N-angle between $p(r)$ and $p(R)$ decreases when r increases.

holds, because the formulas (2) and (7) are identical, so that the proof of Lemma 1 can be repeated.

Let us give an algebraic illustration of Theorem 1. The following calculation makes reference to the left eigenvectors of A, which have not been considered up to now. Their introduction is unnecessary but natural, because the left vector u_i associated with eigenvalue λ_i is orthogonal due to the right vectors v_j for all eigenvalues λ_j, $j \neq i$. Therefore, when a vector x is decomposed into basis $\boldsymbol{B} = \{v_j, j = 1,\ldots,n\}$ as $x = \sum_j x_j v_j$, its ith component x_i in the basis is obtained as the inner product $<x, u_i>$. Consider the matrix

$$10A = \begin{bmatrix} 2 & 2 & 4 \\ 3 & 5 & 0 \\ 0 & 2 & 6 \end{bmatrix}$$

The roots of A are (0.8, 0.3, 0.2) and the corresponding left-hand vectors are $(1, 2, 2)/3$, $(3, 1, -4)/\sqrt{26}$ and $(1, 0, -1)/\sqrt{2}$. The Perron-Frobenius right-hand vector is $(1, 1, 1)/\sqrt{3}$, with a maximum profit rate R = 25%. Define $\pi(r) \equiv Np(r)$ and $\lambda \equiv Nl$, where N displays the left-hand vectors of A. Simple calculation shows that the non-Euclidean angle θ_N between $p(r)$ and $p(R)$ is such that

$$\tan^2\theta_N = \left(\frac{\lambda_2}{\lambda_1}\right)^2 \left(\frac{2-8r}{7-3r}\right)^2 + \left(\frac{\lambda_3}{\lambda_1}\right)^2 \left(\frac{2-8r}{8-2r}\right)^2. \tag{8}$$

Provided that λ_2 and λ_3 are not both zero (case $\lambda_2 = \lambda_3 = 0$ corresponds to a labour vector proportional to the Perron-Frobenius eigenvector: then the organic composition is uniform and the relative prices do not change with distribution), it is clear from expression (8) that θ_N declines monotonically as r increases up to 25%.

5. GEOMETRIC INTERPRETATION

Let us descend from these heights of abstraction and propose an interpretation of the result in economic terms. What has been established? First, there are two aspects to the monotonicity property stated in Section 3, *i.e.* concerning the Euclidean angles. For $n = 3$ commodities, consider the family of cones defined by their axis $p(R)$ and a given Euclidean angle (Figure 2).

Figure 2 :
A family of attractive « circular » cones

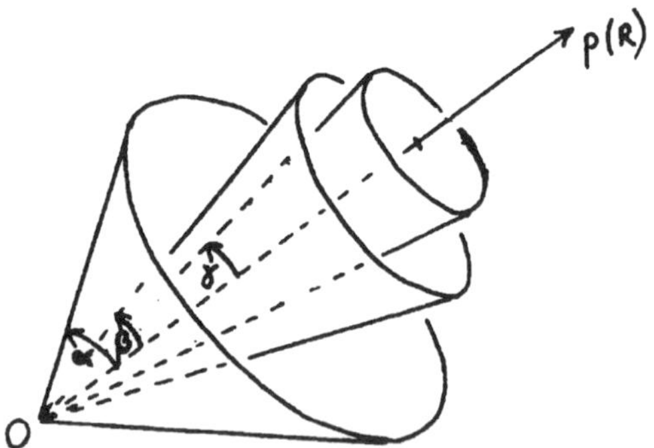

One aspect is that the family is « attractive » once a price curve has entered into a cone, it remains inside it until $r = R$. The other aspect is that every cone is « circular ». For the monotonicity properties we are looking at, the important aspect is the first property, the circular nature of the cones being only a secondary matter. Since, when A is not symmetric, the attractiveness property is lost for circular cones, we will be content if it is maintained for some other simple family of non-circular cones.

This is indeed the result stated in Theorem 1. If matrix A is diagonalizable and admits real eigenvalues, the attractive cones are defined by a constant (non-Euclidean) angle with the axis $p(R)$. What is their exact shape? These cones, which are « circular » *according to the notion of N-angle*, are somewhat distorted according to the familiar Euclidean view. The equation of the cone which makes a given N-angle θ_N with vector $p(R)$ is:

$$< p(R), x >_N = \cos\theta_N \; \|p(R)\|_N \; \|x\|_N = \cos\theta_N \; \|x\|_N \qquad (9)$$

As $p(R)$ is the first vector of B, the explicit algebraic equation of the cone is

$$(x_1)^2 = \cos^2\theta_N \left(\sum_i x_i^2\right) \qquad (10)$$

where the x_i's are the components of vector x in a basis made of the eigenvectors of A. (It is not surprising to find once more formula (2), since the whole endeavour consists in giving a more general interpretation to a unique basic formula.) Knowing the eigenvectors, it is possible to transform equation (10) and write down the algebraic equation of an attractive cone in the natural basis $\{e_1,..., e_n\}$. A quadratic relationship between the natural coordinates is then obtained. This means that, for people wearing Euclidean glasses, the family we have found is a family of quadratic cones.

Let there be $n = 3$ commodities for the sake of simplicity. In order to visualize the movement of relative prices, we may normalize them by choosing a given basket d as numeraire. A normalized price vector is then represented by a point P in the simplex $dp(r) = 1$ (Figure 3). The trace of the attractive cones in a family of attractive conics. As the Greeks knew, the exact shape of these conics depends on the intersection plane, i.e. on the normalization.

Figure 3 :
Traces of attractive « elliptic » cones

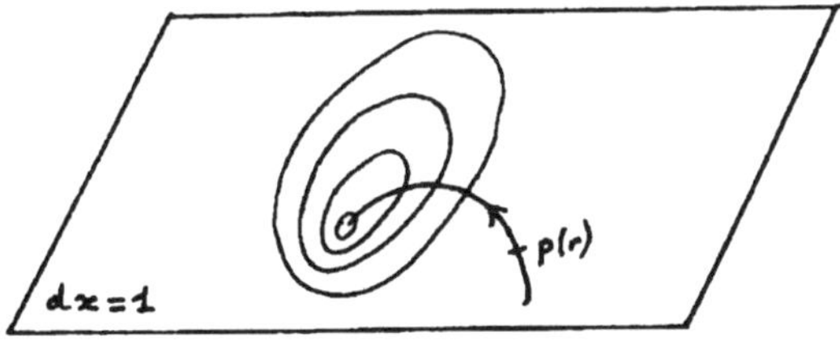

6. EXTENSIONS

Three types of extensions are considered:

1. It has been shown that, for the family F of diagonalizable matrices with real eigenvalues, the N-angle between $p(r)$ and $p(R)$ varies monotonically with r. The notion of N-angle is associated with matrix A. Let us retain it, but consider more generally the N-angle between $p(r)$ and $p(s)$, r and s being two feasible rates of profit. Then it can be shown that the N-angle between $p(r)$ and $p(s)$, $r < s$, is a monotone function of r and s. The principle of the proof is easily understood, once the notion of N-angle is mastered. It consists in decomposing each vector $p(r)$ and $p(s)$ in a basis made of eigenvectors of A (i.e., $p(r) = \sum p_j(r) v_j$, and similarly for $p(s)$), then calculating their N-angle by means of formula

$$\cos^2(p(r), p(s))_N = \left(\sum p_j(r)\, p_j(s)\right)^2 / \left(\sum_j p_j^2(r)\right)\left(\sum_j p_j^2(s)\right) \quad (11)$$

Finally, one calculates the partial derivatives of the second member of equality (11) with respect to r and s (only one calculation is necessary, since the formula is symmetric) in order to check that the N-angle varies monotonically.

2. Assume now that matrix A admits complex eigenvalues. The previous calculations can be generalized. Let us start from the simplest case, which is a direct extension of Lemma 2 to the complex field.

Lemma 3. Let matrix A be normal $\left(AA^T = A^T A\right)$. The Euclidean angle between $p(r)$ and $p(R)$ decreases as r increases ($r \leq R$).

Proof. A normal matrix is diagonalizable in a (complex) unitary basis $B = \{\ldots, f_i, \ldots\}$ (Horn and Johnson, 1990). Given real or complex vectors α and β decomposed in a unitary basis

$$\alpha = \sum_i \alpha_i f_i \text{ and } \beta = \sum_i \beta_i f_i$$

their inner product is defined by formula

$$<\alpha,\beta>=\sum_i \alpha_i \overline{\beta_i} \quad . \tag{12}$$

In particular

$$\|\alpha\| = <\alpha,\alpha>^{1/2} = \left(\sum_i |\alpha_i|^2\right)^{1/2} \text{ and } \|\beta\| =<\beta,\beta>^{1/2}. \tag{13}$$

The Euclidean angle between real vectors is still defined as:

$$\cos(\alpha,\beta) = <\alpha,\beta>/\|\alpha\|\|\beta\|. \tag{14}$$

The only difference from the proof of Lemma 2 is that the diagonalized matrix and the components of the labour vector in the basis B are complex. In geometrical terms (Figure 1) the angle is now obtained as

$$\cos^2(p(r), p(R)) = \sum_i |p_i|^2 \Big/ |p_1|^2 = \sum_i (|L_i|/|L_1|)^2 (MI/MC_i)^2$$

hence the result. ◆

If matrix A is diagonalizable but not normal, the construction seen in Section 4 for the real case can be extended to the complex field. It consists in decomposing the price vectors in a complex basis made of eigenvectors, then calculating their N-inner product and N-norms by formulas (12) and (13) and, finally, their N-angle by expression (14). The result is a real scalar θ_N. The reason why this angle decreases when r increases is that, from the non-Euclidean point of view, the basis made of the eigenvectors of A is unitary and, therefore, all happens as if matrix A were normal. No supplementary calculations are required, since they are the mere reproduction of those made in the normal case. The attractive cones thus defined are still of the elliptic type. To sum up, Theorem 1, which has been enunciated in Section 4 under the restrictive hypothesis that the eigenvalues of A are real, also holds if they are complex. The other restriction concerning the possibility to diagonalize the matrix is statistically non significant and might also be dropped. Theorem 1 has therefore a general value, provided that it is adequately interpreted.

3. Finally, consider the N-angle between $p(r)$ and $p(s)$ when A admits complex eigenvalues. Its cosine is defined by

$$\cos^2(p(r), p(s))_N = \left(\sum p_j(r)\,\bar{p}_j(s)\right)^2 / \left(\sum \|p_j\|^2\right) \left(\sum \|p_j(s)\|^2\right) \tag{15}$$

The principle of the calculation is the same as for matrices with real eigenvalues. This time, however, complications occur: due to the interactions between complex numbers and their conjugates, the derivative with respect to r of the second member of (15) is much more intricate than it was for (11). It can be shown that the derivative has a constant sign (therefore, the variations of the N-angle are monotone) if there is at most *one* pair of complex eigenvalues. With two pairs the sign becomes unclear, though we conjecture that the monotonicity property holds in all generality.

7. CONCLUSION

If the input-output matrix A is normal then the Euclidean angle between $p(r)$ and $p(R)$ falls monotonically as r rises to R. Unfortunately, there is no reason why A should be normal and this nice result fails to hold in general. However, one can redefine the angle, in a way completely determined by the characteristic vectors of A, so as to restore the montonicity result in terms of the newly defined angle. The behaviour of relative prices as the rate of profit changes is thus simpler and more systematic than sometimes seems to be thought.

REFERENCES

Bidard, C. and Krause, U. (1996), A Monotonicity Law for Relative Prices, *Economic Theory*, 7, 51-56.

Bidard, C. and Steedman, I. (1996), Monotonic Movements of Price Vectors, *Economic Issues*, 1, 41-44 (and: editor's corrections in *Economic Issues*, 2, 85-6).

Horn, R.A. and Johnson, C.R. (1990), *Matrix Analysis* (Cambridge, Cambridge University Press).

Sraffa, P. (1960), *Production of Commodities by Means of Commodities. Prelude to a Critique of Economic Theory* (Cambridge, Cambridge University Press).

Steedman, I. (1999), Values do Follow a Simple Rule!, *Economic Systems Research*, 11, 5-14.

THE ROLE OF SAMUELSON'S *ECONOMICS* IN THE PRODUCTION OF A KEYNESIAN ECONOMIST

*Michael Emmett Brady**

ABSTRACT:

The effective role played by Samuelson's textbook, *Economics*, in presenting a version of Keynes' theoretical model that could be taught to, and grasped by, introductory - intermediate economics students can't be overestimated. This effectiveness is demonstrated by examining the role this textbook played in the author's intellectual development and understanding of the paradox of thrift.

1. INTRODUCTION

This paper examines Samuelson's success in integrating a valuable, reconstructed version of Keynes' original 1936 model into the principles of macroeconomics course that an undergraduate student could grasp and understand. The absolute need for such a reformulation of Keynes' original construction was due to the fact that Keynes meant for his book to be a contribution to pure economic theory which would rival the contribution of his colleague, A.C. Pigou, who had come out with his *The Theory of Unemployment* in 1933. Keynes never meant for his General Theory to be used as a college or university teaching text.

The technical analysis in Pigou's and Keynes' books requires the reader to have a good working knowledge of basic differential calculus, optimization theory, intermediate microeconomic theory (elasticity analysis), as well as the new terminology used by Keynes in conveying his theoretical approach.

---

* Department of Mathematics, Statistics and Economics, University of California, U.S.A.

No introductory or intermediate college or university student, in 1936 or 1996, could be expected to obtain an understanding of Keynes' theory without some degree of simplification and modification.[1] Samuelson succeeded in accomplishing this task while at the same time giving the anti-Keynes side.

The paper consists of this introduction, plus four additional sections. Section 2 examines the role of Samuelson's text in producing a Keynesian economist. Although there are many possible descriptions of what it means to be a Keynesian, the operational definition used is that a Keynesian economist is one who does not accept the argument that economic systems have operating within them internally a naturally self-correcting, self-adjusting price mechanism that will automatically maintain or bring the economic system back to the boundary of the PPF. There is no Invisible Hand. Three particular parts of Samuelson's textbook played an important role in the author's intellectual development. The impact of each part is discussed.

Section 3 argues that the 45° Cross Model is pedagogically superior to the AD-AS Model. The AD-AS Model is, in fact, a modified version of the 45° Cross Model. However, the problem of equilibrating Investment with Savings at a point on the boundary of the PPF, static or dynamic, is swept "under the rug". The importance of exhibiting graphically the paradox of Thrift is one of the 45° Cross Model's important features.

---

[1] It should be noted that while the author has a very positive view of Samuelson's presentation of Keynes' theoretical *conclusions* in his *Economics* textbook, he strongly disagrees with some of Samuelson's negative critical comments about the technical and analytic skills used or exhibited by Keynes in the presentation of the theoretical argument in the General Theory. Keynes, unfortunately, presented his conclusions, in Chapter 3 of the General Theory first, while waiting until Chapters 19, 20, and 21 to present his technical argument.

Keynes himself must have realized that the *form* his analysis took in the GT failed to make any impact. However, Keynes was an *idea* man. He wanted his *ideas* to get through. And they did, not only in Samuelson's path breaking textbook, but in the vast majority of later principles textbooks that followed Samuelson. Thus,

> "I am more attached to the comparatively simple fundamental ideas which underlie my theory than to the particular forms in which I have embodied them, and I have no desire that the latter should be crystallized at the present stage of the debate. If the simple basic ideas can become familiar and acceptable, time and experience and the collaboration of a number of minds will discover the best way of expressing them." (Keynes, 1937, pgs. 211-212).

The best way for expressing Keynes' simple basic ideas is through the use of the 45° Cross. The AD-AS Model simply does not measure up.

Section 4 contrasts Samuelson's 8th edition handling of the paradox of Thrift with Mankiw's "discussion", a discussion that is unclear and incomplete. It appears Mankiw never fully grasped or understood the discussion of the paradox of Thrift as contained in Samuelson's text. If he had understood, then he would never have removed the 45° Cross Model from his own principles text.

Section 5 demonstrates that all of the "big" Keynesian issues in macroeconomics are still viewed as important. There is no consensus supporting a downplaying of Keynes' (or Samuelson's) contributions.

2. PRODUCING A KEYNESIAN ECONOMIST IN 1970

In 1970, the author took the principles of macro and micro economics at Cerritos Junior College in Norwalk, California, U.S.A. The textbook used was Samuelson's *Economics*, 8th edition. After finishing the principles courses, the author decided that Keynes was, for the most part, correct while his neoclassical critics were, with a few exceptions, incorrect. What were the crucial parts of Samuelson's presentation, in the macro portion of the principles course, that led to the production of the Keynesian output? There were three sections. These are the same three sections that the author makes sure all his principles' students cover. These crucial portions are discussed under subsections 2a, b, and c.

2a Production Possibilities Frontier Analysis

Samuelson covered this on pages 17-26 and 147-151. The conclusion the author reached was that neoclassical theory essentially was a special theory of an economy always, or in a stochastic version, the average or mean position of the economy, operating on the boundary of its PPF at a natural rate of unemployment. On the other hand, Keynesian economics dealt with the general case of an economy operating in the interior of the PPF. The difference between the interior point and the boundary point was a theoretical measure of involuntary unemployment existing in an economy at any particular point in time.

2b The 45° Cross Model (Chapters 11, 12, and 13)

Samuelson's coverage, at the very beginning of Chapter 11, concerning the problem of investment spending (pages 193-196) made a very deep impression. The deflationary gap, or GNP gap, is almost always an *investment gap*. This problem was the *core* problem of any and every capitalist economy. Let me quote Samuelson's text:

> "The amount of investment itself is *highly variable* from year to year and decade to decade."
>
> .
> .
> .
>
> "The extreme variability of investment is the next important fact to be emphasized."
>
> .
> .
> .
>
> "Unless proper macroeconomic policies are pursued, a laissez faire economy cannot guarantee that there will be exactly the required amount of investment to ensure full employment: not too little so as to cause unemployment, nor too much so as to cause inflation. As far as total investment...is concerned, the laissez faire system is without a good thermostat." (Samuelson, 1970, p. 195).

Nor did Samuelson ignore monetary policy, the Federal Reserve System or interest rates, as was alleged in a *Time* business note:

> "While a realist must recognize that an economy like ours of 1929 or of the 1970's will not *by itself* maintain stability of prices and full employment, critics should still recognize that there are certain elements in a pricing economy that can work toward stability if given a chance to operate and if helped by vigorous public stabilizing actions. AS we shall see later, *the structure of interest rates*—which determines how costly and hard it is to get credit for investing activities—can be helped by Federal Reserve monetary policy to play a *stabilizing* role in moderating investment fluctuations. Also, to a considerable extent the frictions that keep various prices inflexible and sticky in a modern mixed economy can be offset by public fiscal actions. This, then, is one of our most important economic lessons."
>
> "Where the stimulus to investment is concerned, the system is somewhat in the lap of the Gods. We may be lucky or unlucky; and one of the few

> things you can say about luck is, 'It's going to change'. Fortunately, things need not be left to luck. We shall see that perfectly sensible public and private policies can be followed that have greatly enhanced the stability and productive growth of the mixed economy." (Samuelson, 1970, p. 196).

2c The Paradox of Thrift

Samuelson covered this topic on pages 224-226. I can't put it better than Samuelson did:

> "An increased desire to consume—which is another way of looking at a decreased desire to save—is likely to boost business sales and increase investment. On the other hand, a decreased desire to consume—i.e., an increase in thriftness—is likely to reduce inflationary pressure in times of booming incomes; but in time of depression, it could make the depression worse and reduce the amount of actual net capital formation in the community. *High consumption and high investment are then hand in hand rather than opposed to each other*." (Samuelson, 1970, p. 224).

Samuelson's explanation on pages 224-225, although he does not explicitly say so, amounts to the following: If an economy is operating on its PPF boundary, then more investment requires more savings and less consumption. The relationship between consumption and investment is a *negative* one. On the other hand, if an economy is operating in the interior of its PPF, increased savings leads, not to increased investment, but to reduced consumption (C), a fall in sales, an increase in inventories, a reduction in investment (I), a negative multiplier effect, a fall in national income, and further movement into the interior of the PPF. Thus, as stated above by Samuelson, in the interior of the PPF, the relationship between C and I is positive, not negative. The analysis on these two pages, logical, straightforward and precise, yet written out clearly for an introductory student, cemented my Keynesian perspective. Samuelson's decision to remove this discussion in later editions was, in my opinion, a mistake, especially since it goes to the heart of Keynes' General Theory. The reader can find practically the exact same conclusion stated by Keynes. See Keynes' *Evening Standard* article of March 19, 1929 in CWJMK, Vol. 19, pages 804-808, or the letter to R. Kahn of September 28, 1931 in CWJMK, Vol. 13, pages 374-375. Keynes presented a correct mathematical analysis of the PPF in this letter that Kahn was unable to comprehend. Samuelson's discussion is identical.

3. SAMUELSON'S 45° KEYNESIAN CROSS VERSUS THE AD-AS MODEL

Consider the following statement of Mankiw about the 45° Cross Model:

> "When I was writing my text, I made a lot of hard decisions about what to leave out and, sometimes, had to battle my editors over these choices. The biggest battle was over my decision to leave out the Keynesian cross (sometimes called the income-expenditure model), which has been at the center of teaching macroeconomics since Samuelson introduced it into the principles course in 1948. I am not opposed to the substance of this model, and I include it in my intermediate text, but I felt that it was not worth covering in a principles course. The model is often hard for students to understand. Moreover, the big ideas of Keynesian economics can be presented more simply using only the model of aggregate demand and aggregate supply." (Mankiw, 1998, p. 519).

Not worth covering in a principles course? Often hard for students to understand? This author completely disagrees. First, the reader should briefly consider Figures 1, 2, and 3. The notation has been defined in the figure title. It is standard and should cause no problems.

The differences in the two models range of analysis are minor. First, the price level is implicit in the Y(AS) axis (abscissa) of the 45° Cross, while the price level is explicit in the AD-AS Model in the p axis (ordinate). Second, the 45° Cross Model excludes the S(Synthesis) range in the interests of parsimony. The primary, fundamental differences between Keynesians and Neoclassicals are explicitly exposed in the 45° Cross, with Neoclassicals arguing that the economy is generally on the boundary of the PPF. The main problem is inflation. There is no problem of waste or inefficient use of resources *in the private sector* in the aggregate. On the other hand, Keynesians argue that the main problem is a waste, misallocation or underutilization of resources in the private sector. Economic growth is non-optimal because of insufficient private investment. The economy is operating in the interior of the PPF. The main problem is an unemployment rate greater than the natural rate of unemployment (NRU). Adam Smith's argument (Wealth of Nations, 1776, Part IV, Chapter 2, pages 421-426) that the private sector always maximizes private sector inputs is rejected. There is no Invisible Hand, in 1776 or 1996.

The 45° Cross presents both arguments in an evenhanded manner. It leaves it up to the student to decide who was right or wrong in the debate. In the opinion of the author, based on having taught some 5,000 principles students, the 45° Cross is grasped in a straightforward fashion by the vast majority of students *if* the instructor is willing to do some model construction and curve shifting on the blackboard or overhead projector. Finally, the AD-AS Model can't deal in a satisfactory manner with the Investment Saving problem. Contrary to Mankiw, the question is not "spending more time on...the role of financial markets in equilibrating savings and investment" (Mankiw, p. 521). The question is why the equilibration does not occur on the boundary (optimal state) of the PPF. All too often what is equilibrated, in the short run or the long run, is saving and speculation at a interior position inside the PPF.

4. THE PARADOX OF THRIFT

Again consider the following statement of Mankiw:

> As a sign of how times have changed, imagine asking a group of principles students the following question: If Americans decided to save a larger fraction of their income, how would this change affect the economy? The answer I learned as a freshman in 1976 was based on the Keynesian cross and the paradox of thrift: Higher saving rates would depress aggregate demand, lead to lower national income, and in the end fail to result in higher quantities of saving. By contrast, the first answer I teach as an instructor today is based on classical growth theory: Higher saving means more investment, a larger future capital stock, and a higher level of national income. Both answers have some degree of truth, depending on the circumstances, but I have no doubt that the classical answer is more central to current discussions of practical public policy." (Mankiw, pages 502-503).

Yes, in Keynes' General Theory, as in Samuelson's 45° Cross, "Both answers have some degree of truth, depending on the circumstances". Unfortunately, Mankiw begs the question grievously. The correct appraisal is that classical growth theory assumes the private economy to be always on the boundary of its static, and dynamic, PPF, or that the mean or average GNP outcome is on the boundary. *If* this assumption is correct, *then* Mankiw's second answer is true (not "some degree of truth"). On the other hand, if the economy is operating in the interior of the PPF (static or dynamic), then Mankiw's second answer is correct.

Mankiw claims that "I have no doubt that the classical answer is more central to current discussions of practical public policy." (Mankiw, page 523). If he has no doubts, then he should present both sides and allow the student to make up his own mind. The 45° Cross approach presents both sides. However, in my teaching experience, I have found very few students who will accept Mankiw's answer *at the principles level.* I suspect that this is the real reason for Mankiw's decision to eliminate the 45° Cross. Too many Keynesians are being produced at the principles level.

Lodewijks (1997) has previously noted what appears to be Mankiw's incomplete understanding of the paradox of thrift in his critique of Mankiw (1992):

> "It is useful at this point to mention Okun's views on the promotion of economic growth, given Mankiw's comments about stagnation and excessive savings. First, we need to make a sharp distinction between an increase in potential output and changes in real output relative to potential. In 1961 and 1962 the priority was gap-closing." (Lodewijks, 1997, p. 37).

and

> "Mankiw's view that discretionary policy in the end, simply leads to higher inflation without lower unemployment...is unlikely to be acceptable to most modern Keynesians" (Lodewijks, p. 38).

Lodewijks correctly argues that "what Mankiw is presenting is the 'Treasury View' that Keynes so devastatingly attacked..." (Lodewijks, 1997, p. 142). Any student who used Samuelson's 8th edition could not help but be sympathetic to the Keynesian position and reject the Treasury View, which was that the private sector naturally operates at an optimal position on the boundary of the PPF unless disturbed by "government interference" in the form of unemployment compensation, minimum wage laws, the legalization of unions, and social security legislation.

5. CONCLUSION

Mankiw's comment about "how times have changed" is not borne out. The American Economic Review's Paper and Proceedings session of 1992, titled "Is There a Global Economic Consensus", presented empirical findings by Alston, et al., Ricketts and Shoesmith, and Frey and Eichenberger that supports Keynesian policy proposals that follow directly from an understanding of the 45° Cross Model. For instance, in response to the following assertion,

> "An economy in short run equilibrium at a real GNP below potential GNP has a self-correcting mechanism that will eventually return it to potential real GNP", (Alston, et al., 1992, p. 204).

47.6% generally disagreed, 29.5% agreed with provisos, while only 21.3% agreed. In response to the assertion that,

> "Fiscal policy has a significant stimulative impact on a less than fully employed economy", (Ricketts and Shoesmith, 1992, p. 214).

The average weight of opinion was +1.1. A weight of +1.0 meant "agree with reservations". In my opinion, Samuelson's 8th edition with the 45° Cross Model and discussion of the paradox of thrift, was a winner in 1948 (or 1998). There is no reason to change to Mankiw's approach.

Figure 1 :
Samuelson's 45° Cross Model

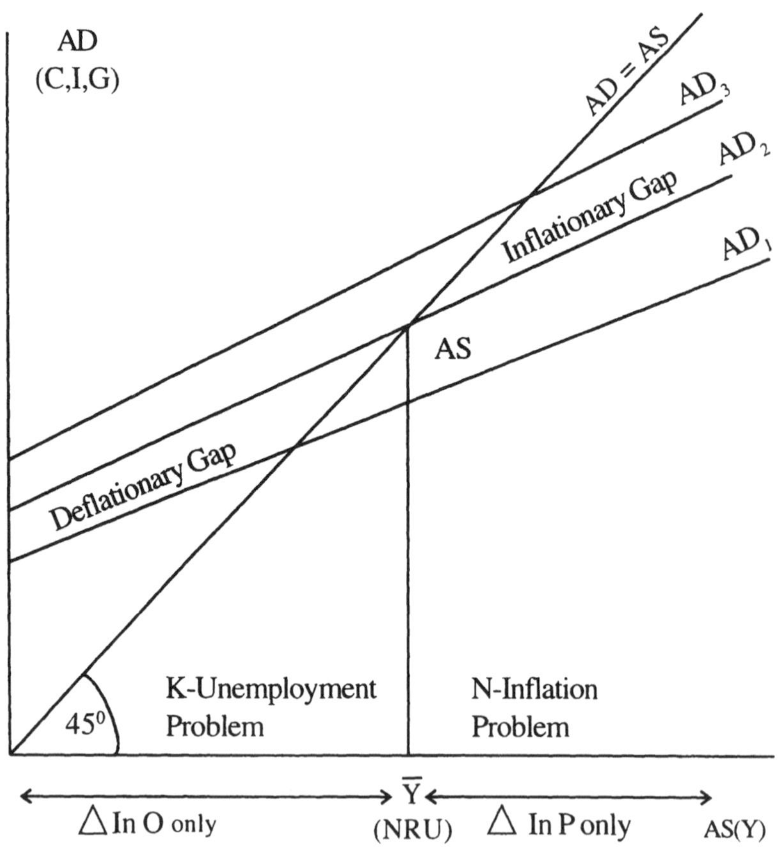

K=Keynesian range, N=Neoclassical range, Y=Potential GNP, NRU=Natural rate of Unemployment (on boundary of PPF), O=real output, p=price level, Y=pO=nominal GNP=AS=Aggregate supply, C+I+G=AD= Aggregate Demand. Δ=change in.

Figure 2:
Modified AD-AS Model

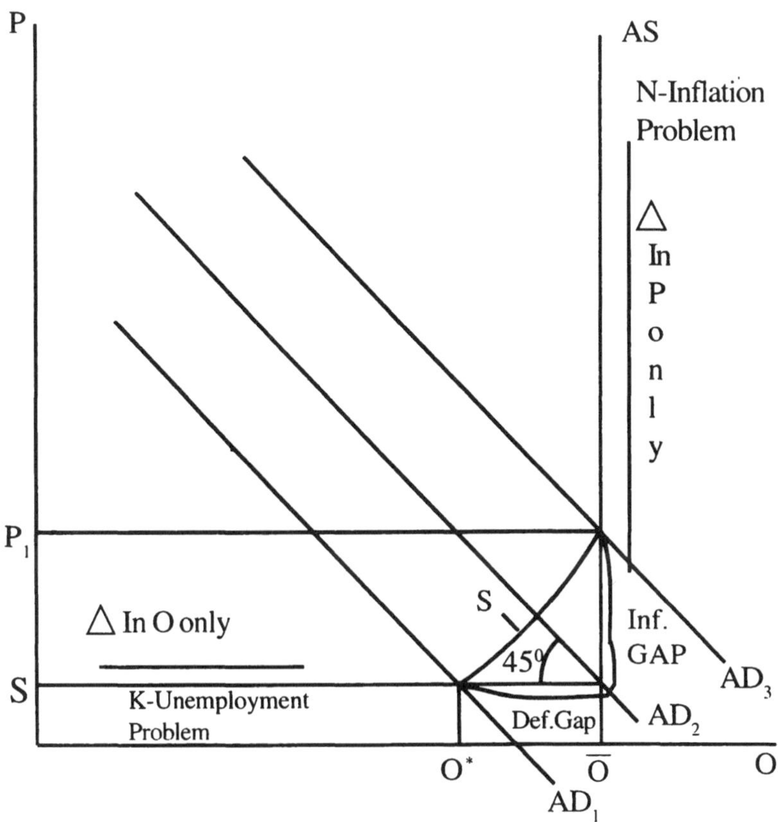

K=Keynesian range, N=Neoclassical range, S=Synthesis range, represented by red line, O=real GNP, p=price level, Y=pO=nominal GNP=AS, AD=Aggregate Demand, AS=Aggregate supply, AS=O=real aggregate supply, O=potential real GNP, NRU=natural rate of unemployment.

Figure 3:
Samuelson's I=S (Investment equals Savings).

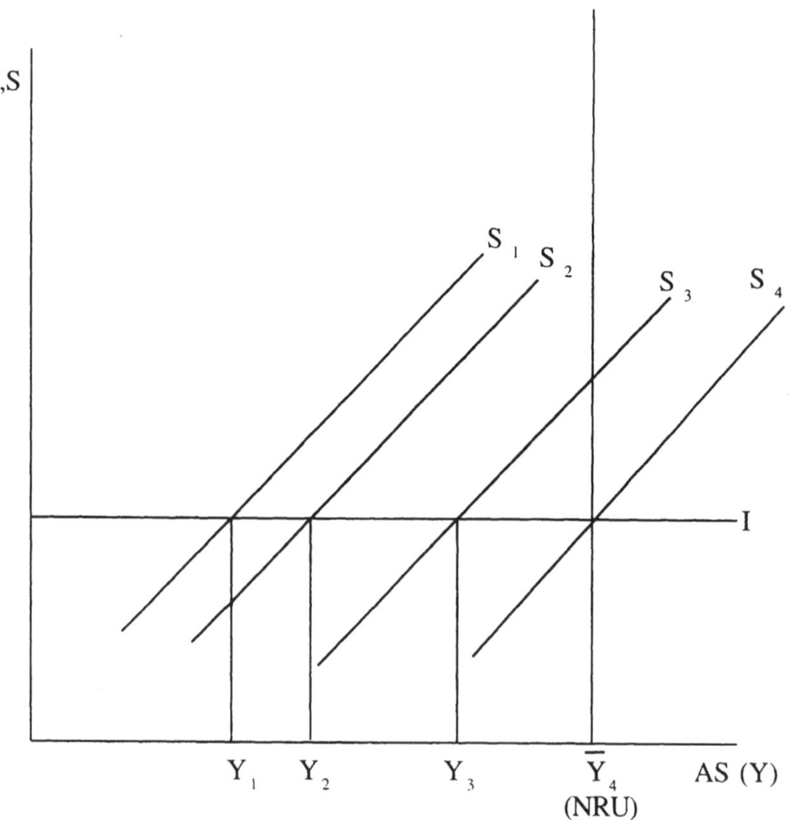

Difference between Y's ($Y_1Y_2Y_3$) and Y_4 represent different deflationary gaps.

REFERENCES

Alston, R., Kreal, J.R., and Vaughn, M.B. (1992). "Is There A Consensus Among Economists in the 1990's?" *American Economic Review, Papers and Proceedings*, 82, 203-209.

Business Notes. (1985). "Updating a Classic", *Time*, March 4,1985, p. 68.

Frey, B.S. and Eichenberger, R. (1992). "Economics and Economists - A European Perspective", *American Economic Review, Papers and Proceedings*, 82, 216-220.

Keynes, J.M., (1964). *The General Theory of Employment, Interest and Money*. Harcourt, Brace and World, New York.

Keynes, J.M., (1973, '79). *The Collected Writings of John Maynard Keynes*, Vols. 13, 14, 29. Edited by D. Moggridge, London: Macmillan.

Lodewijks, J. (1997). "Old and New Keynesians", *Indian Journal of Applied Economics*, 6, 27-40.

Lodewijks, J. (1999). "Hicks and the Crisis in Keynesian Economics", *Indian Journal of Applied Economics*, 8, 141-146.

Mankiw, N.G. (1992). "The Reincarnation of Keynesian Economics", *European Economic Review*, 36, 559-565.

Mankiw, N.G. (1998). "Teaching the Principles of Economics", *Eastern Economic Journal*, 24, 519-524.

Ricketts, M. And Shoesmith, E. (1992). "British Economic Opinion: Positive Science or Normative Judgment", *American Economic Review, Papers and Proceedings*, 82, 210-215.

Samuelson, P.A. (1970). *Economics 8th edition*. New York: McGraw Hill.

Contributors

Seyed Ahmad, Professor Emeritus, Department of Economics, McMaster University, Ontario, Canada

Carlo Benetti, professor, Université Paris X, Nanterre, France

Christian Bidard, professor, Department of Economics, Université Paris X, Nanterre, France

Michael Emmett Brady, professor, University of California, USA

Jean Cartelier, professor, Université Paris X, Nanterre, France

Frank Hahn, professor, Churchill College, Cambridge, United Kingdom

O.F. Hamouda, associate professor, Department of Economics, Glendon College, York University, Toronto, Canada

Lawrence R. Klein, Nobel Laureate in Economics (1980), Benjamin Franklin Professor of Economics, Emeritus, School of Arts and Sciences, University of Pennsylvania, Philadelphia, USA

Vittorangelo Orati, professor Universita della Tuscia, Facolta di Economia, Instituto Economico, Viterbo, Italy

B.B. Price, professor, Department of Economics, Glendon College, York University, Toronto, Canada

K. Puttaswamaiah, editor-in-chief, *International Journal of Applied Economics and Econometrics*, Emeritus Professor in Applied Economics and Chairman of the Scientific Committee of the International Institute of Advanced Economics and Social Sciences, Cremona, Italy

Robert M. Solow, Nobel Laureate in Economics (1987), Professor Emeritus, Department of Economics, Massachusetts Institute of Technology, Cambridge, USA

Ian Steedman, research professor, Department of Economics, Manchester Metropolitan University, Manchester, United Kingdom

Albert E. Steenge, professor, Faculty of Public Administration and Public Policy, Department of Economics, University of Twente, The Netherlands

Richard van den Berg, Holborn College, London, United Kingdom

ANNEX

PAUL A. SAMUELSON : PUBLISHED WRITINGS

1939 1. "*Interactions between the Multiplier Analysis and the Principle of Acceleration*", Review of Economics and Statistics, Vol. 21, 1939, pp. 75-78.

1943 2. Wold, H. (1943-44) "*A Synthesis of Demand Analysis, I-III*", *Skandinavisk Aktuarietid-Schrift* 26, pp. 85-118, 220-263, and 27 pp. 69-120.

1947 3. *Foundations of Economic Analysis*, Cambridge, Harvard University Press, 1947 (See under 1983).

1948 4. *Economics: An Introductory Analysis*, Mc-Graw Hill, 1948.

1949 5. "*International Factor-Price Equalisation Once Again*", Economic Jour. 59: 181-197 Reprinted in CSP chap. 68, vol. 2.

6. "*Market Mechanisms and Maximization, Part III, Dynamics and Linear Programming*," The RAND Corporation (June). Reprinted in CSP chap. 33, vol. 1.

1950 7. "*Probability and the Attempts to Measure Utility*" (English and Japanese). Economic Review (Keizai Kenkyu) 1 (Tokyo, Hitotsub shi University): 167-173. Reprinted in CSP Chap. 12, vol. 1.

1951 8. "*Abstract of a Theorem Concerning, Substitutability in Open Leontief Models*", In: Activity Analysis of Production and Allocation. ed. T.C. Koopmans (Cowles Commission for Research in Economics). New York: John Wiley. Reprinted in CSP chap. 36. Vol. 1.

1952 9. "*Utility, Preference, and Probability*", Brief abstract of paper given at conference on "Les Fondements et Applications de la Theorie du Risque en Econometrie" (May), Reprinted in CSP chap. 13, vol. 1.

10. "*Probability, Utility and the Independence Axiom*", Econometrica 20: 670-678. Reprinted in CSP chap. 14, vol. 1.

International Journal of Applied Economics and Econometrics, Oct.–Dec., 2001,
Vol. 9, No. 4, pp. 493–499

1957 11. "*Wages and Interest: A Modern Dissection of Marxian Economic Models*", American Economic Review 47: 884-912. Reprinted in CSP chap. 29. Vol. 1.

1958 12. "*Linear Programming and Economic Analysis*" (with Robert Dorfman and R.A. Solow), New York, McGraw Hill, 1958, 1964, 14th printing 1981.

13. "*Problems of United States Economic Development*", Committee for Economic Development, New York, 1958.

1960 14. "*The St. Petersburg Paradox as a Divergent Double Limit*", International Economic Review 1: 31-37, Reprinted in CSP chap. 15, vol. 1.

15. "*An extension of the Lechatelier Principle*", Econometrica 28: 368-379. Reprinted in CSP chap. 42, vol. 1.

16. "*Structure of a Minimum Equilibrium System in Essays in Economics and Econometrics: A Volume in Honour of Harold Hotelling*", ed. Ralph W. Pfouts. Chapel Hill: University of North Carolina Press. Reprinted in CSP chap. 44, vol. 1.

17. "*Efficient Paths of Capital Accumulation in Terms of the Calculus of Variations*", In: Mathematical Methods in the Social Sciences, 1959, ed. K.J. Arrow. S. Karlin, and P. Suppes, Stanford, Calif: Stanford University Press, Reprinted in CSP chap. 2, vol. 1.

1961 18. "*A New Theorem on Nonsubstitution: In: Money*", Growth and Methodology, published in honour of Johan Akerman (Lund Social Science Studies, 20). Lund, Sweden: CWK Gleerup. Reprinted in CSP chap. 37, vol. 1.

1962 19. "*Parable and Realism in Capital Theory: The Surogate Production Function*", Review of Economic Studies, 29: 193-206. Reprinted in CSP chap. 28, vol. 1.

1964 20. "*A Brief Survey of Post-Keynesian Developments*", in Keynes General Theory: Reports of Three Decades, ed. R. Lekachman, St. Martin's Press, New York, 1964.

1965 21. "*Using Full Duality to Show That Simultaneously Additive Direct and Indirect Utilities Implies Unitary Price Elasticity of Demand*", Econometrica 33: 781-796. Reprinted in CSP chap. 134, Vol. 3.

22. *Postscript in CSP*, vol. 1, p. 124.

23. "*Rational Theory of Warrant Pricing*", and "*Appendix: A Free Boundary Problem for the Heat Equation Arising from a Problem in Mathematical Economics*", by H.P. MaKean, Jr. Industrial Management Review, 6: 13-39. Reprinted in CSP chap. 199, vol. 3.

24. "*A Theory of Induced Innovation along Kennedy-Weizsacker Lines*", Review of Economics and Statistics, Vol. 47, 1965, pp. 343-356.

1966 25. "*The Fundamental Singularity Theorem for Non-joint Production*", International Economic Review, 7: 34-41. Reprinted in CSP chap. 145, Vol. 3.

26. "*The Collected Scientific Papers of Paul A. Samuelson. Cambridge*", Mass: MIT Press, vol. 1, ed. Joseph E. Stiglitz, 1966, vol. 2, ed. Joseph E. Stiglitz. 1966.

27. "*Rejoinder: Agreements, Disagreements, Doubts and the Case of Induced Harrod-Neutral Technical Change*", Review of Economics and Statistics, Vol. 48, 1966, pp. 444-448.

28. (with Modigliani, F.) "*The Pasinetti Paradox in Neo-classical and More General Models*". Review of Economic Studies, Vol. 33, 1966, pp. 269-301.

1967 29. "*General Proof That Diversification Pays*" Journal of Financial and Quantitative Analysis, 2: 1-13. Reprinted in CSP chap. 201, vol. 3.

30. "*Efficient Portfolio Selection for Pareto-Levy Investments*", Journal of Financial and Quantitative Analysis, 2: 107-122. Reprinted in CSP chap. 202, vol. 3.

31. "*A Turnpike Reputation of the Golden Rule in a Welfare-Maximising Many-Year Plan*", In: Essays on the Theory of Optimal Economic Growth, ed. K. Shell, Cambridge, Mass.: MIT Press. Reprinted in CSP chap. 137, vol. 3.

1970 32. "*Classical Orbital Stability Deduced for Discrete Time Maximum Systems*", Western Economic Journal, 8: 110-119. Reprinted in CSP chap. 158, vol. 3.

33. "*The Fundamental Approximation Theorem of Portfolio Analysis in Terms of Means, Variances, and Higher Moments*",

Review of Economic Studies, 37: 537-542. Reprinted in CSP chap. 203, vol. 3.

34. "*Law of Conservation of the Capital-Output Ratio*", Proceedings of the National Academy of Sciences, 67: 1477-79. Reprinted in CSP chap. 142, vol. 3.

1971 35. "*Stochastic Speculative Price*", Proceedings of the National Academy of Sciences, 68: 335-337. Reprinted in CSP chap. 206, vol. 3.

36. "*Understanding the Marxian Notion of Exploitation: A Summary of the So-called Transformation Problem between Marxian Values and Competitive Prices*", Jour. of Economic Literature, 9: 399-431. Reprinted in CSP chap. 153, vol. 3.

37. "*The 'Fallacy' of Maximizing the Geometric Mean in Long Sequences of Investing or Gambling*", Proceedings of the National Academy of Sciences, 66: 2493-96. Reprinted in CSP chap. 207, vol.3.

38. "*On the Trail of Conventional Beliefs about the Transfer Problem*", In: Trade, Balance of Payments, and Growth: Papers in International Economics in Honour of Charles P. Kindleberger, ed. J. Bhagawati et al. Amsterdam: North-Holland Publishing Co. Reprinted in CSP chap. 163, vol. 3.

39. *Ohlin was Right*, The Swedish Journal of Economics, vol. 73, No. 4, 1971, pp. 365-384.

1972 40. "*Unification Theorem for the Two Basic Dualities of Homothetic Demand Theory*", Proceedings of the National Academy of Sciences, 69: 2673-74. Reprinted in CSP chap. 212, vol. 4.

41. "*Mathematics of Speculative Price*". In: Mathematical Topics in Economic Theory and Computation, ed., R.H. Day and S.M. Robinson. Philadelphia: Society for Industrial and Applied Mathematics. Reprinted in CSP chap. 240, vol. 4.

42. "*A Quantum-theory Model of Economics: Is the Co-ordinating Entrepreneur just Worth his Profit*", (Development and Planning: Essays in Honour of Paul Rosenstein-Rodan), Bhagwati and Eckaus, Edited, Allen and Unwin, 1972.

43. "*The Collected Scientific Papers of Paul A. Samuelson*", Vol. III, edited by Robert C. Merton, The MIT Press, 1972.

1973 44. "*Optimality of Profit Including Prices Under the Ideal Planning: Marx's Model*", Proceedings of the National Academy of Sciences, 70: 2109-11. Reprinted in CSP chap. 226, vol. 4.

1974 45. With Robert C. Merton. "*Generalized Mean-Variance Tradeoffs for Best Perturbation Corrections to Approximate Portfolio Decision*", Journal of Finance, 29: 27-40.

46. "*Fallacy of the Log-Normal Approximation to Optimal Portfolio Decision Making over Many Periods*", Journal of Financial Economics, 1, No. 1, 67-94.

1975 47. "*Addenda on Compact Probabilities: Gaussian Surrogates in the Capital Asset Pricing Model and Convergence Pathologies,*" MIT Working Paper.

48. "*Limited Liability, Short Selling, Bounded Utility, and Infinite-Variance Stable Distributions*", Journal of Financial and Quantitative Analysis, 11: 485-503. Reprinted in CSP chap. 247, vol. 4.

49. "*Economics of Forestry in an Evolving Society*", Economic Inquiry, 14: 466-492. Reprinted in CSP chap. 218, vol. 4.

1977 50. "*St. Petersburg Paradoxes: Defanged, Dissected and Historically Described*", Journal of Economic Literature, 15: 24-55.

51. "*The Collected Scientific Papers of Paul A. Samuelson*", Edited by Hiroakai Nagatani and Kate Gowley, Volume IV, the MIT, 1977.

52. "*The Political Economy of the New Left, An Oversiders view*", Assar Lindbeck, Foreword by Paul A. Samuelson, Harper and Row, London, 1977.

1978 53. "*Interest Rate Equalization and Non-Equalization by Trade in Leontief-Sraffa Models*", Journal of International Economics, 8 (Feb.), pp. 21-27.

54. "*Free Trade's Intertemporal Pareto-Optimality*", Journal of International Economics, 8 (Feb.), pp. 147-149.

55. "*Readings in Economics*", 6th Edition, McGraw Hill Book Co., First published in 1955, 1970; reprinted in 1978, 1982.

1979 56. "*Why we should Not Make Mean Log of Wealth Big Though Years to Act are Long*", Journal of Banking and Finance, 3: 305-307.

1980 57. "*A Corrected Version of Hume's Equilibrium Mechanisms for International Trade*", chap 9 in J.S. Chipman and C.P. Kindleberger, eds. Flexible Exchange Rates and the Balance of Payments, Amsterdam, North-Holland.

1981 58. "*Summing Up on the Australian Case for Protection*", Quarterly Journal of Economics, 96 (Feb.), pp. 147-60.

59. "*Bertil Ohlin (1899-1979)*", Scandinavian Journal of Economics, Vol. 83, No. 3, 1981, pp. 355-371.

1982 60. "*The Normative and Positivistic Inferiority of Marx's Values Paradigm*", Southern Economics Journal, 49: 11-18.

61. "*Rigorous Observational Positivism: Klein's Envelope Aggregation; Thermodynamics and Economic Isomorphisms*", L.J. Klein Festschrift, Cambridge, Mass.: MIT Press.

62. "*Variation on Capital/Output Conservation Laws*".

63. "*Marx without Matrices: Understanding the Rate of Profit*", A. Erlich Festchrift, Cambridge, Mass.: MIT Press.

1983 64. "*Foundations of economic Analysis*", (Enlarged Edition) Harvard University Press, 1983.

65. "*Economics in a Golden Age*", in Paul Samuelson and Economic Theory, edited by E. Cary Brown and Robert M. Solow, McGraw Hill, 1983.

66. "*Thunnen at Two Hundred*", Journal of Economic Literature, Vol. 21, December 1983, pp. 1468-1488.

1984 67. (with Ryuzo Sato) "*Unattainability of Integrability and Definiteness Conditions in the General Case of Demand for Money and Goods*", American Economic Review, Vol. 74, No. 4, Sep. 1984, pp. 588-604.

1986 68. "*The Collected Scientific Papers of Paul A. Samuelson*", Edited by Kate Gowley, Vol. V, MIT, 1986.

1988 69. "*Mathematical Vindication of Ricardo on machinery*", Journal of Political Economy, vol. 96, No.2, April 1988.

1990 70. "*Economics in My Time*" in Breit, William and Spencer, Roger W., Ed., *Lives of Laureates*, Second Edition, 1990, pp. 58-76.

1992 71. "*Economics*" (with William D. Nordhaus), Fourteenth Edition, Mc-Graw Hill, 1992, and the revised Fifteenth Edition - An Inernational Edition, 1995.

72. "*Maximum Principles in Analytical Economics*", Nobel Memorial Lecture on December 11, 1970 published in Lindbeck, Assar., Edited, *Economic Sciences — 1969-1980*: Nobel Lectures, World Scientific, published for the Nobel Foundation, 1992, pp. 62-77.

73. "*My Life Philosophy: Policy Credos and Working Ways*" pub. in Szenberg, Michael., Ed., *Eminent Economists: Their Life Philosophies*, Cambridge Univ. Press, 1992, pp. 236-247.

1996 74. "*Tribute to Tinbergen : One Exact Match for Economics and Physics*" (Special issue in Reverential Memory of Jan Tinbergen), *Indian Journal Applied Economics*, Vol.5, No.3, April-June, 1996, pp. 1-16.

1998 75. "*How Foundations Came To Be*", *Journal of Economic Literature*, Vol. XXXVI, No.3, Sept. 1998, pp 1375-1986.

76. "*My John Hicks*", Indian Journal Applied Economics, Special Issue in Respectful Memory of John Hicks, Vol. 7, No.4, Oct.-Dec.1998, pp. 1-4.

2000 78. "*The Collected Scientific Papers of Paul A. Samuelson*", Vol. 6 & 7 (In press).

Index